D0153876

About the author

Francisco Panizza is Senior Lecturer in Latin American Politics at the London School of Economics and Political Science. He was born in Montevideo, Uruguay, and studied politics in Brazil and England. He has taught in universities in Uruguay, Brazil, Mexico and England, where he has lived since 1979. His research interests are populism, democracy and the politics of economic reform. He combines his academic career with consultancy and journalism. He is a frequent contributor to the BBC, Bloomberg TV and several Latin American newspaper and radio networks.

Contemporary Latin America

development and democracy beyond the Washington Consensus

Francisco Panizza

Zed Books

LONDON | NEW YORK

Contemporary Latin America: development and democracy beyond the Washington Consensus was first published in 2009 by Zed Books Ltd, 7 Cynthia Street, London N1 9JF, UK and Room 400, 175 Fifth Avenue, New York, NY 10010, USA

www.zedbooks.co.uk

Set in OurType Arnhem and Futura Bold by Ewan Smith, London
Index: ed.emery@thefreeuniversity.net
Cover designed by Rogue Four Design
Printed and bound in the UK by the MPG Books Group

Distributed in the USA exclusively by Palgrave Macmillan, a division of St Martin's Press, LLC, 175 Fifth Avenue, New York, NY 10010, USA

A catalogue record for this book is available from the British Library
Library of Congress Cataloging in Publication Data available

ISBN 978 1 84277 853 1 hb
ISBN 978 1 84277 854 8 pb

Contents

Introduction

This book is about political change under democracy. The first decade of the twenty-first century has been a time of great political transformation in Latin America. After a long period of hegemony of forces of the right and centre-right, political forces of the left and centre-left (henceforth left-of-centre, LOC) have made strong advances in the region. The trend began in 1998 with the triumph in Venezuela of Hugo Chávez – then perceived more as an anti-establishment candidate rather than a radical left-winger. It was followed by the victory of Socialist Party candidate Ricardo Lagos in Chile in 2000 and by the emblematic triumph of Luiz Inácio Lula da Silva in Brazil in 2002. By the second half of the decade it looked as though, if not a red tide, at least a pink one was sweeping throughout the region, as different shades of LOC governments held office in Argentina, Bolivia, Brazil, Chile, Costa Rica, Guatemala, Ecuador, Nicaragua, Paraguay and Uruguay. The so-called turn to the left has not been uniform across the region, while electoral results have revealed deeply divided societies. But altogether Latin America's political map looks very different from that of the 1990s, when centre-right governments dominated the political landscape of the region.

The LOC political forces that have become ruling parties throughout the region are highly heterogeneous entities whose political differences raise difficult questions concerning their categorization, however loosely we define the left. The answer to these questions depends in turn on more fundamental theoretical questions: How do we define the left? Where do we trace the dividing line between the centre-left and the centre-right? Does it make sense to group together such moderate political forces as Chile's Socialist Party (PSCh) with more radical forces such as Bolivia's Movimiento al Socialismo (MAS)? Are not Venezula's Hugo Chávez, Bolivia's Evo Morales and Ecuador's Rafael Correa populists rather than leftists? And, what is meant by populist?

I deal with the definitions of the left and populism and other related questions in the body of this book. But while there are significant questions concerning the scope and nature of LOC governments in the region, there appears to be a strong consensus on what is behind their political ascendancy, namely a backlash against the economic policies that were implemented throughout the region in the late 1980s and 1990s. Attacks against 'neoliberalism', 'the Washington Consensus (WC)' or simply 'the model', as the free market economic reforms of the 1990s are often indistinctively referred to in political discourse, has been a central element of the political appeal of LOC candidates, whether radicals or moderates.

And yet, a decade earlier the political mood in the region was strikingly different. As noted in Chapter 3, by the early 1990s Latin America appeared to be on the verge of leaving behind its history of political and economic turbulence as a mix of liberal democracy, economic liberalization and regional integration achieved significant consensus throughout the region. The formula had considerable support both at elite and at popular level, as shown by the electoral victories of economic reformers such as Carlos Menem in Argentina in 1995, Ernesto Zedillo in Mexico in 1994, Fernando Henrique Cardoso in Brazil in 1994 and 1998, and Alberto Fujimori in Peru in 1995. There were few significant challenges to liberal democracy in a region in which elections were becoming the only game in town, where a centrist consensus prevailed over political polarization, and 'human rights' was part of the new common language if not yet the common practice. The turnaround in economic performance appeared to vindicate the free trade economic reforms that were being implemented throughout the region. *From Despair to Hope*, the subtitle of a book on crisis and reform in Latin America by the Chilean economist Sebastian Edwards, reflects the belief that free market economic policies were working. Published in 1995, the book hailed the new vision of economic policy based on market forces, international competition and a limited role for the state in economic affairs, and mapped its implementation throughout the region (Edwards 1995).

Optimism about the impact of the free market reforms proved premature and short lived. The so-called Tequila crisis of 1994 in Mexico was the first in a series of financial crises that affected the main economies of the region in the second half of the 1990s and the first years of the new century (Brazil 1999, Argentina 1999 and 2001/02, Uruguay 2002). Economic volatility made 1997–02 a new lost half-decade for development after the so-called 'lost decade' of the 1980s. During that period, GDP per capita fell throughout the region and poverty that had fallen in the first half of the 1990s again increased in both relative and absolute terms. Equally important to the social and economic consequences of the financial crises were their intellectual and political repercussions. Economic stagnation and its social impact in terms of poverty and unemployment provided the common ground for the emergence of new development discourses that challenged the Washington Consensus. As will be seen in Chapter 7, these discourses, which are part of what is here referred to as the post-Washington Consensus (PWC), differed significantly among themselves in the ways in which they related to the WC and in the extent to which they advanced new alternatives. But even for the more staunch supporters of the free market reforms, the perceived failures of the reforms opened a period of debate and introspection in which different explanations were offered about how and why things went wrong, and what to do to put them right. Edwards's *From Despair to Hope* was followed by his 'Latin America at the end of the century: more of the same?' (Edwards 1999), which perhaps should have been subtitled 'From despair to [crushed] hopes'. In this process of reflection and self-criticism, the international financial institutions (IFIs) that, as argued in Chapter 2, were the intellectual and financial driving force behind the WC sought to take on board some of their critics' objections and, as shown in Chapter 7, elaborated a more comprehensive development framework that acknowledged the importance of institutions for economic development, promoted a more active role for the state, and highlighted the importance of reducing poverty and inequality as part of the development process. Arguably, the agenda, if not necessarily the IFIs' proposed means to achieve its goals, shifted the development debate to a terrain more favourable to the traditional concerns of the left.

The period between 2003 and 2008 saw new economic and political developments in the region. As noted in Chapter 10, the commodity boom allowed the region to grow at its highest rate for the preceding forty years. Partly as a result of high economic growth, but owing also to the implementation of new social programmes, poverty fell to its lowest level since 1980 in relative terms, and there was also a fall in inequality. LOC governments took advantage of the new economic conditions in order to adopt an increasing distance from the International Monetary Fund, which had seen its influence in the region decline. But, as argued in the same chapter, the increased margins of policy autonomy allowed by a favourable international context between 2003 and 2008 also highlighted significant differences between LOC governments' approach to

3

development; some governments have followed broadly orthodox economic policies, while others have sought more fundamental transformations of their countries' economies and societies. The maintenance by some LOC governments of some of the main tenets of the free market reformation has led to disillusionment among sectors of the left that envisaged a more decisive break with neoliberalism, but on the whole, LOC governments have maintained strong popular support, as shown by the re-election of Presidents Lula da Silva and Hugo Chávez in 2006.

This book addresses the intellectual and political journey from the Washington Consensus to the post-Washington Consensus and beyond in the context of uneven processes of democratization and the parallel rise of LOC forces in the Latin American region. Two central questions frame the analysis of the historical, and at times contradictory, economic and political changes in Latin America over the past two decades.

The first question concerns the role of interests, institutions and ideas in processes of political and economic change. While running throughout the book, the issue is specially addressed in Chapters 2, 3, 7 and 10. To establish the relationship between the three is not an easy undertaking, but I believe it makes obvious sense to seek to do so: reforms have distributive effects and produce winners and losers. It is thus important to understand who benefited from the free market reforms, how reforming coalitions were set up in support of the reforms, and how governments acted to neutralize or compensate losers. Institutions provide the formal and informal rules of the game which shape political and economic activity. Among the institutions to be examined are those characteristic of democracy: political parties, the state and social organizations. How could processes of change under democracy overcome institutional inertia and veto points, and in the process displace the powerful political and economic actors that control political and economic institutions? The state is another key institution that needs to be taken into consideration when analysing change. The redefinition of the role of the state has been at the heart of the free market reformation, both as a subject of reform and as a key actor in the process of reform. Lately a reconsideration of the role of the state in economic development under LOC governments has raised new questions about the limits to state intervention in a globalized economy. I deal with the changing role of the state in the PWC and under LOC governments in Chapters 7 and 10.

Interests and institutions cannot be understood independently of the

4

influence of ideas in processes of change. Political learning transforms perceptions of interests and redefines the terms of political discourse. How do certain ideas, such as those of the WC, become the common sense of the time and how do they lose their hegemonic status? How does the framing of an economic problem affect the options available to policy-makers? Through processes of identification, discourses constitute interests: we define what we want in relation to how we perceive ourselves. Context-dependent interpretation makes institutions work in everyday life: we cannot understand the rules of the game which shape human action without considering how those rules are defined, interpreted and subverted by political discourses.

The second question explored by this book concerns the relationship between political change and democracy. As noted above, in any process of change there are winners and losers, and the losers may resist change by all means at their disposal, and this is capable of generating considerable conflict. History shows that any political regime is vulnerable to extreme conflict, and that democracy may be particularly vulnerable since the institutions that are part of a democratic polity can suffer or yield under the pressures of political polarization. The chequered history of democracy in Latin America shows how vulnerable democracy is to political conflict, particularly when dominant groups perceive that their fundamental interests are under threat. Marxists have a point when they argue that a radical transformation of the social order can be achieved only through revolutionary means: understood in their own terms, 'the system' cannot be transformed, it must be destroyed through revolutionary class struggle. As revolution, at least violent revolution, appears to be off the agenda in Latin America, this brings particular relevance to the examination of the means and limits for change under democracy which are explored in Chapters 8, 9 and 10.

If democracy cannot withstand extreme polarization, it also cannot survive without political conflict. Paradoxically, the insight that a healthy democracy needs 'the right kind of class struggle' (i.e. the right balance between conflict and accommodation between contending social sectors) comes from Seymour Martin Lipset (1959), a scholar who sought to develop an alternative theory of political development to Marxism but who wrote under its shadow. The question of what is the 'right kind of class struggle' for the survival of capitalist democracy, however – that is, of demands from below that advance democracy and social justice but

5

do not threaten the fundamental interests of the dominant classes – has also been highlighted by scholars who are otherwise critical of Lipset's modernization theory, most notably Rueschemeyer et al. (1996: 62–3) (Chapter 5).

The notion that democracy can prosper only if the dominant classes are reassured of their place in society suggests that there are limits to change in a democratic environment. But these limits are not set in stone, and the tension between conflict and accommodation should not be understood in crudely economic terms. Social changes have made conflict much more complex and fragmented than Marx's traditional view of the industrial working class against the bourgeoisie. The 'fundamental interests' of the dominant classes, or of any social actor for that matter, are defined and redefined politically. Above all, social actors are political actors, and political actors' identities and interests are mediated and redefined by history and institutions: political parties, electoral rules, forms of political representation, forms of state organization and state intervention are crucial for understanding how conflict is processed in society. Leadership also counts.

The analysis of the relationship between conflict, accommodation and democracy is particularly relevant for understanding LOC politics in contemporary Latin America. As the most unequal region in the world, with just over 34 per cent of the population living below the poverty line in 2007 (ECLAC 2008a), Latin America hardly appears as the most fertile soil for the 'right kind of class struggle' under which liberal democracy thrives. In countries such as Venezuela, Ecuador and Bolivia, society is deeply divided along socio-economic, ethnic and regional lines. While democracy has survived socio-economic polarization, institutions have been unable to process conflicts in times of crises, as seen by the number of presidents in the region who have been unable to complete their con-stitutional mandate in the 1990s and early 2000s. As argued in Chapter 9, elections in the second half of the first decade of the twenty-first century have shown a clear polarization in term of voting preferences between the poor and subordinated social groups on the one side supporting candidates of the left, and the middle and upper classes on the other side voting for candidates of the centre and centre-right. Political polarization has in certain circumstances spilled over into the streets with occasion-ally violent confrontations between supporters and opponents of LOC governments, particularly in Venezuela and Bolivia. Democracy has not only survived, however, it has also enabled political change in the region, although the nature and extent of change are matters for debate.

In seeking to explore the above issues I work more as a bricoleur, bringing together concepts from different theoretical approaches that share *a certain regard of society*, rather than as a follower of a particular school of thought. Institutionalism in its historical and discursive variations (Hall, P. 1993; Hay 2001) has influenced my analysis of the emergence and crisis of the Washington Consensus. In the analysis of that crisis I have found particularly insightful Colin Hay's concept of crisis narrative which argues that crises are not defined in terms of objective factors, but in subjective terms as the perception of the need for rapid and decisive intervention in the context of widely experienced accumulation of political and economic contradictions (Hay 2001: 203). As noted above, the analysis of the relation between conflict and democracy is influenced by the otherwise very different insights of Lipset and of Rueschemeyer et al. My understanding of populism is grounded in the seminal work of Ernesto Laclau (1997, 2005b) and in my own writings on the topic (Panizza 2005a).

A book that seeks to map political change throughout such an eventful period in Latin American history will unavoidably neglect some relevant issues and fail to do justice to the diverse political experiences of individual countries. Concerning LOC governments, in 2008 at least nine governments had reasonable claims to be included within the category. It would have been impossible to give all LOC governments equal treatment in this book and some of them are hardly covered at all. I particularly regret not having been able to look in more detail at the cases of Chile and Bolivia, two of the most interesting case studies at opposite ends of the LOC political spectrum.

In the treatment of each of the issues addressed by the book I have sought to combine a region-wide analysis with more detailed references to specific country cases. The structure of the book is as follows. Chapter 1 looks at the emergence of the Washington Consensus in the context of the regional economic crisis of the 1980s. Chapter 2 discusses the intellectual thinking and political role of the International Monetary Fund (IMF) and the World Bank (WB) in the free market reformation. Chapter 3 analyses the domestic institutional settings and political bases of support for the reforms. Chapters 4 and 5 look at the condition of democracy in Latin America and at the impact of the free market reforms on the region's polities and societies. Chapters 6 and 7 analyse the unravelling of the Washington Consensus and the emergence of the post-Washington Consensus. Chapters 8, 9 and 10 discuss the rise of the left in the region and assess political and economic change under LOC governments. The conclusion reflects on the book's main themes in the context of a rapidly changing international economic environment.

This book brings together ten years of writing and postgraduate teaching on democracy and development in Latin America. During this period I have had the privilege of working in the intellectually challenging and cosmopolitan environment of the London School of Economics and Political Science and of teaching some of the brightest and most enthusiastic students I have met in my academic career. This book is dedicated to them. Emily Mulville has been of great assistance in the preparation of the manuscript and I want to state my gratitude to her. Last but not least, I would like to thank my wife Sara for her patience and support during the long days taken up with the writing of this book, more appreciated because it was so often understated.

1 | Paradigm found: in search of the Washington Consensus

What was the Washington Consensus?

Over the past twenty years, Latin America has gone through fundamental economic changes, which by common agreement have been characterized as the implementation of neoliberal reforms. Labelling these changes as *neoliberal* reforms makes it easier to identify what has been otherwise a complex, uneven and at times contradictory process. But if labelling a process makes it easier to give it an essence, it also risks obscuring some fundamental questions about its nature, or indeed makes more difficult a questioning of its internal logic and temporal unity.

We can try to address these questions if we move from labelling to definition and beyond. In public debate, neoliberalism seldom exists in its pure form, but coexists with other discourses embedded in economic and political institutions. As such, neoliberalism should not be conceived as a closed totality of ideas diffused across nations and through time, but rather as a loosely connected set of concepts, distinctions and arguments that gained meaning as they were articulated and then stabilized in specific ways, depending on the particular discursive and political contexts in which this occurred (Kjær and Pedersen 2001: 221).

Neoliberal discourse is not just concerned with the economy. It has achieved its current status by drawing on ideological, cultural and symbolic elements from different social, political and moral discourses, such as those concerning family relations, cultural values, consumer choice, individual responsibility, etc. As an ideational frame, neoliberalism is a mental structure that shapes the way its holders see the world (Lakoff 2004). It is grounded in a loose set of beliefs associated with laissez-faire capitalism, such as the notion that the health of the economy depends on the ability of rational individual actors to pursue their self-interest through free exchanges in competitive markets, that competition among private actors is the main source of innovation and growth, and that government intervention undermines efficient market activities (Campbell 2001: 171; Jessop 2002: 453). As an economic theory, neoliberalism has its roots in the classical economic thinking of Adam Smith, David Ricardo and John Stuart Mill, and in the present-day writings of Milton Friedman, Friedrich Hayek and many others. Its status within the economic profession and academic circles gives it a scientific dimension, subject to the protocols of scientific enquiry such as the use of the scientific method, reproducibility, contestation and falsifiability.

As a set of policy prescriptions, neoliberalism helps actors to frame concrete solutions to economic problems. Neoliberal prescriptions range from broad guiding principles, such as the benefits of reducing state intervention in economic affairs, the advantages of promoting free trade and the desirability of low taxation, to more specific policy proposals, such as that state-owned enterprises should be privatized. Neoliberal economic thinking has its institutional home in academic departments, in states' financial agencies such as the ministry of the economy and the central bank, in advisory boards, think tanks and consultancy firms, in economic research departments within private firms and the public sector, and in international financial institutions (IFIs) such as the International Monetary Fund (IMF) and the World Bank (WB).

There is a considerable distance between the highly formalized formulations of modern neoclassical economists, which at best reach a selected number of peers, and political initiatives that seek to translate the loose principles of laissez-faire capitalism and supply-side economics into public policies. The difference is even broader between the terms of academic and technical debate on the one hand, and the terms of political debate that promotes or disqualifies economic policies in parliamentary discussions, political speeches and party manifestos. Politicians are usually hardly aware of the fine points of academic debate. They tend to borrow ideas from the most varied sources without particular concern for origins or orthodoxy, and they pragmatically adopt, adapt or discard ideas according to their own political calculations. And although inspired by economic ideas, policies are more often than not the result of messy compromises between contending interests rather than the transparent expression of a given intellectual orthodoxy. The diverse and uneven nature of neoliberal ideas means that their meaning cannot be asserted in the abstract, but can be provisionally fixed only by certain discourses, which are themselves subject to challenge and contestation. This means that neoliberalism is a relational construct, whose contested meaning is defined and redefined by the political struggles between its defenders and detractors, and to which specific policies are contingently articulated according to the history and contexts in which battles for hegemony are fought.

Fixing the meaning of neoliberalism appears to be less problematic in Latin America than in other regions of the world, as in this region neoliberal dogma has been strongly identified with the so-called Washington Consensus (WC). It is therefore important to consider in some detail what the WC was and was not about, what are its relations with neoliberalism, and how it has changed through time. In 1990, the British-born economist John Williamson edited a book entitled *Latin American Economic Adjustment: How Much Has Happened?* In this book, which included contributions from a conference convened by the Washington-based Institute for International Economics in 1989, Williamson (1990) listed a set of policy prescriptions, which in his own words embodied 'the common core of wisdom embraced by all serious economists of the time' (Williamson 1994: 18). He labelled these prescriptions 'The Washington Consensus', after the city in which the main IFIs of the modern global era, such as the IMF and the WB, as well as the US Treasury, are located. In its original formulation, the WC was a decalogue for economic development, summarized in the following headings:

- Fiscal discipline.
- A redirection of public spending priorities towards fields offering both high economic returns and the potential to improve income distribution, such as primary healthcare, primary education and infrastructure.
- Tax reform (to reduce marginal rates and broaden the tax base).
- Interest rate liberalization.
- A competitive exchange rate.
- Trade liberalization.
- Liberalization of foreign direct investment inflows.
- Privatization.
- Deregulation (in the sense of abolishing barriers to entry and exit to markets and services).
- Secure property rights.

Williamson validated the consensual nature of these principles with an appeal to the authority of both reason and history. He argued that the key to successful economic development was to emulate the market-oriented and relatively open policies preached (although not always practised) by developed nations, and that the universal benefits of these policies were proven by the successful development experience of the East Asian countries (ibid.: 12). And yet, the consensual nature of the WC principles was soon to be hotly disputed no less than among Washington insiders. On a more detailed look, under the appearance of a closed totality, the WC had a more partial, open and flexible nature than is suggested by its label. In the brief formulations that followed the headings detailed above, the WC combines highly specific recommendations (e.g. an operational deficit of no more than approximately 2 per cent of GDP) with much more flexible ones (e.g. import tariffs of between 10 per cent and 20 per cent, to be reduced over a period ranging from three to ten years), and combines general normative principles (e.g. the legal system should provide secure property rights) with programmatic ones (e.g. a unified and competitive exchange rate).

The contested issues that Williamson (ibid.: 17–18) lists in his review of the original document include some key issues of economic development, among others the desirability of maintaining capital controls, the usefulness of income policies and wage and price freezes, the proportion of GDP to be taken in taxation, and whether there is a role for industrial policy in economic development. It is worth noting that some of Williamson's contested issues, such as capital controls and industrial policy, are part of development programmes that are often presented as alternatives to neoliberalism. Perhaps more strikingly, Williamson notes that the wisdom of the Washington Consensus does not extend to addressing how to reinitiate growth after stabilization has succeeded, which was surely the key issue for Latin American economies following the 1982 debt crisis.

Williamson also disputes the identification of the WC with neoliberalism. Significantly, he notes that there is no *consensus* among economists on the best model of capitalist economy to be followed by developing nations – whether it should be the Anglo-Saxon model (the one more traditionally associated with neoliberalism), the European social market model, or Japanese-style corporate capitalism based on the responsibility of corporations to multiple stakeholders (ibid.: 18). He denounces the technocrats' 'blind faith in markets' as 'an idiosyncratic ideology', and leaves open the question of whether competitive markets and an open trade policy are good for welfare (ibid.: 16). Against those who regard the WC as a right-wing decalogue, he argues that the policies of the WC, such as the need for fiscal discipline in order to combat inflation, the redirection of public investment towards primary health and education, trade liberalization and the defence of property rights, are pro-poor, although he notes that the impact on the poor of reforms is sensitive to the ways in which those policies are implemented. He also accepts that the original formulations of the WC need to be supplemented by more comprehensive poverty reduction and income redistribution initiatives (Williamson 2000).

There is little question that under any conventional definition of neoliberalism, an economic programme that includes among its main prescriptions trade liberalization, privatization, deregulation and the liberalization of foreign direct investment should be considered part of what is conventionally known as a free market economic discourse, as it is equally true that other elements of the WC, such as the redirection of public spending towards social programmes, have a broader discursive affiliation. It is not my purpose here, however, to dwell on the true nature of the WC, whether neoliberal or otherwise. For the reasons expressed above, this attempt is ultimately meaningless, or rather its meaning is given by the political struggles to establish its ultimate significance.[1] The issue is not to determine the neoliberal nature of the WC, but to show how, under the appearance of a highly codified and prescriptive policy agenda, there was a surplus of meaning that left it open to interpretation, contestation and redefinition by friends and foes alike (and even by its own author). Some of the WC's core prescriptions, such as the importance of fiscal discipline and the benefits of low inflation, have now become part of conventional economic wisdom and have been incorporated into the policy decisions of many of those who campaigned against neoliberalism. And today, few would doubt the advantage of eliminating indexation or would argue in favour of wage and price freezes, which Williamson considered open questions at the time. A better understanding of the politics of the WC will not be achieved, however, through an analysis of its discrete policies or by giving too much respect to the privileges of authorship. Rather it is necessary to look at how the WC emerged as an attempt to address the key problems of the time, how its main institutional backers reacted to the model's failures, and how it adopted and adapted some of the key elements of its critics' agenda.

13

The historical roots of the free market reformation

The WC established itself as the hegemonic economic discourse of the era of capitalist globalization by redefining the terms of political debate against the old Keynesian–corporatist consensus. In the specific context of Latin America, the WC acquired its meaning in relation to the crisis of the dirigiste economic model based on a closed economy that dominated policy-making in the region between the late 1940s and the late 1970s, known as Import Substitution Industrialization (ISI), and its political correlate, the national popular state (Prebisch 1949; De Ipola and Portantiero 1989; Cavarozzi 1992).

For a period of time that ran from the late 1960s to well into the 1980s, no single economic narrative was able to impose its own version on the roots, nature and degree of the ISI crisis and the best alternatives to overcome it. A complex and contested process of change ensued, in which crisis narratives competed for hegemony while elements of the ISI settlement were dismantled, deepened or adapted throughout the region according to each country's political and economic realities. The dimension and direction of changes were influenced by economic factors, such as the size of each country's internal market and the availability of financial resources, for instance oil rents, that cushioned distributive struggles, and political factors, such as the capability of the state to mediate social conflicts, the degree of radicalization of the popular sectors, the economic elites' perception of the threats posed to the established order by popular mobilizations, the military's reaction to said threats, and the ability of governments to insulate themselves from corporatist pressures.

Free market ideas influenced to different degrees the economic policies promoted by technocratic sectors within the Argentinian, Chilean and, to a lesser extent, Uruguayan military regimes of the 1970s. These governments, particularly the Chilean government, represented the earlier and more radical attempts at dismantling the ISI settlement and at reorganizing the economy and society on alternative economic principles. For the military, the dismantling of the ISI model had above all a political objective. They identified the ISI model with economic stagnation, inflation and political corruption. They believed that the distributive struggles brought about by the model's inbuilt dislocations resulting from extensive state intervention favoured the growing influence of the unions and were a breeding ground for communist and other subversive organizations. Thus, ISI-corporatist-style political arrangements were discarded in favour of technocratic policy-making and the deactivation and repression of working-class organizations.

Chile's military government, the first and more radical of the free market reformers, is an early and extreme example of the two dimensions – political and economic – of the process leading to the imposition of free market reforms. Economically, it was in Chile that the survival of the capitalist system itself was perceived as more under threat from the policies of the socialist government of Salvador Allende (1970–73). As Jeffrey Frieden (1991) argued, the high degree of class conflict in Chile in the early 1970s encouraged most entrepreneurs, some of whom, particularly small and medium-size ones, would suffer to a greater or lesser extent under the impact of neoliberal reforms, to support the Pinochet regime. Radical free market reforms were imposed by Pinochet, not so much because the military were free market believers but as the best option to impose an alternative social, political and economic order that would make impossible the return of the left.

But with the exception of Pinochet's Chile, economic failures, political opposition and internal contradictions within the military prevented the Southern Cone military regimes from effectively setting up the foundations of a new political and economic order. When implemented, economic liberalization policies affected a relatively narrow range of policies, particularly centred on partial trade and financial liberalization and in the enactment of gradualist, orthodox, monetarist anti-inflationary programmes based on wage restrictions and fiscal austerity. Even in terms of core policies, results were often modest. Many formerly state-controlled prices were left to the market, but the state still intervened extensively in the allocation of resources. External tariffs were reduced substantially, but from extremely high levels. In Argentina the combination of the overvaluation of the currency and the rapid reduction of import tariffs decimated the highly protected industrial sector, particularly small and medium-size firms. A not unwelcome result of deindustrialization for the military was the weakening of the traditional Peronist working class.

But the new tariff ceilings were still considerably higher than those in the industrialized world: in Argentina the top rate of 94 per cent was cut to 35 per cent in 1981, while in Uruguay the 100 per cent top rate was lowered to 35 per cent in 1985. In contrast, in Chile top tariffs were reduced from 94 per cent in 1973 to 10 per cent in 1979 (Schamis

15

1991: 208). Moreover, in Uruguay and Argentina market liberalization policies coexisted with policies typical of ISI – for instance, in the case of Argentina, with the growth of the state-owned military-industrial sector. Overall, state reform in Argentina was strictly limited. Few state firms were privatized, as the military repeatedly vetoed economy minister José Alfredo Martínez de Hoz's proposals for reducing the state's holdings in the economy. Fiscal austerity was abandoned in the late 1970s: the 1978 World Cup brought an increase in public spending, as the military government used the event to showcase the 'new Argentina' and blocked the technocrats' attempts at cutting resources linked to the military and security apparatus (Cavarozzi 1997). The military government was not even able to keep inflation under control. In the 1980s, economic recession eroded tax revenue and the result was an upsurge in fiscal deficits, which in turn impacted on inflation, which reached 310 per cent in 1983, the last year of military rule (Lewis 1993: 561–2).

In other countries of the region, such as Brazil, Mexico and Peru, the 1970s and early 1980s saw a deepening rather than a retreat in the state-led model of economic development. Between 1950 and 1980 Brazil was Latin America's most successful developmental state.[2] Over the period, annual gross domestic product (GDP) growth averaged 7.4 per cent, or almost 4.5 per cent in per capita terms. The industrial sector grew at more than double the average rate for agriculture (8.4 per cent against 4.1 per cent). Industry employed a quarter of the labour in 1980, against 12 per cent in 1950. Exports of manufactured goods represented nearly 60 per cent of the total in 1980, against 12 per cent in 1950. By 1981 Brazil had 900 state enterprises generating 40 per cent of all investment, employing 1.4 million people and providing indirect employment to an additional 4.2 million (Baloyra 1986: 41).

Over the same period, Mexico was another highly successful case of state-led development. Under the generic name of *Desarrollo Estabilizador* (Stabilizing Development), the policies followed by successive administrations between the mid-1950s and the mid-1970s achieved high economic growth with low inflation and relatively high social inclusion, particularly in the urban sector. The model shared the broad general characteristics of ISI, but in contrast to similar economic policies elsewhere in Latin America it was characterized by strict measures to control public spending and the promotion of domestic savings and foreign investment. From 1960 to 1970, average GDP growth was 7 per cent per year, while average inflation was only 3.5 per cent. In spite of a high rate of population growth, average incomes grew steadily over the period (Enríquez 1988: 24).

Peru, a country historically characterized by a weak state and a highly divided and unequal society, was a latecomer to ISI, which effectively started in the 1960s under President Fernando Belaunde Terry (1963–68). In contrast to the Southern Cone military regimes, the so-called Revolutionary Government of the Armed Forces (RGAF), which ruled the country from 1968 to 1980, greatly expanded the state sector, particularly between 1968 and 1975, when nationalist General Juan Velasco Alvarado was in office. State-owned enterprises that accounted for just 1 per cent of GDP in 1968 were responsible for almost 20 per cent of GDP by 1975 (Wise 1994: 90). The expansion of the state was financed by borrowing, which also covered balance of payments shortfalls. But as foreign lenders became increasingly reluctant to finance the country's deficits, already in the second half of the 1970s the military government was forced to request the assistance of the IMF, which promoted an orthodox structural adjustment programme aimed at reducing state intervention.

The late 1970s and early 1980s were a period of divergent and often inconsistent economic policy-making in the region. Elements of the ISI model subsisted well into the 1980s, but the second half of the 1980s brought fundamental changes in Latin America's economic and political landscape. The 1980s debt crisis, triggered by Mexico's default on its external obligations on 13 August 1982, represented a critical juncture in the history of the region. The crisis narrowed economic policy options and played a major role in the paradigm shift that brought with it the hegemony of free market economics. By their very nature, crises provide the opportunity for radical change as dominant ideas become discredited, existing institutions lose their ability to structure society, and the political repercussions of the crisis weaken the ability of powerful actors to uphold the status quo (Olson 1982). It is at times of crisis that crisis narratives change the terms of political discourse and redefine actors' perceptions of their own interests. But crises only open the possibility for change; they do not determine its direction, shape or pace.

Democratization, economic crisis and economic reform

Free market ideas did not become hegemonic in the region until the late 1980s. The political and ideological progress of market reforms in

17

the 1980s was a protracted process, the outcome of which was the product of region-wide trends mediated by country-specific factors. But in order to understand their ascendancy we need to enquire why, of all alternative models of economic development, free market reforms were perceived as the best solution for the problems of the region. Ideologically, the ascendancy of neoliberal ideas in Latin America was part of a broader ideational shift that took place in both the developed and the developing world. Changes in the economic common sense of the time were rooted in the crisis of the Keynesian economic order in the developed world, brought about by the end of the post-war long cycle of economic expansion of the 1950s and 1960s. In the industrialized countries, economic slowdown in the 1970s was followed by an inflationary surge in the early 1980s. These economic developments established the background for the political ascendancy of the Anglo-Saxon, free market model of capitalism represented by the Reagan administration in the USA and the Thatcher government in Britain. Also, fundamental social, political and economic changes were at work in the 1980s, driving the process of capitalist globalization whose full dimensions would become apparent only in the 1990s. The adoption of neoliberal ideas in Latin America, however, cannot be understood as the unmediated effect of the free market drive that originated in the developed world. Nor can it be understood as the forced imposition of international financial organizations, such as the IMF and the WB, on helpless national governments. This claim does not amount to denying the influence of powerful international actors, be they the US government, private investors or the multilateral financial agencies, whose influence will be discussed in more detail in Chapter 2. It is also not meant to deny that financial constraints resulting from the debt crisis and the subsequent strengthening of the IMF and the WB's power as lenders of last resort weighed heavily on the Latin American governments' decisions. Rather, it is to claim that the adoption of free market reforms was a decision taken by the governments of the region, which, with the exception of Chile and the partial exception of Mexico, were democratically elected, for their own political considerations, including an assessment of the political costs and benefits to be drawn from the imposition of the reforms.

The ascendancy of free market ideas in the 1980s cannot be separated from the process of democratization that took place over the same period. This book argues that free market economics, liberal democracy and regional integration came to define the broader meaning of the WC in the 1990s. The collapse of the Soviet bloc in the late 1980s contributed to make democracy safe for capitalism by reassuring the right that there would be no new 'communist threats' in the western hemisphere and making the left revise its views on the feasibility and desirability of wholesale alternatives to capitalism. But the view that free market economics and political democracy go hand in hand was not prevalent in the early 1980s, during which, if anything, democracy and free market economics were regarded as incompatible. Although in most countries of the region democratization took place against the background of severe economic crises, the economic debate was not central to transitions to democracy, a process that was dominated by issues such as the human rights abuses of the military regimes and the need to set up forms of political representation that would guarantee democratic governability. Democracy rather than economic reform was regarded as the foundation for a better and more prosperous society. The belief in democracy as a solution for the countries' economic problems was encapsulated by the claim by President Raúl Alfonsín of Argentina during the 1983 electoral campaign that 'democracy feeds, cures and educates' (Cavarozzi 2004: 210).

To the extent that economic issues were part of the public debate, particularly in the Southern Cone, free market economics were associated with the economic policies of the right-wing military regimes of the 1970s. As such they were identified with attempts at imposing liberalizing economic reforms through state terror and repression. In the countries in which these attempts had badly failed, as was the case in Argentina and to a lesser extent in Uruguay, pro-market reforms were seen as part of an authoritarian past that could not, and should not, be repeated under conditions of democracy. More broadly, orthodox stabilization programmes raised familiar concerns that the political impact of these packages could potentially destabilize fragile democracies. Economic liberalization was seen as having a conservative bias that favoured capital at the expense of labour, multinational interests at the expense of domestic industry, and economic stability over economic growth (Armijo and Faucher 2002: 3). Again quoting President Alfonsín:

> Those who talk about the reorganisation of the economy, who say
> that the market should prevail, that prices, salaries and the currency

exchange should be liberalised; they are at least politically irresponsible because they intend to put a time bomb on democracy. (*El Bimestre*, 10, p. 98, quoted in Barros 2002: 104)

The initial economic diagnosis of Argentina's first democratically elected government after more than seven years of military dictatorship was that in spite of the current problems the country's economy was basically sound and did not require structural reforms. Rather, it was thought that the crisis had been brought about by the politics and policies of the military regime ('*El Proceso de Reorganización Nacional*'), particularly by the liberalizing and orthodox anti-inflationary policies of the regime's economics minister, José Martínez de Hoz. In the first years of the new democratic administration of President Alfonsín (1983–89), the reduction of inflation was a goal to be achieved within a broader strategy that effectively assigned higher priority to improving income distribution and to the restoration of economic growth. Answering his critics, President Alfonsín denounced 'the technocrats of failure [...] who get scared and claim that these goals [fighting inflation, increasing real wages and promoting economic growth] are incompatible with each other' and expressed confidence that his government would rise to the challenge (*El Bimestre*, 13, p. 54, cited in ibid.: 142). Concerning the country's external obligations, the government's preferred option was that the refinancing of debt should be collectively negotiated by all Latin American nations on the basis of rejecting any agreement that could have recessionary effects (Camou 1997).

In Brazil the political crisis of the military regime was accelerated by faltering economic growth between 1978 and 1980, and economic recession between 1981 and 1983. The return to democracy in 1984 was greeted with expectations of social and economic change. But the critique of the military regime's economic model was centred on its gross economic inequality and high unemployment, and on the military governments' inability, particularly since the late 1970s, to control inflation without affecting economic growth, rather than on the role of the state in economic affairs or the high levels of economic protectionism. The economic and social chapters of the 1988 constitution illustrate the enduring influence of developmentalist ideas. The new constitution, which was drafted through a highly participatory process, sanctioned state monopolies in the oil and telecommunications sectors and placed restrictions on foreign investment in mineral extraction, health, telecommunications and oil exploration and refining. The constitution also established a generous system of social security and labour rights under the principle of universal coverage. (80s)

In a region that was going through a decade of negative economic growth per capita, the Peruvian economy was one of the worst performers. Between 1976 and 1989 economic growth averaged only 1 per cent annually, with per capita domestic product declining for half of that period. In the early 1990s real average wages had shrunk to 40 per cent of their 1980 level (Mauceri 1995: 11). Attempts by the conservative second administration of President Belaunde Terry (1980–85) to promote fiscal adjustment, liberalize the economy, stimulate private investment and reduce the number of state-owned enterprises made little progress, as the government lacked the political capital necessary to drive through the reforms. As the unions resisted the government's liberalizing attempts, politics became increasingly polarized, with widespread social unrest (Crabtree 1998). Political radicalization took an extreme turn with the emergence of the Shining Path (Sendero Luminoso) armed organization that sought to overthrow the political order and instal a Maoist-inspired regime. President Belaunde Terry's successor, Alan García (1985–90), promoted a return to the politics and policies of state interventionism and heterodox anti-inflationary packages. The new government's economic programme was based on the assumption that the IMF programmes had misunderstood the Peruvian economy's problems and that, as a result, they had made the economic situation worse (Stallings 1992: 75). In contrast to the IMF's monetarist orthodoxy, the government assumed that inflation was not caused by fiscal deficits but by production bottlenecks that created scarcity. To remedy the problem, President García, who had inherited an economy suffering from inflation of over 200 per cent, pursued stabilization through expansionary means. Shortly after assuming office his government instituted the so-called 'Inti development plan', which consisted of a price freeze, increases in wages and public spending, tax cuts, and the pegging of the exchange rate. In order to finance extra spending, payments on foreign debt interest were reduced unilaterally to approximately 10 per cent of exports (Edwards 1989: 184). The success of the plan was short lived, as high inflation soon turned into hyperinflation. Peru was cut off from foreign loans, and business withheld investment. The result was stagflation, the combination of economic recession, scarcity and hyperinflation. By the time García left the presidency in 1990, his heterodox economic experiment was a dismal failure (Weyland 1999: 178).

The economic crisis of Peru was paralleled by that of Bolivia. One of the early democratizing countries in the region, Bolivia returned to constitutional rule in 1982 when Hernán Siles Suazo was elected as president. Siles headed a left-of-centre administration led by the Unidad Democrática y Popular (UDP) party, a precarious alliance of left and left-of-centre political parties that included Siles's own party, the Movimiento Nacionalista Revolucionario de Izquierda (MNRI), the Movimiento de Izquierda Revolucionaria (MIR) headed by Vice-President Jaime Paz Zamora, and the Communist Party of Bolivia (PCB). His government (1982–85) was internally divided, it had no majority in Congress, and suffered the opposition of the militant Confederación Obrera Boliviana (COB), the country's powerful umbrella union organization. Attempts to stabilize the dire economic situation inherited from the military-narco dictatorship of General Luis García Meza (1980–81) through a mixture of heterodox economic packages and watered-down agreements with the IMF failed, as much because of the government's political weaknesses as owing to the policies' flawed economic principles and inconsistent implementation. Affected by a mixture of economic mismanagement, falling tin prices and the weight of the external debt, GDP shrank by a cumulative 10.5 per cent between 1982 and 1985. Over the same period inflation rose from an annual average of 185 per cent in 1982 to 11,800 per cent in 1984, while the public sector deficit reached 22.9 per cent of GDP in 1984 (Smith et al. 1994: 104). The collapse of political and economic order prompted Congress to call early presidential and parliamentary elections in 1985, which resulted in the election of the Movimiento Nacional Revolucionario (MNR) leader, Víctor Paz Estenssoro, who promptly introduced one of the earliest and most radical free market packages in the region.

Political order, economic crises and the new economic narrative

The terms of economic discourse started to change in the second half of the decade. By then it had become increasingly evident that heterodox attempts at controlling inflation and restoring economic growth while increasing real wages and maintaining public spending were condemned to failure. The depth of the economic crisis of the late 1980s in Latin

America can only be compared to that of the 1930s, and arguably it was in many ways more devastating. During the 1980s, GDP per capita for the region dropped almost 10 per cent, and by 1990 the average annual inflation rate for the region had reached over 1,000 per cent (CEPAL 1990: 26–7). High inflation and hyperinflation produced deep social dislocations. As Nobel Prize winner for Economics John Hicks has pointed out, money is not just a device, an M1 or M2 or an equation, but is essentially one of the most notable of human institutions.[3] As such, it is more than just a measure of value: it is one of the most crucial elements of a national identity. The acceleration in the speed of circulation of money associated with hyperinflation deeply affects notions of social time and undermines the institutionalization of collective and individual practices. In the countries affected by hyperinflation, incomes and jobs were obliterated. State revenue fell drastically, resulting in deep cuts in public sector wages and public services. More fundamentally, the economy lost its institutional moorings in the national currency, state institutions and the tax system (Panizza 2005b: 11). The breakdown in social order, the debasing of local currencies and the fall in tax revenue meant that the state lost the ability to hold society together.

In Argentina, Bolivia, Brazil and Peru, the failure of heterodox economic programmes to prevent the escalation of inflation into hyperinflation turned what was originally an economic crisis into a wider question of social order. The breakdown of the economic order translated in these countries into crises of the political order, understood as the failure of the state to regulate social relations, as the loss of the political system's capacity to represent its citizens, and as a threat to political stability posed by mass street protests against the economic crises. The gravity of the situation was summed up in the words of President Alfonsín in a speech in 1985: 'If the economic problem is not solved, the political life of the Nation is at serious risk.'[4] In a similar vein, in a speech dated 28 February 1986, President José Sarney of Brazil summed up the impact of inflation on Brazilian society by stating: 'Inflation is society's worst enemy,' and further added: 'Inflation has become people's main enemy' (cited in Pinto 1989: 76).

Given the depth of the economic crisis of the 1980s, it is not surprising that, as in the 1930s, the crisis led to changes not just in the model of economic development but also, more fundamentally, in the ways of looking at the history of the region. Crucially, the shape and direction of these changes became part of the political struggles for the construction of alternative crisis narratives. As happens with any crisis, the 1980s crisis meant that things could not go on as before. But what was meant by 'before' and 'after' and where the dividing line between the two should be traced was a matter for ideological struggles and political contestation. The political relevance of these ideological struggles was that by assigning responsibility for the crisis to different economic and political factors, the reinterpretation of the history of Latin America had a significant bearing on the politics of the present.

As a part of these ideological struggles, the crisis was construed as both 'new' and 'old': new, because it was interpreted as a product of the specific economic conditions of the 1980s; old, because it was also seen as the manifestation of deeper, long-term, economic and political factors affecting the Latin American countries.[5] In the Southern Cone, the crisis was initially framed by the new democratically elected governments as the legacy of the region's military regimes' failed attempts at dismantling the old interventionist state and replacing it with an economically liberal and politically authoritarian one (O'Donnell 1981). In other countries that had not experienced a right-wing military dictatorship – for instance, Peru under the García administration – the crisis was construed as the consequence of an unfair and illegitimate debt imposed on the people by spurious economic interests. But these interpretations of the origins and nature of the crisis soon became politically untenable, as it became evident that the social dislocations produced by hyperinflation and economic recession could not be materially overcome or symbolically repaired by the policies and discourses of ISI. Instead, the crisis made possible the emergence of new interpretative frameworks that sought to make sense of it, and to advance solutions for the reconstruction of social order.

For the organic intellectuals (Gramsci 1971) of the free market reformation, the threat that hyperinflation posed to the political order became part of a broader narrative that linked politics and economics to a more general crisis of social order. Concerning the economy, the new narrative moved decisively away from the developmentalist discourse that still framed the policies of the Alfonsín, Sarney and García administrations. Instead, free marketeers argued that hyperinflation was rooted in the structural problems of the ISI model. This view was in line with the monetarists' early critique of the ISI's failures of the 1960s (Hirschman 1981; Helwege 1994: 147). But it was now argued that the 1980s crisis could not be solved by orthodox IMF-inspired fiscal adjustment packages alone. Thus, monetarism, the narrow economic orthodoxy of the 1970s centred on combating inflation through orthodox fiscal and monetary policies, broadened into a much wider economic and political reform agenda. It was claimed that without structural reforms that would significantly alter relations between states and markets, there could be no end to hyperinflation and no resumption of economic growth. In an ironic twist, the heirs of the orthodox economists who had confronted ISI's 'structuralists' in the 1970s turned into the new structuralists, but the structural reforms they advocated were opposite in nature to those favoured in the 1960s by the structuralists of national-popular ISI persuasion.

Politically, the failure of the new democratic governments to secure economic order delegitimized incumbents and undermined relations of representation between citizens and their political representatives. By 1987, President Alfonsín had already changed the terms of his political discourse. Confronted with the failure of the heterodox Austral anti-inflationary plan, the Argentinian government performed a volte-face and sought to implement some of the liberalizing economic policies that it had denounced in the past as a danger to the democratic order. In the words of Alfonsín's economics minister, Juan V. Sourrouille, the government's new economic programme was directed 'against the populist and *facilista* [easy option] [economic] model that was holding up the development of the country' (*El Bimestre*, 34, pp. 36–7, cited in Barros 2002: 143). The government's change of economic strategy was, however, too little and too late to stabilize the country's polity and economy. With an administration depleted of political capital and economic credibility, the reforms lacked political support and inflation spiralled out of control. In the 1989 presidential election the candidate of the ruling Radical Party, Eduardo Angeloz, was heavily defeated by the Justicialista (Peronist) candidate Carlos Menem. As riots and protests against the economic chaos threatened social order, President Alfonsín, who had come to power as the embodiment of Argentina's democratic hopes, was forced to hand over office early to his elected successor, Carlos Menem.

Elsewhere in Latin America, the failure of heterodox stabilization plans had the effect of discrediting incumbents and opening the way for free market reformers. In Brazil, the high popular expectations that in 1985 greeted the birth of the so-called 'New Republic' that succeeded the military dictatorship soon foundered in view of the failure of President José Sarney's heterodox economic policies. In 1989 a political outsider, Fernando Collor de Mello, who campaigned on an anti-corruption, anti-establishment, pro-economic modernization platform, beat the candidate of the left-wing Partido dos Trabalhadores (PT, the Workers' Party), Luiz Inácio Lula da Silva, to become Brazil's first democratically elected president in twenty-nine years. President Collor's economic programme combined yet another heterodox anti-inflationary plan, the so-called *Plano Collor*, which included the freezing of all bank accounts over 50,000 cruzeiros (about US$1,300) for a period of eighteen months, with the start of what was to be an uneven and protracted process of privatization and economic liberalization.

In Mexico, the fallout from the debt crisis did not undermine the economic and political order to the extent that it did in Argentina, Brazil, Bolivia or Peru. Rather it led to a gradual process of economic reform that started under President Miguel de la Madrid (1982–88). After 1983, the government eliminated import licence requirements, official import prices and quantitative restrictions. Stabilization measures adopted in 1983 were largely abandoned in 1984, but the oil crisis of 1985–86 made the status quo unsustainable (Philip 1993). In spite of the de la Madrid administration's economic failures, the ruling PRI maintained control of the political order by appealing to traditional corporatist-style agreements to secure political and economic stability. In 1986 Mexico acceded to the General Agreement on Tariffs and Trade (GATT), now the World Trade Organization (WTO) (Stallings 1992: 80), and in 1987 it agreed to a major liberalization of bilateral trade relations with the United States. Also in 1987, the government negotiated a new programme of stabilization and reform with the unions and business organizations. While the PRI regime survived the crisis, popular discontent with the economic situation and opposition to de la Madrid's reforms resulted in splits within the PRI and in the first real challenge to the PRI's hegemony by the left-of-centre presidential candidate, Cuauthemoc Cárdenas, in the 1988 election. Although the PRI's candidate, Carlos Salinas de Gortari, was declared the winner of the election by a narrow margin, accusations of electoral fraud further eroded the regime's legitimacy and initiated a process of broader political and economic change that would lead to a transition to democracy in the 1990s.

The failure of the new democratic administrations of the 1980s to live up to the promises of a better life and, crucially, to uphold economic order brought about a change in the relations between democracy and free market economic policies. After being perceived as the legacy of the 1970s military regimes and as a threat to democracy, free market economics now offered embattled democratic governments a clear diagnosis of the economic problems of the time and an agenda for the restoration of political and economic order. Denunciations by economic liberals of the inefficiencies of ISI resonated with a population that was weary of corruption and an arbitrary, predatory and inefficient state. This new political context of economic liberalism and mistrust of the state, and ultimately of politics, resonated with popular disillusionment with the failed promises of a better life under democracy. Free market reforms were presented as a forward-looking programme of modernization that embodied 'change', a key political signifier at times of crisis.

A seminal book at the time, Hernando de Soto's (1989 [1986]) *El Otro Sendero* (The Other Path), popularized the crisis narrative that was formulated in a more technocratic key by neoliberal economists. De Soto argued that in Latin America the true capitalists were not the wealthy entrepreneurs but the self-employed poor who were making a living in the informal sector. He painted an image of the poor (street vendors, van and taxi drivers, small traders) as the unsung heroes of a subterranean free market economy. Holding down these popular entrepreneurs was a privileged political and economic elite that benefited from state protectionism and from a legal system set up to perpetuate their social privileges and economic rents. Far from protecting the poor from the dangers of the market, the state was an instrument for their political and economic exclusion at the hands of the business elite. He labelled this undemocratic and unfair system as *mercantilist*, rather than capitalist. As one of the co-authors of *El Otro Sendero* put it in a later article celebrating the success of free market reforms in the region:

> Private property, free enterprise, and competition, as inherent rights of the poorest among the poor, have been vindicated. The individualistic ethic is shown to have existed in the Latin American in the past: The law does not limit power, it only reflects it; and the state is a means of oppression of all citizens. (Ghersi 1997: 101)

The case of Chile is illustrative of the ideational shift that took place in Latin America in the late 1980s and early 1990s. Under the dictatorship of Augusto Pinochet, Chile was the trailblazer in the introduction of free market reforms as a mean to solve a crisis of order, which in very different degrees and in different political contexts would affect other countries of the region in the 1980s. But even when in the late 1970s and early 1980s the Chilean economy was the fastest-growing economy in the region, its politics were out of step with the rest of Latin America as the advance of democracy dominated the political landscape of the region. Critics of Pinochet's neoliberal policies argued that these policies could be introduced only through force and repression, and noted the high social costs of Chile's conversion to neoliberalism. The Chilean economy was seriously affected by the 1982 crisis, which was taken as confirmation that neoliberal economic policies had failed even in that country. As the Chilean economy recovered strongly from its 1982 slump in the second half of the 1980s, however, and the democratic opposition committed itself to largely follow the free market policies of the dictatorship in the run-up to the 1989 election, Chile's economic success could not simply be dismissed as just an authoritarian imposition. And while critics of neoliberalism continued to stress the increase in inequality brought by free market economics to Chilean society, supporters of the free market reformation would present Chile as an example to follow under democracy.

The failure of the heterodox anti-inflationary plans of the 1980s set up the conditions for the emergence of new forms of political representation centred on leaders who represented a break with the past and were prepared to take decisive action to impose radical economic reform. By the early 1990s, free market economic reforms had largely lost their historical association with the politics of the military regimes of the Southern Cone of the 1970s, and became instead articulated to new political discourses. Prominent among these was that of the 'politics of anti-politics' enunciated in different ideological codes by free market technocrats and a new generation of populist leaders alike. In this new narrative, the failure of incumbent governments (most of them first- or second-generation post-military regime democratic governments) became part of a long historical period of failure, which paradoxically bound together the embattled democratic governments and the military regimes that preceded them as upholders of an outdated 'populist' economic model.

Within this new political context, economic liberalism's mistrust of the state and ultimately of politics resounded with popular disillusion-ment with the status quo. Neoliberalism's promise of a better future was upheld against a tired and failed interventionist model that, allegedly, had produced only misery and corruption. Instead, the new language of choice, competition, decentralization and the empowerment of civil society offered the prospect of a more efficient economy and a more accountable democracy. Economic liberalization connected with the spirit of the time, in which the Anglo-Saxon economic model was in the ascendancy, as the USA and Britain were presented as the most successful economies in the developed world, and in which the failure of socialism was regarded as evidence that there was only one road to global modernity: free market capitalism.

Promoting this vision of the future divide were a new type of forward-looking, 'can do' political leaders best represented by Carlos Menem in Argentina, Alberto Fujimori in Peru and Fernando Collor de Mello in Brazil. Few among these leaders were true believers in free market economics, or campaigned on a free market platform. Some of them, particularly Menem and Fujimori, originally presented themselves as alternatives to candidates more identified with free market economics. But it would be a mistake to regard their electoral victories as a mandate against reform. Menem did not win because he advocated a specific set of economic policies, but because he told the Argentinian people '*síganme, que no los voy a desfraudar*', 'follow me, as I will not let you down' (Gantman 2003: 263). The people believed him and gave him an enabling mandate to exercise his leadership. In doing so, these new leaders adopted free market reforms because they represented a set of clear and relatively simple-to-enact policy prescriptions with which to address the most pressing problem of the time: the restoration of political and economic order.

Conclusion

The conjunction of transition to democracy with the economic crisis of the 1980s overdetermined relations between the politics and the econom-ics of the period. The re-signification of the crisis by the propagandists of free market economics as the manifestation of the long-term failure of an entire model of economic development (ISI) had important political implications. The new political frontier set up by the free market crisis narrative between economic populism and free market economics was

29

very different from the one that dominated transition to democracy at the beginning of the decade, namely the divide between authoritarianism and democracy. As Woods (2006: 69) has put it:

> In the 1980s the Washington Consensus offered a simple, intuitively appealing set of ideas and a vision of future competitiveness and wealth. In many ways this mindset fulfilled the role of an ideology in attributing blame and letting off steam, creating morale and optimism about the future, engendering solidarity or a particular identity and permitting advocacy. Old nationalist identities and solidarity were replaced with a new identity of entrepreneurialism, modernisation and integration to the world economy. Specific economic goals were prioritised and policies advocated. Neoliberal ideas offered not just a clear way to respond to a crisis but a whole new social language and rationale for reform.

If a credible crisis narrative and decisive political leadership were necessary, the conditions of the radical reform process, narratives and leadership alone were not sufficient to explain the hegemony of free market economics. Economic ideas crystallize into policy-making decisions in response to deeply felt political demands that require the backing of powerful interests in order to be addressed. In the late 1980s and early 1990s, free market reforms had the backing of a powerful coalition of interests, comprising the technocratic elite, the business sector and the international financial community. Moreover, in a democracy, elite support alone is not enough to secure the success of a reform process. An element of popular consent is necessary, even in largely top-down processes of reform. The following chapters look at the role of international and domestic actors in the process of reform.

2 | The organic intellectuals of the Washington Consensus

The power of international financial institutions

A common outcome of the debt crisis throughout Latin America was the increase in the power and influence of international financial institutions (IFIs), particularly the International Monetary Fund (IMF) and the World Bank (WB), which was greatly diminished during the years of easy private credit of the late 1970s.[1] As private sector lending dried up following Mexico's default in 1982, the IMF turned from its traditional role of lender of last resort to the only available source of external financial assistance and became the leading agency in the management of the crisis. As part of this process, the IMF went through a fundamental transformation from its traditional role of providing short-term funding to governments experiencing balance of payments problems to assuming a key role in restructuring the countries' foreign debts, conditioning financial assistance to the promotion of structural reforms along free market principles. Similarly, the WB changed its role from lending money for developing projects in areas such as physical infrastructure (road building, agricultural projects, etc.) to the promotion of structural reforms that involved fundamental changes in economic policy. As a result of these role changes, the IMF and the WB's relations with the countries of Latin America became highly politicized and open to the charge that unaccountable multilateral institutions were forcing democratically elected governments to adopt policies that hurt the poor and privileged the interests of foreign companies and foreign banks over the welfare of the people. We need to examine these allegations in some detail.

There is little doubt that in the aftermath of the debt crisis the IMF's position as overseer of relations between indebted Latin American countries and international financial lenders significantly increased the Fund's influence over the countries of the region. It is also the case that the IMF and the WB's voting systems reflect the power and interests of their larger shareholders, particularly the US, Japan and western European governments, and that the Fund and the WB's relations with developing countries crystallize an unequal international power structure. A better understanding of the nature and limits of the IFIs' influence requires, however, an analysis of the nature of their power, of the institutions' changing goals and objectives, of the reasons for which these institutions became the guardians of the free market reformation, and of the mechanisms by which the IFIs sought to promote free market reforms.

Defenders of the IMF point out that strictly speaking the Fund has no real power to impose policy (Edwards 1989), and that its authority derives from the free consent of its member nations within the legally binding rules of its charter. Furthermore, the IMF's economic programmes are voluntary undertakings agreed by borrowing governments as outlined in the letters of intention they submit to the Fund's authorities. Arguably, the conditions imposed by the Fund as part of its negotiations with borrowing countries are nothing more than would be required from any prudent lender with responsibility to its shareholders, which, in the case of the IMF, derive from the member countries' reciprocal obligations as partners in the regulatory regime administered by the institution.

The IMF has no compulsory power to force countries to comply with the economic programmes agreed with the organization. As will be shown in the next sections, a very high proportion of these programmes are not implemented or are only partially implemented, with little by way of negative consequences for the borrowing nations. The IMF authorities are also right in stressing the voluntary nature of the relationship between the Fund and borrowing countries, and in highlighting the legitimacy bestowed to the Fund's actions by the borrowers' consent. Moreover, even if the USA and the Western industrial nations have a controlling share of the votes in the IMF's board, it does not automatically follow that the IMF would necessarily serve their interests or that everyone that gains at the expense of others is dominating the other part.

The nature of the IMF's relations with borrowing nations is not, however, exhausted by references to consent and legitimacy. To have power over others is more than just the ability to force somebody to do something backed by the use of force or by the threat to use force. Power is an asymmetrical relation in which the dominant actor can secure the compliance of the dominated one not just by force but also through its ability to set the agenda and manipulate preferences (Lukes 2005). As is shown in the next sections, the IFIs were highly influential in setting the agenda of economic reform in Latin America in the late

1980s and early 1990s. It could also be argued that through their superior technical knowledge and other forms of influence, the IFIs shaped the preferences of borrowing countries to extract consent for policies that were not necessarily in those countries' best interests. The manipulation of preferences (Lukes's third dimension of power) takes us, however, to the uncertain terrain of actors' values, preferences and interests, and raises the difficult issue of how to identify an actor's 'true interests'. If we discard the definition of interests in terms of false consciousness, 'objective' class attribution or – in the case of the borrowing nations – of the national interest, there is no easy answer to this question. We can, however, seek to understand how interests are formed. Actors' interests are at least partly exogenously defined by their place in society: the interests actors defend are at least partially constructed by the institutions that determine distributions of gains and losses. Given that institutional rules and procedures are not neutral, this would almost certainly mean that those who control institutions will seek to define the interests these institutions shape (Dowding 2006: 141). If this is the case, the question is then how the interests of those who control the IMF shape the Fund's policies towards borrowing countries.

Questions about the legitimacy of those who control the IFIs to impose their preferences on other members, about who defines the institutions' rules and procedures, and about how can we determine the winners and losers from its policy decisions also become relevant. The restrictions placed by the IMF on sovereign nations' policy-making autonomy can be legitimized in terms of the higher costs of following alternative policies and by the benefits that can be obtained from the IMF monetary regime as a whole (Thirkell-White 2005: 39). This in turn, however, raises questions about the cost–benefit calculation of the IMF's programmes and about their distributional impact. The issue for our purpose is whether the IFIs' relations with the countries of Latin America were so distorted by the disparity of economic alternatives on offer as to be a relation of domination rather than a consensual one.

The changing role of the World Bank and the International Monetary Fund

The IMF and the WB are public institutions created not to advance the interest of foreign banks or to promote global capitalism, but to step in where markets fail (Woods 2006). By the very nature of its mandate, the IMF is expected to deal with short-term economic problems rather than with long-term economic change. As such, the Fund did not take into consideration issues of economic development or, less so, of poverty alleviation. Although the role of the IMF began to change following the shift to floating exchange rates in the early 1970s, the catalyst for a more radical change in the Fund's role and outlook was the 1982 Mexican debt crisis. The crisis represented a systemic threat to international commercial banks heavily exposed in Latin America, and a potentially destabilizing threat to the region's economic and political order. In assuming a central role in managing and coordinating the markets' response to the crisis, the Fund changed its mode of intervention, from helping countries with short-term balance-of-payments problems to a much more comprehensive policy-making role in economic development. This shift, however, did not take place immediately after the crisis, but developed through the 1980s as the shortcomings of the IMF's traditional short-term approach to solving financial crises became more apparent and the indebted countries' resumption of economic growth became the priority for both the IMF and the World Bank.

The 1982 debt crisis was initially addressed by the Fund on a case-by-case basis in which financial support was provided to countries willing to adjust their economies according to the IMF's traditional stabilization package of tightening monetary, fiscal and wage policies, while bringing exchange rates to competitive levels. But even allowing for the recessive effects of the IMF's stabilization packages, this was not a traditional crisis that could be solved through the Fund's usual policy prescriptions. High interest rates, high inflation, deep economic recessions, a hostile global economic environment and massive debt repayments meant that indebted countries were in no condition to restart economic growth while continuing to meet their debt obligations (ibid.).

By the mid-1980s, the evident failure of the Fund's strategy to pull countries out of their debt-cum-recession mire prompted multilateral agencies to incorporate economic growth into the stabilization agenda, which materialized in the so-called growth-oriented structural reforms (Pender 2001). As happened with past IMF initiatives, the US government was the leading force behind this change in strategy. In a speech in Seoul, Korea, on 6 October 1985, the then US Secretary of the Treasury, James Baker III, suggested that the IMF, in conjunction with the World Bank, should play a central role in promoting the adoption by debtors of market-oriented policies for growth. The goal of the new plan was the promotion of 'comprehensive macroeconomic and structural policies to promote growth and balance of payments adjustment and to reduce inflation' (Boughton 2001: 417). Debtors were now required to embark on new, deeper, 'structural adjustment' policies, emphasizing supply-side reforms rather than purely demand-side measures. Private banks would in turn support the new policies with fresh lending, amounting to around US$20 billion over three years.

The Baker plan, as the new strategy came to be known, allowed private banks to reduce their debt exposure to the region but failed to restore economic growth. Debtor countries continued to be burdened by debt payments incompatible with the resumption of growth, particularly as private banks failed to provide new lending on any significant scale. In light of the shortcomings of the Baker plan, in 1989 the US Secretary to the Treasury, Nicholas Brady, advanced a new initiative that incorporated a powerful incentive for the implementation of market liberalization reforms. The so-called Brady plan included debt buy-backs and the replacement of existing bank loans with bond swaps, which would reduce the countries' overall debt liability. Debt reduction was to be conditioned to the implementation of structural reforms, such as the liberalization of prices, the privatization of state enterprises and the simplification of economic regulations.

The WB played a leading intellectual and financial role in the promotion of the new growth strategy throughout Latin America. The Bank's main financial instrument for the advancement of the free market agenda was its Structural Adjustment Loans (SALs). This type of loan was first used in the 1980s in response to balance-of-payments problems of developing countries, and to what the Bank's authorities perceived as policy weaknesses in the borrowing countries. They represented a significant change from the Bank's traditional project lending for infrastructure, and the move closely aligned the Bank's lending goals with the IMF's policies.[2] The loans' conditions combined macroeconomic and microeconomic elements based on an agenda of economic stabilization and the restoration of economic growth. Macroeconomic policies included measures to limit money and credit growth, reduce the fiscal deficit and implement a real devaluation. The broadening and deepening of the WB's agenda in the second half of the 1980s in line with free market reforms were even more significant in the microeconomic reform agenda.

Here, changes involved tax reform, the promotion of economic opening by reducing export taxes and removing import quotas, and institutional reforms to eliminate public sector inefficiencies.

Imposition, persuasion and consent

As a result of the broadening of their remit in the late 1980s and 1990s, the IMF and the WB, together with the domestic technocrats who shared their views, became the collective 'organic intellectuals' of the reform process (Gramsci 1971).[3] The formal mechanism through which the IMF exercised its influence was conditionality, an exchange of policy changes for external financing (Kahler 1992: 89). The rationale for imposing conditions to borrowing countries is that the IMF lends money to its member countries to be used in accordance with the Fund's goals as determined in its mandate. The Fund must also ensure that the loans are repaid promptly in order to be able to assist other member countries in time of need. To ensure that these conditions are fulfilled, it is in principle a legitimate part of the Fund's purpose to attach conditions to its lending, particularly as, in the Fund's view, conditions would merely be a statement of the policies that a deficit country should adopt in any case (Thirkell-White 2005: 21–2). The legitimacy of the IMF's conditionality mechanism has, however, been challenged on three grounds: the way in which conditions are imposed, their content, and the interests they serve. The former managing director of the IMF, Michel Camdessus, claimed that the IMF does not *impose* conditions on governments, arguing that if programmes were to be imposed from the outside their chances of being implemented would be minimal (Camdessus 1993: 51). Camdessus's claim is formally true, as conditions are agreed following a process of negotiations between IMF representatives and the government of the borrowing country. And yet it would be difficult to explain the parallel and simultaneous drive towards privatization and liberalization of the late 1980s without taking into account the asymmetry of resources and the dearth of alternatives that the Latin American countries faced if they refused to agree to the IMF's policy prescriptions. This unbalanced relationship placed the Fund in a clearly dominant position (Stallings 1992).

An acknowledgement of the IFIs' power to promote the reform agenda does not amount, however, to claiming that the IFIs' influence was *the only or even the main cause* of the reforms, and tells us nothing about the borrowing countries' governments' attitudes towards the reforms. The IFIs' influence varied considerably depending on the international financial context, the issue area, the political salience of the policy options, the condition of the national economy in question, and the governments' institutional characteristics, including the technical capacity of government officials to negotiate with IMF and WB technocrats. Leverage, the direct use of power with a promise of reward (or the threat of punishment) for carrying out (or not) a desired policy, is most effective when resources are scarce, creditors are unified, and the incentives they offer are credible, all of which conditions were present in the late 1980s. Conditionality was at its strongest on issues of debt service in the early 1980s, and shifted towards structural reform in the late years of the decade. The IFIs' influence was also stronger in the case of smaller countries and those with limited state capabilities (Kahler 1992: 98; Stallings 1992: 55).

To the IFIs' hard power grounded on financial asymmetry and the use of conditionality should be added the soft power of policy learning and the construction of ideological consensus (Nye 1990). IFIs regarded the educating of governments and transforming the parameters of domestic policy debate by furthering and entrenching ideas about economic policy as part of their role (Woods 2006: 99). External and internal consensus would most likely result in a more robust implementation of the free market reforms, and minimize internal opposition on the grounds that they were the result of an external imposition. Through their combined influence, hard and soft power contributed to the redefinition of domestic actors' preferences in accordance with the IFIs' policy prescriptions. The IFIs had significant symbolic as well as material resources with which to build up consensus on the rightfulness of their policies. Many technocrats were appointed to top positions within the national governments' financial agencies after having worked in the World Bank and the IMF, with the purpose of negotiating with their former colleagues (Haggard and Kaufman 1992a: 13). The IFIs' research departments produce large quantities of position papers, technical reports and policy documents that give intellectual substance to the agencies' policies. Both the IMF and the WB encourage policy dialogue between their staff and economists from borrowing countries. Dialogue brings together epistemic communities (Haas 1989) of like-minded international and domestic technocrats, most of whom have already shared an intellectual framing that privileges neoclassical ideas over alternative approaches. National and international economic think tanks elaborated and systematized these agreements in the new economic agenda crystallized in the Washington Consensus.

While technocrats often occupy key bureaucratic positions within the governments' economic agencies, it is necessary for the transition from elite consensus to policy reform to persuade the technocrats' principals (normally the president) to adopt the IFIs' economic vision and empower technocrats to enact the reforms. This is more likely to happen at times of economic crisis and uncertainty, in which politicians are unlikely to have strong ideological preferences about a specific course of action but are willing to adopt any given policy that in their perception has a significant chance of solving the crisis. Negotiations on the crisis-solving policy packages are usually conducted in a highly elitist environment, typically including a technical delegation from the IMF and domestic technocrats embedded in the financial agencies of the state (ministry of the economy and the central bank). Given the narrow circle of participants in these discussions and the closed nature of the meetings, it is difficult to back up the theoretical discussion on the respective weight of leverage and consensus on policy decisions with empirical accounts of the negotiating process. The cases of Peru, Venezuela, the Dominican Republic, Bolivia and Mexico provide good examples of the mix of coercion and consent that characterizes the ambiguous political games that are often played by key actors in the negotiating process.

Alberto Fujimori of Peru and Carlos Andrés Pérez of Venezuela campaigned for the presidency of their countries in 1990 and 1988 respectively on political platforms that took a distance from the free market orthodoxy of the time, only to implement shock liberalizing packages once in office, a process that Susan Stokes (1997) has labelled 'policy switches'. The two presidents' policy turnaround could be construed as prima facie evidence of pressure from the IMF overriding their electoral commitments. In accounting for Fujimori's policy switch, Stokes (ibid.: 217–18) relates a meeting that took place in New York in June 1990, shortly after Fujimori had won the second-round election. The meeting brought together the newly elected Peruvian president, the managing director of the IMF and the presidents of the WB and the Inter American Development Bank (IADB), Michel Camdessus, Barber Conable and Enrique Iglesias respectively. According to one of Fujimori's advisers present at the meeting, the Peruvian president was told in no uncertain terms that if his government tried to avoid an immediate, painful adjustment, his administration would risk the same fate as that of Alan García's disastrous outgoing administration, in which case he ought not to turn to the Fund for help. He was also advised that if he undertook a combination of stabilization measures and structural reforms, the IFIs would support him. In other words, if the government did not adjust, it would face continued isolation; if it did everything the international financial institutions wanted, it could count on them for full support.

The elected president also received strong advice to reach an agreement with the IMF from high-ranking members of the Japanese government, including the prime minister, during the Japan leg of the same trip. Some members of Fujimori's campaign and transition teams believe that the meeting with the heads of the IFIs led Fujimori to change course on economic policy. Other advisers, however, believe that Fujimori was already wavering in his opposition to fiscal adjustment during the electoral campaign. One of them recalls advising Fujimori that some kind of adjustment was unavoidable and calling him to 'think more like a statesman, not only like a politician', to which Fujimori reportedly replied, 'If I don't think like a politician now, I'll never get to be a statesman' (ibid.: 218).

The case of Venezuela's Carlos Andrés Pérez shows some similarities with but also significant differences from that of Fujimori's meetings with the representatives of the international financial agencies.[4] At the time of the 1988 electoral campaign, Venezuela was not experiencing the hyperinflation of Peru. Towards the end of the outgoing Jaime Lusinchi administration (1984–89), however, the fiscal deficit amounted to 7.6 per cent of GDP and the deficit on the current account had reached 9.9 per cent of GDP (DiJohn 2004). Like Fujimori, Pérez ran a presidential campaign based on an ambiguous political message. He attacked the Fund's policies of economic adjustment and promised a return to the good old days of high economic growth that characterized his first administration (1974–79). He also talked, however, about the need for profound changes to modernize the Venezuelan economy, without specifying the nature or the magnitude of the changes he envisaged. In early 1989, in the aftermath of Pérez's electoral victory, a team of officials representing both the outgoing and incoming governments went to Washington for discussions with the IMF. In the meetings, IMF staff were told straightforwardly by the elected president's advisers that the new government was planning to enact a strong fiscal adjustment and a programme of economic liberalization. The incoming government's policy commitments facilitated a swift agreement between the Fund and the Venezuelan authorities on the economic programme that would serve as the basis for the financing of Venezuela's financial requirements in the years ahead. In exchange for the reforms, the Fund committed US$4.5 billion to support Venezuela's economy. Once in office, Pérez appointed US-educated technocrats with no party affiliation to the main economic ministries. In a televised speech of 16 February 1989, shortly after assuming office, President Pérez announced a dramatic shift in economic policy ('the great turnaround'). The new economic programme included, among other measures, the end of interest rate ceilings, the unification of exchange rates, the doubling of fuel prices, the reduction of food subsidies, and a broadening of the tax base. The policy announcement triggered some of the worst riots in modern Venezuelan history, with more than three hundred people dead.

Sections of the Venezuelan press blamed the IMF for imposing the policy shift, a view that was not discouraged by the government. President Pérez called the IMF a 'conspiracy of the great powers against the Third World'. He sent an open letter to the then IMF managing director, Michel Camdessus, linking the riots to the 'unjust terms' imposed by a global system in which the Fund stood at the 'apex' (quoted in Boughton 2001: 694). Camdessus's terse reply was that '[i]t is a prerogative of sovereign states to decide themselves what measures are required for recovery, however unpleasant those measures may be', adding that '[i]t does them honour if they take responsibility for policies in the eyes of their people, even in the most adverse circumstances',[5] presumably a reference to the gap between the president's public rhetoric and his government's earlier private agreements with the Fund.

In the case of the Dominican Republic, the Fund approved in 1983 an Extended Fund Facility loan arrangement but, according to the IMF's official historian, James M. Boughton, from whom this version of events is taken, the programme went off track before the end of the year. In negotiating a programme for 1984, the Fund demanded the unification of the exchange rates and a large increase in controlled and subsidized prices, especially for petroleum and basic foodstuffs. Reportedly, the Dominican Republic authorities alleged that although they were willing to implement the adjustment demanded by the Fund, they feared that they lacked the necessary political support at home. In January 1984, President

Salvador Jorge Blanco sent a personal letter to the IMF's managing director, Jacques Larosière, arguing that the programme requested by the IMF was 'excessive and ... could not be absorbed in the short period of one year, without provoking social shocks which would threaten the stability which it has cost the Dominican Republic so much effort to obtain and preserve' (quoted in ibid.: 691). Negotiations remained deadlocked for another three months, during which time President Blanco travelled to the USA to unsuccessfully appeal to the US government for economic assistance and to the IMF for an easing of economic conditionality. On his return from Washington, the president announced a policy pack that partially met the Fund's conditions but warned about its high social costs. The president was right: his announcement triggered a wave of riots and street protests that were harshly repressed by the police. Measured in human lives the costs were an estimated sixty to eighty deaths. Following the riots, President Blanco backtracked from his commitment to raise oil prices. Negotiations between the Fund and the authorities continued for several months, after which the extended arrangement was cancelled (ibid.: 691–2).

In other cases, relations between Latin American governments and the IFIs were distinctly more collaborative, grounded on shared ideas and common interests. The cases of Bolivia and Mexico, although very different in themselves, show how the two governments established close working relations with the WB and the IMF.

The new government that took office in Bolivia in 1985 faced a near economic catastrophe, with inflation running at around 25,000 per cent a year. Immediately after taking office, the new administration of President Paz Estenssoro embarked on a radical programme of economic stabilization and free market reform that received strong backing from the IMF and the WB. The WB created a brand-new unit and engaged a new team to back up the Bolivian government's initiatives with policy advice and finance. The IMF and the WB put together what was then a wholly new WB/IMF instrument, the Policy Framework Paper (PFP), with the goal of persuading the international aid community to address what was understood to be an impossible debt situation and justify higher financing, especially from the International Development Association (IDA).[6] In her study of the World Bank, Katherine Marshall describes the relations between the IFIs' representatives and members of the Bolivian government in the following terms:

While frictions sometimes occurred among the development partners and between them and government officials, this was a heady time full of energy and hope. The partnership was in important respects exemplary, as it was grounded in mutual respect and in a fairly clear idea of comparative advantage among the participating agencies. There was no question about who was in the driving seat: the Bolivian government. (Marshall 2008: 115)[7]

The acknowledgement that everyone involved in the early planning days had barely considered the social implications of drastic economic reforms, including the fate of thousands of miners and their families who were largely left to fend for themselves as a result of the drastic downsizing of the state-owned tin mining company, Corporación Minera de Bolivia (COMIBOL), also captures the spirit of the time.

The case of Mexico shows a more complex relationship between the IMF, the WB and the national authorities.[8] In the 1980s, the Mexican economy entered an enduring crisis that started in 1982 and dragged on for most of the decade. Mexico had a strong state and an authoritarian, centralized political regime, however, in which power was concentrated in the presidency and the core state financial agencies, such as the ministries of finance and planning, as well as a highly capable technocracy. This allowed the Mexican technocracy a relatively high degree of domestic autonomy in their dealings with external actors (Teichman 2004). Negotiations between the IFIs and the Mexican government lasted for most of the decade and covered a broad range of issues. The history of the negotiations shows how the IMF and the WB combined financial incentives and intellectual persuasion to promote fundamental policy changes. It also shows how the IFIs' willing technocratic interlocutors within the Mexican government used the IFIs' conditions to overcome resistance to the reforms, while at the same time furthering their political careers. Following the 1982 crisis, the United States government and the IMF offered Mexico substantial financial assistance in exchange for an orthodox debt management package. After some difficult negotiations, the Mexican authorities agreed to abide by an economic programme supported by the Fund. For most of the decade, however, the de la Madrid administration (1982–88) remained divided between nationalists, who controlled the political agencies of the government, such as the Secretaría de Gobernación (Ministry of the Interior), and the ruling PRI party apparatus and liberal technocrats embedded in the finance ministry and the central bank. While the nationalists defended a more inward-looking economy and an arm's-length relationship with the IFIs, the technocrats were keen on working in close collaboration with the Fund and the WB to modernize the Mexican economy. During the negotiations, technocrats often used the opposition from nationalist members of the cabinet and the threat that a nationalist economic backlash would impose to financial stability as a tool to extract concessions from the Fund and the WB.

In the course of the decade, the WB sought to deepen its policy dialogue with the Mexican government, focusing on areas such as fiscal policy, trade and public enterprises. The Bank backed its ideological offensive with offers of structural and sectoral adjustment loans. The WB's efforts found willing partners within the Mexican government technocracy. As part of the process of persuasion, the Bank funded high-profile conferences in which IMF and WB staff presented papers on the benefits of trade liberalization and other issues, and gave technical support to liberalizing technocrats in areas such as agricultural reform. As a World Bank document put it, the Bank and the Mexican government shared 'a common vision about required reforms and Mexico needed external financial assistance'.[9]

The above case studies show that beyond the 1980s regional trend of increasing financial and ideological influence by the World Bank and the IMF, there were significant differences in the balance between coercion and consent that characterized relations between the IFIs and borrowing countries. The cases of Mexico and Bolivia show how domestic technocrats and politicians used the IFIs' support to promote programmes of reforms that they substantially owned, and in the process furthered their political careers. In contrast, the case of the Dominican Republic shows the IMF at its most imperious, as it was the case in which the asymmetrical power of the IMF vis-à-vis a small country with a highly vulnerable economy was more evident. The history of the negotiating process between the Dominican government and the IMF shows that the Fund sought to dogmatically impose a programme of adjustment on a reluctant government with no regard for the programme's social and political costs. It is clear that the dearth of alternatives made it impossible for the Dominican Republic government to make a meaningfully free choice.

The cases of Fujimori and Carlos Andrés Pérez show the blurred dividing lines between constraints, ownership and persuasion. Both Fujimori and Pérez were pragmatic politicians, who gained office in countries suffering economic crises of different degrees of gravity. The case of Fujimori is the most ambiguous one, as it could be interpreted as involving a mixture of learning from the mistakes of the previous administration, persuasion from the IFIs, and naked political calculation. Negotiations took place in a context in which economic constraints left the incoming administration with very little room for manoeuvre. The depth of the crisis made it easier for Fujimori to play the politics of 'there is not an alternative' and persuade the Peruvian people that it was worthwhile to pay the costs of the adjustment. The success of the economic shock in rapidly bringing down inflation was capitalized by Fujimori to consolidate his grip on power and further advance a programme of economic reform without any significant internal opposition. On the surface, the case of Pérez's Venezuela appears similar to that of the Dominican Republic, and yet the two were significantly different. The Venezuelan people's reaction to Pérez's broken promise of a return to a better yesterday made President Pérez appeal to the politics of scapegoating. While the riots did not deter Pérez from pushing ahead with his programme of reform, the liberalizing reform drive proved unsustainable in the face of strong domestic political and social opposition. After surviving two coup attempts in 1992, Pérez was impeached for corruption and thrown out of office in 1993.

The limits and impact of the IMF's and the WB's policy prescriptions

The Brady plan and its aftermath represented the high-water mark in the power of the IFIs in the region. It combined the leverage provided by the debt reduction package with the institutional and ideological authority of the Fund and the WB that allowed the two agencies to frame the new development agenda. Paraphrasing Woods (2006: 90), the WB and the IMF offered a simple, ready-made solution to governments disenchanted with the ideas behind the old economic model and without the finances to continue it. It is not by chance that it was in this period that the expression the *Washington Consensus* originated; this was an intellectually confident paradigm that was aggressively promoted by powerful institutions. As such it became the new common sense that brought together IFIs, domestic technocrats and embattled presidents, although arguably governments adopted liberalizing policies more for pragmatic reasons than because of ideological conversion.

And yet, at the time when they were more powerful the IFIs also became more vulnerable. By assuming an intellectual and financial leadership in the promotion of free market reforms, the IFIs became increasingly involved in political decisions and exposed to the consequences of their failure. Intellectually, the IFIs' free market policy consensus was subject to significant criticisms from mainstream economists. I will deal with these in some detail in Chapter 7. More importantly, the IFIs' intellectual assertiveness obscured important known unknowns and unknown unknowns about their own policy prescriptions.[10] Among the known unknowns there is no firm evidence that the IMF and the WB knew what was good for their borrowing countries (ibid.: 6). Also among the known unknowns was the relation between adjustment and economic growth and the impact of adjustment on income distribution and the poor. Not surprisingly, these questions became politically more salient as the number, depth and length of IMF interventions increased in the late 1980s and early 1990s.

The Fund itself was constrained by its own charter on the growth-promoting policies that it could impose, and divided on whether it should advance a particular growth strategy. In the early 1980s the Fund did not have a model for making adjustments more conducive to economic growth, and paid little attention to the impact of adjustment programmes upon the poor. A report by the Fund's Exchange and Trade Relations Department for the 1986 conditionality review argued that, despite the persistence of public perceptions, conventional adjustment programmes were already well designed to promote sustainable growth (IMF 1985). A review paper submitted to the Executive Board in the same year claimed that the Fund's neoclassical emphasis on liberalization and macroeconomic stabilization provided the economic strength needed to pursue longer-run growth-oriented policies, as growth would follow the restoration of external balances (IMF 1987: 32–5). The claim that the neoclassical strategy of economic liberalization and export promotion was a necessary and sufficient condition for economic growth was, however, highly simplistic, and showed a lack of awareness of both the history of development and of the complex relations between the economy, politics and society in processes of economic development. The IMF's market reductionism was questioned both by a new generation of development economists, such as Jeffrey Sachs and Joseph Stiglitz, and by IMF directors from developing countries, who disagreed with the view that market liberalization and the reduction of institutional constraints would necessarily improve economic efficiency or raise economic growth (Boughton 2001: 609–13).

The impact of adjustment and structural reform on economic growth, poverty and income distribution became core elements of the intellectual and political battles between defenders and critics of the IFIs' policies. The multilateral agencies themselves were unable to provide conclusive evidence about the effects of their policies on the borrowing countries' economies. The task was the more difficult because internal and external reviewers of IFIs' policies used different evaluation criteria, starting points, economic indicators and counterfactuals in their assessments. The IMF's own reviews found that the effects of the Fund's programmes on the key goal of restoring balance-of-payments equilibriums were moderate at best (ibid.: 615). If the effects of structural adjustment on economic growth and its impact on the poor were taken into consideration, it became even more difficult to find agreed criteria between defenders and critics of the Fund's policies. In a study on the effects of the IMF programmes in eighteen Latin American countries, Manuel Pastor (1987) found that IMF policies had improved the balance of payments, had not improved the current accounts, and had reduced labour shares in real incomes. Pastor also found that IMF programmes had a negative effect on income distribution. With regard to economic growth, he found no clear-cut evidence concerning the impact of IMF policies.[11] Studies by the Fund's staff found no statistically significant effects on overall economic performance derived from adjustment programmes. On the whole, internal studies concluded that successful adjustment and sustainable growth were elusive goals (Boughton 2001: 615).[12] Independent studies were equally inconclusive. A review of these studies suggests modest economic effects at best: greatest on balance of payments and the current account, negligible on the rate of inflation, and uncertain on the growth rate (Kahler 1992: 95). As has been noted above, the social dimensions of economic adjustment had been historically overlooked by the Fund. The human costs of the policies were considered by the Fund as a short-term price worth paying for policies that were necessary and sufficient conditions for the restoration of growth, which was regarded as the best mechanism to lift people out of poverty. Criticisms about the effects on the poor of the IMF's traditional package of fiscal discipline, cuts in subsidies, devaluation, and wage restraints, however, became politically more difficult to ignore as the IMF's intervention widened in scope and lengthened in time. The Fund's response to its critics was to deny that adjustment programmes damaged income distribution, arguing that distributional effects were a domestic matter and claiming that conventional adjustment policies benefited all sections of society.[13]

To the economic debate about the effects of the IMF policies on the economies and the people of Latin America should be added the political debate about the expanding role of the IMF and the WB. As seen above, the power of the IFIs in the region was not the same if the different dimensions of power are taken into consideration. Increasingly, the World Bank and the IMF dictated the economic agenda in the region, even if its implementation was uneven and often far from transparent. They were also able to secure the consent of often sympathetic governmental elites to their programmes of reform. But the IFIs' increasing influence concerning Lukes's second and third dimensions of power (agenda-setting and interest-shaping) was not matched by an equal increase in the first dimension of power: the ability to enforce policy conditions. Paraphrasing Kahler (ibid.: 128), technocratic consensus failed to translate into policy implementation when consensus did not extend up (to the political principals), laterally (to the implementing agencies) and downwards (to representative institutions and public opinion). Success became more and more difficult as policy-making was opened up to a greater number of participants, more interest groups and further debate (Woods 2006: 5). Moreover, the more complex and extended the conditions, the more difficult it was for the IFIs to use the threat to withdraw funding as a way of forcing policy implementation.

A long-term study of the IMF's policy packages in Latin America between the 1950s and the mid-1980s found that 'the dominant theme to emerge from this analysis of IMF programmes (1954–84) was not that of success but of failure', and that '[u]nsuccessful implementation of IMF recipes has been the norm in Latin America, not the exception' (Remmer 1986: 21). Broader research on IMF programmes found that programme breakdown was running at over 60 per cent in the early 1990s (Killick 1995).[14] For IMF and WB critics, however, there was little distinction to be made between the IFIs' considerable responsibility for the agenda, and their more limited responsibility for its implementation.

In the same way that for critics of socialism the failures of the Soviet Union signified the failure of an economic model rather than the distorted implementation of a specific version of an abstract model, for these critics it was the neoliberal model which had failed and not some partial and distorted implementation of said model. Supporters of free market reform reinforced this perception by presenting the reforms as a closed totality ('the Washington Consensus'), which as such became exposed to the risk that every policy failure could be taken as a proof of systemic failure.

The legitimacy of the IFIs' interventions was also put into question. The mode of intervention of the IMF and the WB became more intrusive and technocratic at the time that its agenda was becoming more politicized and the regional political environment was turning more democratic and open to contestation. The reaction of IMF technocrats to the growing political interference with their economic prescriptions is tellingly summarized by Anne Krueger's assertion that 'the challenge for the IMF and the World Bank is that they are likely to have influence where "rational economic policy" can be formulated away from the hurly burly of politics' (Krueger 2003, quoted in Woods 2006: 82). In other words, politics was an irrational intrusion into what would otherwise be a rational, technocratic, decision-making process. The Fund found it increasingly difficult to square the claim that it respected political choices and that it took into account the special circumstances facing each country, while ensuring uniformity of treatment (Boughton 2001: 571). The changing nature of the IMF's and WB's relations with the countries of the region also made it increasingly unsustainable to ignore the political implications of the distributional costs of their policies and the contested nature of the balance between short-term costs and long-term gains. The identity of the IMF and the WB as politically neutral, public institutions, able to maintain a degree of autonomy from the interests of their main shareholders, was affected by the shift in their roles and by their close association with the US government in promoting the American model of capitalism in the region. The concentration of IMF borrowing in developing Latin American countries altered the nature of conditionality as a mechanism embedded in a broader set of reciprocal legal obligations common to all IMF members, causing it to become the embodiment of the asymmetries of power within the organization. As the IMF assumed a coordinating role in debt negotiations, it became exposed to accusations that it was acting as a debt collector for the banks based in the countries with the largest votes on the Executive Board, rather than as a neutral mediator promoting the public good (Finch 1989; Kapur 1998; Thirkell-White 2005).

Most of all, the legitimacy of the IMF and WB intervention was undermined by the fact that the impact of the IFIs' programmes on economic growth, poverty and inequality cannot be assessed within a technocratic bubble independently of the political contexts in which these policies were applied, independently of popular perceptions about the interference of the IFIs in a country's affairs and separately from the deeply political nature of the decisions required for their implementation. Whatever the empirical evidence, intellectual merits, caveats and arguments of the defenders of the Fund's policies, opposition to the adjustment was based on perceptions about the heavy-handed imposition of reform packages by an unaccountable external organization dominated by rich nations, and that these packages had brought recession, unemployment and cuts in essential services. While the intensity of opposition to the IMF varied significantly according to country-specific circumstances, opposition manifested itself in protests, strikes and riots in a number of countries in the region, including Argentina, Bolivia, the Dominican Republic, Ecuador, Haiti and Venezuela. Moreover, the social impact of the adjustment policies did not affect solely the poor, but also significant sectors of the middle classes, which were often the main beneficiaries of state spending.

The IMF's and WB's reaction to the political challenges, social impact, intellectual criticisms and economic shortcomings of their programme of reform was twofold: on the one hand they sought to extend and deepen the reform agenda, thus making it even more political in nature and more difficult to control, while on the other hand they sought to take on board some of the criticisms of the Washington Consensus and articulate them to their own agenda. I will look at these changes in Chapter 7.

Conclusion

The changes in the economic and political environment of the 1980s discussed in this chapter greatly increased the power of the IMF and the WB over the Latin American governments. There is little doubt that the external influence of institutions such as the WB and the IMF, as well as other international actors, particularly the US Treasury, was a major factor in explaining the policy changes of the 1980s. International influence was particularly evident in the framing of the reform agenda of the 1980s in accordance with the economic ideas of the IMF and the WB, and in the more or less parallel adoption by different governments of similar economic policies. The limits to both the hard and soft power of the IFIs was apparent, however, in the often large chasm between conditionality-driven agreements and the implementation of the policies that were supposed to enact the agreements, in the different pace and depth of policy reforms in each country, and in the persistence of elements of the state-centred model of economic development and of heterodox economic policies within the new free market model. The five country cases outlined above reveal how imposition, persuasion and political calculation played differently in each negotiation. As the case studies show, the picture of overbearing international agencies forcing radical policy changes down the throats of hapless governments masks more complex games of bargains, resistance and agreements, which often blurred the distinction between external influence and domestic ownership. Chapter 3 discusses the domestic sources of support for the free market reformation.

3 | The ascent of free market economics: an economic reformation with popular support?

In previous chapters we looked at the ideational changes that framed the ascendancy of free market reforms, and at the international context that favoured the reform process. In this chapter we are concentrating on the relationship between institutions and interests as explanatory factors for the enactment of those reforms, and on the sources of popular support for them. Economic reforms have costs that are unevenly distributed throughout society. It is necessary to remember that, historically, opposition to IMF-inspired stabilization packages was grounded in their regressive distributive and recessionary costs, and on the impact that cuts in public spending would have on essential public services. Moreover, free market reforms do not affect just the relatively powerless poor; they also hurt powerful domestic business interests that benefit from the protectionist policies of Import Substitution Industrialization, and significant sections of the middle classes that depend on state jobs and universal social benefits.

Even if, as supporters of the reforms have argued, by making the economy more efficient, free market reforms cause everybody to be better off in the long term, transition costs fall directly on specific groups that are more likely to oppose the reforms than putative, long-term, diffuse winners. Thus, the short-term pain imposed by the reforms should be a powerful disincentive for politicians whose interests are determined by equally short-term electoral cycles. Therefore any account of the implementation of free market economic reforms needs to address an important puzzle: if neoliberal reforms are supposed to hurt the majority of the population, how could these reforms have been implemented against the interests of the majority of citizens in a democratic environment? In seeking to solve this puzzle we need to consider three different types of explanation: the first of these relates to the nature of the electoral mandate of reforming presidents, the second concerns the institutional settings that facilitate or prevent the implementation of reforms, and the third looks at the distributional costs and benefits of the reforms.

Presidential mandates and the politics of reform

In a democracy, governments are supposed to be broadly responsive to their citizens' preferences (Dahl 1971). Given that the economy is usually at the heart of electoral campaigns, radical economic reforms should require a clear electoral mandate, not only for them to be perceived as legitimate but also to make possible their implementation in the face of strong opposition from vested interests. In a number of cases, reforming governments did have such a mandate. This was the case, among others, for the successive Concertación administrations in Chile (1990–), for the two governments of President Fernando Henrique Cardoso in Brazil (1995–2002), of the administrations of Presidents Luis Alberto Lacalle (1990–95) and Jorge Batlle (2000–05) in Uruguay, and that of President Ernesto Zedillo in Mexico (1994–2000). It was also the case for the second administrations of Presidents Carlos Menem of Argentina (1995–99) and Alberto Fujimori of Peru (1995–2000). But this was certainly not the case for the first electoral campaigns of Menem (1989–95) and Fujimori (1990–95), in which they fought free market candidates only to implement shock free market reform packages when in office. Similar – albeit less successful – cases were those of the electoral campaigns of Carlos Andrés Pérez (1989) in Venezuela and Rodrigo Borja (1988) in Ecuador. As seen in Chapter 2, these cases have been regarded as examples of so-called 'bait and switch populists' (Drake 1991; Stokes 1997) – that is, of political leaders who campaigned on an anti-neoliberal platform when in opposition only to enact shock free market reforms when in office.

The case of Fujimori is typical of this strategy. During his 1990 electoral campaign Fujimori vaguely committed himself to following moderate economic policies, to achieve stabilization without recession, and to minimize job losses. Above all, he strongly opposed the shock fiscal adjustment advocated by his economic liberal opponent, Mario Vargas Llosa, under the slogan: 'FREDEMO [Vargas Llosa's political party] is the shock, Cambio 90 [Fujimori's party] is the no shock'. In direct contrast to his electoral promises, however, just ten days after his inauguration, Fujimori announced a shock reform package of economic stabilization and free market reform. Following the enactment of the reforms, gasoline prices increased by 3,000 per cent and similar rises were recorded for other essential goods and public services. Monthly inflation reached 397 per cent and recession followed, along with reduced real incomes for all sectors of the economy (Crabtree and Thomas 1998; Newbold 2003; Pastor and Wise 1992; Stokes 1997).

Shock reform from above was not the only way in which reforms were implemented in the region. In fact, they were the exception rather than the rule. For supporters of the free market, however, reformist leaders such as Alberto Fujimori became emblematic symbols of the importance of leadership, political will and swift action in advancing the reforms. In contrast, for critics of neoliberalism top-down reforms enacted in contravention of electoral promises were the most visible example of the undemocratic manner in which neoliberalism was imposed on an unwilling people. In what was a rather broad generalization from a selective number of cases that none the less captured the spirit of the time, Guillermo O'Donnell (1994) claimed that these governments were typical of a new model of democracy that he labelled *delegative democracy*. In O'Donnell's own words, in a delegative democracy '[t]he policies of [a President's] government need bear no resemblance to the promises of his campaign – has not the president been authorized to govern as he (or she) thinks best?' (ibid.: 60). O'Donnell explains the popular delegation of power to presidents in terms of the ideological-cultural expectations of citizens who regard their presidents as the embodiment of the nation. Because of this cultural mindset, the presidents/leaders are trusted by the people to do what they believe to be best for their country, without being hindered by the normal institutional constraints of liberal democracies.

Claims that the enactment of policies that contradicted electoral promises constituted a betrayal of the electors' trust must be balanced against wider considerations relating to the nature of the leaders' electoral mandates. Arguably, leaders who campaign in contexts of deep political and economic crises do not receive a narrow mandate to enact a specific set of policies, but a broad mandate to take decisive action for the restoration of social order. For most citizens, the question of finding a way out of the crisis, the need 'to do something', takes precedence over what specifically is to be done. This gives presidents elected in times of crisis a high degree of authority and autonomy to redefine the political agenda in accordance with the urgencies of the time (Palermo and Novaro 1996: 124). In other words, the delegation of powers to presidents to govern 'as they think best' is not so much the result of an ingrained political culture, as O'Donnell suggests, but of highly specific critical junctures determined by the gravity of the crisis.

Again, the case of Fujimori's first presidency illustrates the point. While the Peruvian president's 'Fujishock' policy package consisted of the very same policies that he had strongly opposed during his electoral campaign, the majority of the population did not react to the abrogation of his campaign promises (Newbold 2003; Sheahan 1999). Support for the reforms was strong, even when the immediate effect of the economic package was an increase in hardship for the majority of the population. Arguably, the reason for popular support for the reforms was the widespread perception that there was no other option and the hope that the policies would bring about an improvement in citizens' economic conditions. As Samantha Newbold (2003: 6) has put it, it was desperation, rather than acceptance of a new ideology, which led voters to support Fujimori. Fujimori himself reinforced this perception by claiming that market-oriented policies were necessary in order to allow the government to operate and that 'there was no other alternative'.

When successfully achieved, the restoration of order, as was the case for Menem and Fujimori in the early 1990s, reconstructed relations of representation between the leaders and the citizens, created new political frontiers between the present and the past, and retroactively legitimized the reforms. Not all so-called 'bait and switch' reformers were equally successful, however. Presidents Carlos Andrés Pérez of Venezuela and Fernando Collor de Mello of Brazil were impeached for corruption and forced to abandon office before the end of their mandates. In the case of Collor de Mello, the impeachment was made politically possible by the fall in his popularity because of the failure to restore economic order through his ill-fated economic stabilization plans. In the case of Pérez, the impeachment reflected continuous popular opposition to the shock free market package he introduced in January 1989, shortly after assuming office. Significantly, the economic crisis in Venezuela in the 1980s never reached the gravity of the economic problems of Argentina and Peru that preceded the elections of Menem and Fujimori.

But, as noted above, the introduction of shock economic reforms without an electoral mandate was not the general norm in the region, nor were the reforms universally rejected by the electorate. In most countries, free market reforms were undertaken by presidents of different political persuasions who campaigned on a programme that can be broadly characterized as the policies of free market modernization, although many of these presidents were not ideologically 'neoliberals'. The pace and content of the reforms also varied considerably from government to government and from country to country. In Brazil, the market reform programme was initiated by Fernando Collor de Mello (1990–92), who campaigned on a broad, anti-corruption, modernizing platform and sought to enact the reforms in a swift, top-down, manner. Following Collor's impeachment in 1992, the process of reform took a distinctive gradualist turn under his successor Itamar Franco (1992–95), a traditional politician of nationalist leanings. The programme of economic modernization was deepened under President Fernando Henrique Cardoso, a social democrat, who received a clear electoral mandate on the back of the highly successful *Real* Stabilization Plan, implemented when he was finance minister for President Franco. Different from past stabilization plans, such as the *Plano Cruzado* and the *Plano Collor*, this was not a shock treatment but a product of negotiations and was implemented in stages. In Argentina, President Menem's successor, the radical Fernando de la Rua (1999–2001), maintained the broad elements of Menem's economic programme, as did President Fujimori's successor, Alejandro Toledo (2001–06) in Peru. In Venezuela, the *Agenda Venezuela* economic programme of President Carlos Rafael Caldera (1994–99), successor to Carlos Andrés Pérez, was fundamentally economically orthodox. Elsewhere in Latin America, free market reforms were gradually rather than swiftly implemented in Uruguay and Colombia.

In short, the gravity of the economic crisis, the nature of electoral mandates and the presidents' charisma and personality played a role in the free market reformations. Broader institutional explanations must be brought into consideration, however, in order to account for governments' ability to pass reforms against the collective-action problems posed by well-organized rent-seekers.

The institutional underpinnings of free market reforms

Defenders of the reforms argued that the vested interests of powerful domestic actors opposing the reforms could be overcome only by a highly autonomous executive, insulated from sectoral and popular pressures. In the economically volatile environment of the late 1980s and early 1990s, presidents used the political capital accrued by their electoral victories to stretch their constitutional powers and impose reforms by presidential decree or other forms of extraordinary legislation. At the heart of the reforming forces were 'change teams': internally cohesive technocratic groups that operated outside of routine decision-making channels with the backing of the president (Haggard and Kaufman 1992a: 19).

The two presidencies of Alberto Fujimori of Peru (1990–95, 1995–2000) were an extreme case of this reform strategy. By centralizing power in the presidency with the backing of the armed forces and the advice of a small group of technocrats, Fujimori was able to impose one of the most far-reaching programmes of market reform in the region. Between the start of his first mandate on 28 July 1990 and late 1991, President Fujimori enacted 120 new laws by power of decree. In April 1992 he broke a political stalemate with Congress by closing it down. Although the decision was clearly unconstitutional, according to public opinion surveys taken at the time this action was supported by over 85 per cent of respondents (Philip 1998: 84). Even when he formally restored constitutional order in 1993 following the approval of a new constitution in October of that year, he continued to enjoy almost complete control of the policy-making process, as congressional authority was weakened by the new constitution and the judiciary lacked the necessary independence to check the excesses of the executive.

An analysis of the reform process in different Latin American countries shows, however, that societal actors played a much more significant role in shaping the reforms than is implied by the state-centred approach. The extent of a society's ability to influence the reform process depended on the nature of the reform and the nature of the country's political system. But even in those countries in which there was a high degree of concentration of power in the executive, there were channels opened for social actors to interact with state decision-makers and shape the content of the reforms. As Moisés Arce (2006) put it, while civil society in general may not initiate or even embrace market reforms through electoral choices, it becomes a critical actor as the process of reform moves on. Even under the autocratic rule of President Fujimori, the reforms were not a purely top-down affair. Measures such as tax, health and pension reforms induced a variety of societal responses from interest groups and sections of the state bureaucracy that were affected by the reforms. Organizations representing these social groups engaged in lobbying activities and collective action, and they opened channels of communication with the executive to influence and negotiate policy. As a reaction to societal pressure, the executive amended the original projects, which in cases such as health and tax reform resulted in the reforms falling significantly short of their original goals (ibid.: 46).

The emphasis on the powers of the executive also underplays the role played by parliaments and political parties in supporting the reform process (Geddes 1994; Haggard and Kaufman 1995). As Eduardo Gamarra (1994: 108) has put it, in order to govern, presidents must be able to form and sustain coalitions in Congress to support policy initiatives. This is the case even where presidents used their constitutional prerogatives to enact executive decrees that bypassed the normal legislative process, as in most countries Congress must either pass enabling legislation that allows the president to rule by decree, or have the constitutional power to reject the decrees. Market reforms imposed particularly high political costs on statist ruling parties, which had historically colonized the state and used state resources to consolidate their hold on power. Naturally, these parties tended to resist free market reforms, particularly initiatives aimed at shrinking the state which would drain their pools of patronage and hurt their political bases of support in the public sector. But the attitude of these parties to reform was not fixed in history or determined by their institutional position. Presidents were able to overcome their parties' resistance to reform by following the right political strategies.

In his comparative study of the reform process in Argentina and Venezuela, Javier Corrales shows that a determining factor in the success of the reforming drive in Menem's Argentina and of the failure of a similar process in Pérez's Venezuela lay in the cooperative relationship between the ruling party and the executive in the former, and in the conflictive nature of their relationship in the latter. Corrales (2002: 29–37) argues that while statist, populist parties are normally reluctant to support pro-market reforms, it is possible for the executive to overcome ruling-party resistance to reforms by following a party-accommodating strategy based on negotiations and concessions resulting in second-best, mutually cooperative, options for both actors. While the resulting reform package may be a watered-down version of the original, negotiation is often the best strategy for securing not just the passing of reforms, but more crucially the sustainability of those reforms; support from the ruling party shields the state from the enemies of reform, thus achieving the bridging of the political credibility gap that is necessary in order to secure societal cooperation with the reforms.

Institutional explanations for the success or failure of free market reforms have significant merits, but also substantial limitations. Crisis situations can motivate incumbents to promote reforms that otherwise they would not have contemplated, if they believe that reforms are crucial for the survival of the system. And yet, as was pointed out in Chapter 1, crises open up the possibility for reform but do not determine their content. How do we explain the preferences for reform of *insulated state actors*? Technocrats may provide the ideological inspiration and technical expertise needed to draft the reforms. But ultimately, technocrats derive their power from their political principals, who according to public choice theory have their preferences shaped by their goal to remain in office, and for whom the control of state resources is one of the main electoral assets, and the inflicting of short-term pain for long-term gain is a high-risk electoral strategy. Moreover, it remains to be explained how enlightened technocrats, even with the support of public-minded politicians, can overcome the opposition of well-organized economic groups and the more diffuse opposition of public opinion. The political insulation hypothesis is at best a partial explanation for the successful enactment of a limited number of reforms in certain countries. Executive insulation can work in the initial stages of the reform programme, particularly in relation to reforms that do not require complex implementation, such as the lowering of external tariffs, the elimination of exchange controls, and the freeing of internal prices. Beyond that, empirical studies of the institutional and political insulation of executives in different Latin American countries show contrasting outcomes in the success and failure of reforms.

The role of interests in processes of reform

The limitations of institutional explanations bring into focus the importance of understanding the role of political and economic interests in free market reformation. In the long term, reforms are not sustainable without considerable support from within the political system and from strategic economic interests. As Robert Bates (1994: 31) argues, the empowerment of technocrats and financial institutions in the 1980s and 1990s represented an attempt to institutionalize policies that served particular interests – to stabilize the fortunes and protect the political triumph of particular industries, sectors and regions of the economy that benefited from the new economic policies. Moreover, support for free market reforms needed to include relatively small, well-organized, elite groups, as well as more diffuse popular sectors. A viable reform strategy was needed to compensate losers as well as produce winners. Among the elite groups that had to be taken into account were incumbent politicians concerned about paying the political costs of unpopular reforms and of losing control of state resources, for instance by the privatization of state enterprises. Also, at the elite level, business and labour groups that benefited from the protectionist policies of the ISI era, and which were an important base of support for dominant statist parties, were not ready to relinquish their economic privileges without being compensated for their losses.

At a personal level, state technocrats and private entrepreneurs developed close individual and institutional connections during the reform process, which brought them mutual economic and political advantages (Bartelli and Payne 1995; Cleaves and Stephens 1991; Conaghan et al. 1990; Kingstone 1999; Silva, E. 1996; Silva and Durand 1998). For instance, in Chile, key policy-makers of the Pinochet era served on the boards of large economic conglomerates before and after holding cabinet and central bank positions, leading to collusion between economic and political power. But rent-seeking coalitions were built on more than just a revolving door between state and private sector jobs. Against the assumption that liberalization policies necessarily concentrate costs and produce diffuse benefits, which facilitates opposition to reform, particular combinations of liberalization policies concentrated benefits on well-defined reform coalitions and dispersed costs among more diffuse groups, resulting in a political environment amenable to the reforms.

Reforming governments put in place a number of strategies to compensate or neutralize losers, and to create coalitions of winners. Contrary to the view that the collective problems raised by the reforms could be overcome only by enlightened policy-making elites insulated from societal pressures, an analysis of the coalitions that supported liberalization is crucial for understanding its dynamics. The bargaining process between economic and political elites shows how new economic actors in alliance with the traditional political and economic elite played an important role in the shaping of the reforms. As Hector Schamis (1999: 236, 268) argues, while neoclassical economists believe that rent-seeking[1] can only result from state intervention in the markets, economic liberalization policies generated a different type of incentive for rent-seeking behaviour. In his study of the political economy of free market reform in Chile, Mexico and Argentina, Schamis (ibid.) shows how the governments of these countries actively promoted rent-seeking liberalizing coalitions by, among other strategies, promoting interlocking ownership of privatized utilities by domestic and international firms. Schamis also shows how governments facilitated the transition of traditional economic groups from rent-seeking under ISI to rent-seeking under neoliberalism through the selling of state assets at reduced prices and monopoly conditions.

For instance, in Mexico the powerful Consejo Coordinador Empresarial (CCE), in which financial interests and large firms had a strong representation, was set up in 1975 with the explicit goal of influencing policy-making. The CCE played a crucial role in the Economic Solidarity Pact (PASE), signed in December 1987 by the Mexican government, business and labour. The PASE became the political binding force of a stabilization strategy based on deepening structural reforms and the adoption of a nominal exchange-rate anchor, complemented by concerted income and price controls. In the early 1990s, during the administration of Carlos Salinas de Gortari (1988–94), the traditional arm's-length relationship between the ruling Partido Revolucionario Institucional (PRI) and business was substituted by a close relationship between the government and the private sector. Privatization was used as a key mechanism for reshaping private economic groups. It strengthened traditional groups that adapted to the new environment and facilitated the emergence of new industrial-financial conglomerates (ibid.: 253–6).

A similar process occurred in Argentina under President Menem. Potential losers from the reforms were compensated by the granting of rent opportunities in new economic sectors to these groups, as well as by selective deregulation and the awarding of economically highly profitable contracts with the state. The sale of state-owned public utilities was characterized by the less than transparent selling of badly regulated monopolist or quasi-monopolist utilities to the same economic elite that profited from public work concessions and other state contracts in the 1970s and 1980s, thus facilitating the elite's transition from the *'patria contratista'* to the *'patria privatista'*.[2] Powerful economic interests were also active, however, in opposing indiscriminate economic opening. Their influence was reflected in the less than transparent nature of the process, as trade liberalization contained a number of exceptions, most notably in the car, steel, petroleum and paper industries. As the exceptions were set up at the discretion of the minister of the economy, they exemplify the enduring influence of traditional domestic industrial lobbies (Cavarozzi 1997; Tedesco 1999).

While it is difficult to pass reforms without considerable support from business, it is even more difficult to pass them without at least the acquiescence of political incumbents. In order to understand why politicians supported free market reforms that on paper deprived them of control over crucial state resources, we need to question another assumption of neoclassical economics, namely that political corruption is a by-product of the political control of state resources and of discretionary and excessive regulation. According to this argument, the privatization of state assets and economic deregulation would greatly reduce, if not completely eliminate, the 'old politics' of corruption and its close relatives, patronage and clientelism. An analysis of processes of economic reform in Latin America shows, however, that the 'new economics' of free trade, privatization and structural reform was moulded by the 'old politics', which had effectively adapted to the new economic environment (Panizza 2000a; Weyland 1999).

The cases of two very different economic modernizers, Presidents Fernando Henrique Cardoso of Brazil and Carlos Menem of Argentina, show how the two leaders combined 'old politics' and 'new economics' to promote the political incentives for the approval of the reforms. Cardoso assumed office in 1995 with strong electoral endorsement for his key economic policy, the highly successful 1994 *Real* Stabilization Plan. Even strong electoral mandates need to be implemented and sustained politically, however. Cardoso used the office of the presidency as a lever to construct a loose multiparty coalition in Congress. Although his administration had a large congressional majority on paper, party fragmentation and lack of internal party discipline, characteristics of Brazil's party system, meant that majorities needed to be negotiated for each legislative proposal. The government's predicament was especially difficult in the case of a number of key constitutional reforms that required a qualified majority in order to be passed. The saga of the government's agenda of administrative, social security, tax and political reform, set at the beginning of Cardoso's first term in office (1995–98) and still unfinished at the end of that mandate, illustrates the difficulties his government faced in its relations with Congress.

The administration's attempts to pass the fiscally crucial constitutional amendment on social security reform were typical of the obstacles faced by the overall process of economic reform that dominated parliamentary life between 1996 and 1998. In March 1996, in order to reverse an earlier defeat and win a first-round vote for the constitutional amendment, the government resorted to a barrage of micro and macro patronage. At a 'micro' level, a patronage vote-gathering offensive included, for example, the appointment of a political protégé from Minas Gerais as superintendent of the Federal Railways. At a 'macro' level, it entailed, among other concessions, the release of R$30 million in federal funds for the construction of a highway in Rondonia to win a further eight votes, and the federalization of the R$3.33 billion debt of the city of São Paulo in order to secure the support of a number of deputies from that state. As one legislator put it: '[w]e vote here [in Congress] in favour of the Government's unpopular measures but we want to take something back to [our] states'.[3] In spite of the government's generous use of patronage, a significantly watered-down reform bill took more than two and a half years to be approved by Congress (Panizza 2000a).

In contrast to Cardoso's strong electoral mandate, Carlos Menem's 1989 presidential campaign did not ask for the voters' endorsement for a specific set of policies. As noted in Chapter 1, in accordance with the Peronist tradition, Menem requested that voters grant a blank mandate of trust in his leadership. Once he was elected, the depth of the economic crisis gave Menem a high degree of autonomy to impose top-down re-forms. He used his position of authority to build up a broad political coalition, both within Congress and in the country at large, to provide political support for economic reform. The heart of his strategy was based on an unlikely alliance that cut across the country's traditional political and class lines. It combined traditional Peronist machine politics (its heartland was in the sprawling working-class suburbs of the province of Buenos Aires and in the political machinery of the poorest provinces) with new provincial leaders from outside the political establishment, pro-business national figures and economic reformers both within and outside his party.

Menem's control over his party and the support he received from Justicialista party (PJ) legislators was crucial for the rapid progress of his programme of reform. Initially, he enacted the reforms with a high degree of autonomy from both the Peronist PJ and from Congress by stretching the limits of presidential powers to pass executive decrees (the so-called *Decretos de Necesidad y Urgencia*). The overuse of presidential decrees, however, and the concentration of power in the executive neither rendered the Justicialista party irrelevant nor led to the consolidation of a delegative democracy. The interaction between 'old politics' and 'new economics' shaped the agenda and the timing of the reforms. Characteristically, the area in which reforms were slower and less thorough was in the provincial administrations and in the labour market, since Menem depended on the political support of the governors of the peripheral provinces and on union bosses to control Congress and the Justicialista party. The influence of the unions and their ability to block reforms that were against their interests were evident in the slow progress of labour reform. By 1995 only 30 per cent of the labour market reform had been completed (Etchemendy and Palermo 1997). Provincial governors were also able to trade their influence in Congress for the upholding of the status quo, as provincial government reform was not even on the agenda until after the 1993 fiscal pact, and not much had been achieved in that respect by the end of the Menem era. Not only were the timing and the agenda of the reforms affected by the need to secure the support of the representatives of the old order (provincial caudillos and union bosses), but the design and content of the reforms were also marked by similar considerations. This resulted in the survival of 'illiberal enclaves' and in the suboptimal implementation of the reforms (Panizza 2000a).

Sources of popular support for the reforms

While the political influence of economic elites and interest groups is crucial for understanding policy decisions, ultimately in a democracy it is very difficult to impose reforms without at least some degree of citizen support. In Latin America's fledgling democratic environment of the 1990s, no amount of ideological conversion, executive insulation, 'old politics' and rent-seeking liberalizing coalitions could have imposed economic reforms against overwhelming opposition from public opinion. The belief that orthodox stabilizing policies and their 1980s offspring, liberalizing reforms, inflict high economic costs on the population which disproportionately hurt the poor with potentially destabilizing political consequences was well entrenched in the political mindset, not just of left-leaning critics of the IMF orthodoxy, but also in that of many mainstream Latin American politicians. It is therefore necessary to re-examine these assumptions in the light of the economic and social outcomes of the first half of the 1990s in order to better understand the complex patterns of citizens' support and opposition to the reforms.

Different mixes of free market reforms attracted different degrees of support and opposition, and the balance of costs and benefits changed through time. I deal with the changing politics of the reform agenda in Chapters 6 and 7. In what follows I concentrate on the so-called first-generation reforms, associated with economic stabilization, deregulation, privatization and trade liberalization. As discussed above, there is good evidence that while economic crises were not sufficient conditions for reform, they were an important trigger for their initiation. Kurt Weyland (1998: 562–3) argues that the citizens' hopes for reversing large losses caused by hyperinflation were crucial for generating support for market-oriented reforms in high-inflation countries such as Argentina, Bolivia, Brazil and Peru. The socio-psychological explanation for this inclination is, according to Weyland, that most people attach far greater importance to losses than to gains in making decisions. While economic reforms did inflict considerable hardship upon large sections of the population, losses were acceptable to the extent that they appeared as necessary to avert the even greater pain caused by hyperinflation.

Weyland's arguments help to explain why under certain circumstances citizens are ready to accept a considerable degree of short-term economic hardship. But how significant actually were the economic losses imposed by the reforms? It is not an easy undertaking to establish the balance of pains and gains resulting from orthodox economic stabilization policies, as not all stabilization packages achieve the same results and, as usual, the balance changes from country to country (Philip 1993: 557). Reforms such as privatization, trade opening and the rationalization of the public administration, however, inflicted significant economic costs on large sectors of the population. In most countries of the region, the implementation of the reforms led to higher unemployment, falling real wages and cuts in public services. But the negative impact of the reforms did not materialize equally for all aspects of the reforms, and trade-offs between the gains and losses of stabilization make cost–benefit calculations less straightforward than is assumed by critics.

Against the critics of neoliberalism's assumption that neoliberal reforms were uniformly opposed by the people, the reality of the first half of the 1990s was distinctly more nuanced. The dismantling of the state-centred economic model was less unpopular than a rather nostalgic view of economic protectionism leads us to believe. By portraying trade opening as a price-stabilizing device, protectionism was now linked to inflation, prompting governments to seek broader societal support for liberalization (Schamis 1999: 254). More broadly, supporters of the free market had a plausible argument in the claim that poverty and inequality in the region were the product of half a century of failed policies that, while supposedly aimed at reducing poverty, had actually made it worse. Among the policies that, according to the critics of Import Substitution Industrialization, had failed the poor were agrarian reform, minimum wage legislation, regressive social spending, price controls and labour market regulation.

Reformers argued that, in contrast to the ill-fated interventionism of the 1960s and 1970s, macroeconomic stability and higher economic growth under free market conditions, particularly when supplemented with social programmes targeted towards the neediest, offered the best hope for solving social problems deeply rooted in Latin America's history (Edwards 1995: 252–6). It seems as if the 'bitter pill' of shock economic reforms (Przeworski 1991) had at least a thick sugar coating. There is evidence that in some countries, particularly those afflicted by hyperinflation in the late 1980s and early 1990s, the initial gains from the economic reforms were actually greater than the costs incurred by them (Palermo 1999). The less than anticipated economic costs of shock economic adjustment were related to the benign international economic environment of the early 1990s. Falling international interest rates and the availability of foreign investment in a context of political democratization and economic opening resulted in a virtuous circle of economic stabilization, growing foreign investment, rising consumption and the resumption of economic growth. In contrast to the 1980s, when capital flight exacerbated the effects of the debt-induced recession, in the first half of the 1990s external funds flowed back to the region on the back of strong international liquidity and the attraction of the privatization processes. Latin America became the region of the world that attracted the most foreign investment after South-East Asia. Foreign investment flows to emerging markets grew from US$3.6 billion in 1990 to US$12 billion in 1993 (Bustos 1995: 18). Combined with the reduced burden of foreign debt interest payments resulting from the Brady plan, privatization receipts provided governments with fresh resources to stabilize the economy, while simultaneously lessening the recessionary effects of orthodox stabilization programmes and allowing increases in social spending (Philip 1998: 87).

While personalist leaders bypassed political parties and other formal institutions, those leaders did not act in a political vacuum. They appealed to the unorganized poor who were the main victims of hyperinflation and who lacked access to the social security benefits of those in formal employment. In some countries, particularly in those that were suffering from high inflation in the late 1980s and early 1990s, winning coalitions took the form of an electoral alliance between the popular sectors and the upper classes. In these elections, the very rich and sectors of the popular classes supported anti-establishment candidates committed to stabilization and reform. An electoral alliance of this type was in evidence in the Justicialista (Peronist) party triumph in the September 1991 elections for the Chamber of Deputies and in the May 1995 re-election of Argentine president Carlos Menem (Fraga 1996). Strong support from the popular sectors was also behind Fernando Collor de Mello's 1989 electoral victory in Brazil (Panizza 2000b) and of Alberto Fujimori's 1995 re-election in Peru. The success of the stabilization plans consolidated popular support for the reforming governments, which was further strengthened by the implementation of targeted social programmes that benefited the poor, a policy that was part of the free market reformers' economic transition strategy. In Argentina, the government of President Menem used social spending to create a parallel network of local and provincial authorities loyal to the presidency which dispensed social security assistance to the Peronists' traditional popular base of support (Levitsky 2003: 28). In Mexico, Carlos Salinas de Gortari (1988–94) centralized the allocation of funds under the social emergency fund, Programa Nacional de Solidaridad (Pronasol), and used it to set up a centralized patronage system that circumvented the traditional patron–client networks controlled by traditional PRI bosses (Murillo 2001: 97). And in Peru, a similar process of centralization in the executive of the assignation of funds to lower-class voters took place under Alberto Fujimori (Hagopian 1998; Kay 1995).

New relations between the state and society

The notion that free market reforms equated to the dismantling of the state also needs to be re-examined. During the years of hyperinflation, intense redistributive conflicts made politics a zero-sum game. The combination of street protests and financial speculation that characterized the politics of hyperinflation seriously challenged the authority of states to secure social and economic order. Political turmoil and economic disorganization were a reflection of the state's loss of its basic administrative and coercive powers, including the ability to regulate social relationships, extract resources, and generally use its powers to secure governability (Mauceri 1995: 10–17). The reduction in the size of the state was certainly part of the reform agenda. As part of the reform process, agencies of the state were closed down, public employees lost their jobs, and state firms were privatized. In the context of the fiscal crisis of the 1980s, public spending was curtailed and the new emphasis on fiscal discipline constrained the governments' ability to run budget deficits. Forms of state intervention, such as price controls, were eliminated, and many tasks performed by the state were contracted out to the private sector.

But as Philip Mauceri (ibid.) points out, the strength of the state has less to do with the size, brute force or formal prerogatives of state institutions than with the effectiveness with which its capacities are utilized. Rather than simply shrinking the state and depleting it of resources, free market reforms aimed at transforming the state and its relations with markets and society. The end of hyperinflation contributed to the replenishment of the state's political, institutional and symbolic capital. As one of the architects of free market reform in Bolivia, former planning minister and president Gonzalo Sánchez de Losada, put it:

> More than a strictly economic programme, the NEP [New Economic Policy, the free market reform programme] is a political plan aimed at re-establishing principles that are essential for the operation of the Republic, in the absence of which there is a great risk of falling into a path leading to the disintegration of the Nation State. (Sánchez de Losada 1985: 5, cited in Morales 1994: 134)

In parallel with privatization and deregulation, the reforms set up new forms of state internal organization, state regulation and state intervention. In the early 1990s, resources from privatization and access to foreign credit allowed governments to selectively increase public spending and restructure patronage networks. Perhaps more significantly, the state's political role was also transformed and the restoration of economic order strengthened the authority of the state in different areas of social life. The reforms gained the support of powerful business interests,

67

increased presidential authority, and made possible the setting up of new political alliances. Cooperative conduct between economic agents, impossible under hyperinflation, now became feasible. New institutions began to effectively regulate social activities that were previously operating in an institutional vacuum. Above all, the end of hyperinflation and the restoration of economic growth legitimized reforming governments, as they were seen to have successfully addressed the most pressing problem of the time. The success of economic stabilization also temporarily neutralized popular protest movements and other opposition forces, which were perceived by significant sectors of the population as part of a turbulent past.

Bolivia is a case in point, as left-wing political parties and labour unions suffered a significant erosion of popular support during the 1982–85 hyperinflationary period (ibid.: 133). During that period, the then powerful Confederación Obrera Boliviana (COB) opposed every attempt by the administration of President Hernán Siles Suazo (1982–85) to stabilize the country's economy, the failure of which led to hyperinflation and to Siles's premature resignation. To impose the package of economic stabilization and free market structural reforms, known as the *Nueva Política Económica* (New Economic Policy, NEP), Siles's successor, Victor Paz Estenssoro, decreed in 1985 a state of siege, banishing hundreds of labour leaders and dismissing thousands of mineworkers. The unions were unable to resist the onslaught, as there was strong popular support for Paz's economic policies, and at the same time the union movement paid the price for the discredit they incurred in opposing President Siles's attempts at economic stabilization (Gamarra 1994).

Between 1990 and 1997 there was a steady fall in the proportion of households under the poverty line throughout Latin America as a result of the resumption of economic growth and higher social spending (ECLAC 1998). The gains from economic stability, the resumption of economic growth, the development of new patronage networks, and the increase in social spending made possible by the rise in tax revenue explain why sectors of the popular classes voted for the election or re-election of reforming presidents, as they effectively did in many countries in the first half of the 1990s. Between 1990 and 1994 presidents who supported the reforms were elected or re-elected in Argentina, Bolivia, Mexico and Peru, countries in which there had been significant reductions in poverty from the peak levels recorded in 1990 (ECLAC 1996: 19).

The reforms also brought benefits for some sectors of the middle classes: trade liberalization and the availability of cheap consumer credit made imported consumer goods available for the first time to ordinary middle-class consumers. The rate of import growth in Latin America in 1992 was four times higher than that of the industrialized nations, and 60 per cent higher than that of Asia (Bustos 1995: 18). While many lower-middle-class state employees suffered the loss of their jobs or falls in their income as a result of the restructuring of the state, others with the right skills benefited from well-paid job opportunities provided by the multinationals that took over state utilities and other modern sectors of the economy. As David Hojman (1994: 202) put it with reference to Mexico's maquilas, but which could equally be extended to other countries of the region, the new industries:

> [c]ontributed to the development of a powerful local middle class, formed by executives of transnational corporations and their local affiliates, state bureaucrats, politicians and professionals, and elite consumers among merchants and media people. Local government officials, lawyers, accountants, bankers, customs brokers, labour contractors, owners of factory land and buildings, subcontractors, managers, technicians, journalists, consultants, academics, educators, office suppliers and entrepreneurs in real estate, construction, utilities, newspapers, tourism, communications and car rental activities had to be recruited, trained or imported.

While the economy of Chile continued to perform strongly over the period, the phoenix-like rise of the Argentinian economy made that country the stellar case for free market reforms. Between 1991 and 1994, Argentina's GDP grew at a cumulative rate of 33 per cent, consumption increased by 37 per cent, and investment by 120 per cent. Inflation fell from an annual rate of 4,923 per cent in 1989 to under 4 per cent in 1994. Between 1989 and 1993 Argentina was the fourth-largest recipient of foreign direct investment in the developing world, and the largest in Latin America (Bustos 1995: 25). Figures from Peru also show the positive initial impact of President Fujimori's shock treatment of stabilization and economic reforms enacted in the early 1990s. In 1993, the economy began a process of recovery from the prolonged recession, political unrest and social crisis which had afflicted the country since the mid-1980s. In 1994, the economy grew at a rate of nearly 13 per cent, while inflation slowed to an annual rate of 15 per cent. This was less than half the level of the inflation of 1993, and the lowest to be recorded in the previous fifteen years (ECLAC 1995: 293), and the recovery was accompanied by an increase in real wages. The minimum living wage rose by 30 per cent, while pay levels in the Lima metropolitan area were up by between 15 per cent and 20 per cent (ibid.: 300).

While less positive than those of Argentina and Peru, economic developments in other countries explain the initial popularity of free market reform candidates. In Bolivia, the New Economic Policy imposed by President Paz Estenssoro faced a dire economic situation. The collapse of the tin market in 1985 led to a combined decline of 3.5 per cent in GDP between 1985 and 1986. Real wages were also down by 20.1 per cent and 23.1 per cent respectively over the same period. The reforms had an immediate positive impact on the condition of the citizens, however. The sharp fall in the rate of inflation, from a record level 11,800 per cent in 1985 to 276 per cent in 1986 and 14.6 per cent in 1987, together with the resumption of moderate economic growth in 1987/88, helped attract strong popular support for the three parties that supported the NEP, which together obtained 65 per cent of the votes in the 1989 election (Gamarra 1994; Morales 1994).[4]

In Mexico the reform process was initiated in the 1980s under the authoritarian rule of the Partido Revolucionario Institucional (PRI). Initially, there was strong popular opposition to the reforms, which were implemented only in a limited and ad hoc way by the administration of President Miguel de la Madrid (1982–88). As high inflation and unemployment affected the standard of living of the population, the 1988 election showed strong support for the opposition presidential candidate, Cuauthemoc Cárdenas, who campaigned on an anti-neoliberal platform and may well have been deprived of victory by fraud. After President Salinas de Gortari's (1988–94) reforms stabilized the economy and engineered the return of economic growth, however, market-friendly candidates won the presidential elections of 1994 (Ernesto Zedillo) and 2000 (Vicente Fox). As in other countries of the region, a combination of factors explains popular support for candidates identified with free market economic policies in Mexico. In 1993 inflation fell to single-digit figures for the first time since the 1970s. Part of the proceeds from privatization were used by President Salinas de Gortari to boost support for the ruling PRI among the poor through targeted social spending under the Pronasol programme. The capital flight of the 1980s turned into an inflow of foreign investment in the 1990s as Mexico joined the North American Free Trade Association (NAFTA) and privatized most of its large state industrial sector. While economic growth in the early and mid-1990s was low by Mexico's historical standards, and the standard of living of the majority of the population barely improved during that period, the contrast with the economic decline of the 1980s favoured reforming candidates.

The above overview of the early political successes of free market reforms is not intended to be read as a balance of its economic costs and benefits. As will be shown in Chapter 6, the claim that the costs of the reforms were lower than anticipated and that in some countries the benefits outweighed the costs for significant sectors of the population does not amount to denying that other significant sectors of the population were losers from the reform, including the unemployed and semi-employed, large sectors of the industrial working class, public employees and members of the lower middle class that came to be known as the *nuevos pobres (nupos)*, the 'new poor'. It is necessary, however, to question the assumption that free market reforms were everywhere a top-down process with no popular support, and a process in which the costs for ordinary people massively outweighed its benefits. While it is true that free market reforms were introduced in most Latin American societies through deliberate government policy rather than as any direct reflection of the demands of civil society (Philip 1994: 366), for the reasons outlined above, in the early 1990s there was considerable popular support for reforming governments. In a study of fourteen elections that took place between 1989 and 1999, Armijo and Faucher (2002: 27–8) found that in ten of them the winning candidate took an explicit position in favour of the initiation or continuation of neoliberal reforms. Electoral support for the reforms was not forthcoming in every country, however, and they were strongly opposed from their inception by the parties of the left, trade unions and other popular organizations. We consider opposition to the reforms in Chapter 8.

Conclusion

By the mid-1990s, different variants of free market economics appear to have gained economic and political hegemony throughout the region. Because of the favourable economic environment in which the free market reforms were initiated, rather than inflicting short-term pain for long-term gains, the reforms produced some considerable short-term pains but also significant short-term gains that contributed to their acceptance by significant sectors of the population of Latin America. According to the Economic Commission for Latin America and the Caribbean (ECLAC 1998), between 1990 and 1997 Latin America experienced seven years of uninterrupted economic growth with falling poverty and increasing social spending. By the mid-1990s, supporters of the free market reformation were celebrating the success of the reforms and noting the emergence of a new free market economic consensus in the region. Typical of this mood was Sebastian Edwards's 1995 incisive account of the reform process. In his book, significantly entitled *Crisis and Reform in Latin America. From Despair to Hope*, Edwards wrote that '[t]oward mid-1993, analysts and the international financial media were hailing the market-oriented reforms as a success and proclaiming that some Latin American countries were on the way to becom[ing] a new generation of "tigers"' (1995: 6).

Belief that the free market reformation had become hegemonic was not confined to sympathetic economists. At the other end of the political spectrum, the left-of-centre Mexican political scientist Jorge Castañeda (1993: 3) was equally clear on the scope and meaning of change in the region:

> The United States and capitalism have won [...] Democracy, free market economics, and pro-American outpourings of sentiment and policy dot the landscape of a region where, until recently, Left–Right confrontation and the potential for social revolution and progressive reform were widespread.

And yet even those who celebrated the success of the reforms were aware of its shortcomings. Edwards (1995: 6–7) himself mentions the main negatives: persistent poverty, increasing inequality, outdated political institutions, political unrest, growing current account deficits, and the appreciation of the real exchange rate as a result of large capital inflows that made the external sector increasingly vulnerable to external shocks. But before analysing in more detail the socio-economic impact of the free market reformation, it is necessary to look at the relation between democracy and free market reforms.

4 | Democracy and its promises

The democratic wave that started in the early 1980s has been the longest and most encompassing in the history of the region. Until relatively recently, however, a dominant concern in academic writings on Latin America was the failure of democracy to take hold in a region in which most countries were subject to frequent breakdowns of the constitutional order. Until the 1980s, the failure of democracy to establish itself as a stable regime was self-evident in a region characterized by cycles of short-lived, weak, civilian governments followed by military coups and dictatorships of a civilian or military kind. When in place, democracy was majoritarian rather than pluralist, meaning that there were few checks and balances to restrain the power of the executive. Civil and political rights were not properly enforced, and political systems lacked adequate institutional mechanisms to process political conflicts. Instead, politics was often played as a zero-sum game. Opposition was displayed in the streets at popular level, and at the level of the elites power was sought by 'knocking at the doors of the barracks' rather than through electoral competition.

Cultural, institutional and socio-economic explanations have been advanced to account for Latin America's historical democratic deficit. Political culture explanations delve deep into Latin American history to draw attention to the way in which culture shapes the working of political institutions. Different versions of the cultural argument exist, but they all share in common the assumption that Latin America's anti-liberal political culture is rooted in a hierarchical and authoritarian Iberian colonial heritage built on the foundations of equally hierarchical and centralized indigenous empires (Morse 1982; Pastor, R. A. 1989: 4; Philip 2003: 24; Wiarda 1973).

A second set of explanations for Latin America's democratic deficit concentrates on institutional elements. A lasting political culture must be embedded in institutions, and it is in the working of political institutions that a number of scholars have sought to explain the weakness of democracy in the region. As Alan Knight (1994: 15) put it, 'in general 19th century state building in Latin America was racist, centralising and socially Darwinian'. Douglas Chalmers (1977) argues that the distinctive feature of Latin American politics is not so much the nature of the region's political regimes, but *the politicized nature* of the state. By this he understands the absence or the weakness of widely held and stable institutional rules to guide state action. In weakly institutionalized states, political struggles for the control of the state blur the divisions between the administrative and political elements of the state. Given the lack of political commitment to legal procedures, political action is subject to constant legal violations and redefinition by power players. The historical results were frequent breakdowns of the constitutional order at the macro level and the proliferation of practices of patronage and clientelism at the micro level.

A third line of explanation for the historical weakness of democracy in Latin America centres on the relations between social classes and political institutions. In the nineteenth century these arguments often took the form of discourses about race and immigration, which shared the assumption that Hispanic America was populated by the 'wrong kind of people' (i.e. indigenous and black people) and that it was necessary to promote European immigration in order to construct a civilized society. Later, particular importance was assigned to the analysis of how class relations affect a nation's path towards democracy. The historical sociological tradition has identified the ascent of the industrial bourgeoisie (Moore 1966) or, alternatively, of an alliance between the working class and the middle classes (Rueschemeyer et al. 1996) as conditions for democracy. Conversely, the power of the landed upper classes has generally been considered as an obstacle to democracy. Class-based analyses of democratization in Latin America argue that economic development in the region has shaped the region's class structure in ways that have kept anti-democratic forces, such as the landed elite, strong, and pro-democratic forces, such as the working class, weak (Germani 1962; Ianni 1975: 42; Laclau 1977: 177–80; Rueschemeyer et al. 1996: 156; Weffort 1968).

The region's return to democracy in the 1980s brought high hopes for a new fit between democracy and Latin America's culture, institutions and society. Democratic continuity since the 1980s put into question the historical pessimism about the sustainability of democracy in the region. Democratic continuity notwithstanding, a new pessimism about the prospects for democracy in the region soon dominated analyses of the new democratic polity. But the focus of analysis shifted from the likelihood of democratic breakdowns to the alleged low quality of the region's democratic orders. This chapter looks at the arguments about the condition of democracy in the region.

The rebirth of democracy

The so-called third wave of democratization (Huntington 1991) started in Latin America in the late 1970s, and over the following two decades expanded to all countries in the region with the exception of Cuba. The background to the process of democratization in the region was the crisis of the military regimes that dominated the political landscape of the 1970s. Less obvious than the political defeat of the military, but equally important, were the military defeats suffered by the Cuban-inspired revolutionary movements of the late 1960s and 1970s (Castañeda 2006a; Weyland 1999). Urban and rural guerrilla movements were defeated by the military in Brazil, Argentina, Chile, Bolivia and Uruguay. The defeat of groups such as the Montoneros in Argentina and the Tupamaros in Uruguay did not completely end revolutionary movements in Latin America. In 1979, in Central America, the Sandinistas became the first revolutionary movement to seize state power since the Cuban revolution of twenty years earlier, but their military triumph proved exceptional and their revolution politically short lived. Elsewhere in Central America in the 1980s, revolutionary armed movements in El Salvador and Guatemala engaged in peace processes that led to the abandonment of the armed struggle and a switch to electoral politics. Over the same period in South America, the Fuerzas Armadas Revolucionarias de Colombia (FARC, the Revolutionary Armed Forces) and the Ejército de Liberación Nacional (ELN, the National Liberation Army) maintained their military campaigns against the Colombian state in spite of several failed negotiations and abortive ceasefires. The most important armed guerrilla movement of the period was Sendero Luminoso (Shining Path) in Peru, established in the 1970s by the San Cristóbal of Huamanga University philosophy professor Abimael Guzman. Inspired by Mao Zedong's doctrine of popular prolonged war, Shining Path launched its first armed actions in 1980, burning ballot boxes on the eve of the country's first democratic elections in twelve years. Over the next decade, Shining Path expanded its guerrilla war to large sections of the Peruvian countryside, posing a present danger to the Peruvian state. The armed revolutionary movements of Colombia and Peru were, however, deeply rooted in the two countries' own social and political conditions and, in contrast to those involved in the wave of political radicalization of the 1960s and early 1970s, were not part of a region-wide revolutionary turn. By contrast, elsewhere in Latin America former guerrilla members and armed organizations joined the liberal democratic order.[1]

Democratization brought with it a reappraisal of the arguments about the conditions for liberal democracy in the region. The political defeat of right-wing military dictatorships and the military defeat of left-wing revolutionaries underpinned the primacy of liberal, capitalist, democracy. Historical cultural, socio-economic and class constraints to democracy were downplayed, and instead political craftsmanship and institutional engineering were seen as key for securing democratic transition and long-lasting consolidation. On the politics of transition, scholars have devoted considerable attention to the conditions for successful negotiations between political elites, involving moderate political and military actors that isolated hardliners (Di Palma 1990; Linz and Stepan 1996; O'Donnell et al. 1986). For the goal of securing the long-term survival of democracy, attention focused on institutional changes, since presidentialism was perceived as problematic for democratic stability. Comparative statistical analysis on democratic breakdowns in presidential and parliamentary regimes was used to support arguments concerning the institutional fault lines of presidentialist regimes. Among these were the rigidity of presidential terms of office, the 'winner takes all' logic of presidential elections, the dangers of political gridlock between the executive and Congress, and the claim that presidentialism promotes the election of populist outsiders (Linz 1994).

While democracy cannot be reduced to elections, elections everywhere marked the shift of direction in the region's political compass. The new democratic wave started in 1979 when the Ecuadorean people approved a new constitution and elected Jaime Roldós as president to succeed the military government that had been in power since 1972. Elections in Ecuador were followed by electoral contests in Peru and Bolivia (1980), Argentina (1983) and Uruguay (1984). In 1982 the Bolivian Congress, which had been dissolved in 1980 by the military coup of General Luis García Meza, reconvened and upheld the result of the 1980 election that had chosen Hernán Siles Suazo as the country's new civilian president. In 1985, an electoral college selected the opposition candidate Tancredo

Neves as president of Brazil to end more than twenty years of military rule. The democratic wave continued in the 1980s throughout South and Central America. Countries that had little or no tradition of democracy, such as Guatemala and Paraguay, elected presidents in 1985 and 1989 respectively. Also in 1989, the candidate of the Concertación por la Democracia coalition of opposition parties, Patricio Aylwin, won the first presidential election in Chile since the election of Salvador Allende in 1970. Finally, Mexico ended an idiosyncratic and protracted process of democratization that had been described as 'always in transition and never fully democratic', by electing the Partido de Acción Nacional (PAN) opposition candidate Vicente Fox as president in July 2000.

The process of democratization was not without setbacks. In April 1992, President Alberto Fujimori of Peru closed down Congress. In May 1993, the Guatemalan president Jorge Serrano illegally closed Congress and the Supreme Court before being forced to resign and flee the country in the face of strong popular opposition and lack of military support for his *autogolpe*. In 1996 in Paraguay, only pressure from the United States, the Organization of American States (OAS) and the countries of Mercosur prevented the then army chief, General Lino Oviedo, from deposing President Juan Carlos Wasmosy. In Venezuela, two attempted military coups in 1992 narrowly failed to depose President Carlos Andrés Pérez. Another military coup in 2002 briefly toppled President Hugo Chávez, before he was reinstated on the back of army divisions and popular support (Chávez himself had been the leader of the first, abortive, 1992 coup). In Haiti, President Jean Bertrand Aristide was deposed by a violent military coup in 1991. The country returned to constitutional rule in 1994 with the backing of the USA, but after winning presidential elections in 1995 and 2000, Aristide was again overthrown by an armed uprising in February 2004.

The proliferation of elections and the absence, with the exception of Haiti, of successful military coups during the period attests to the changed domestic and international political climate. But while free and fair elections have been held regularly throughout the region, serious arguments have been raised about the quality of democracy in Latin America. The routine holding of elections masks considerable political instability: over the last twenty-five years, fourteen democratically elected presidents were unable to complete their constitutional terms in office, a number of them because they were impeached by Congress and others because they were forced to resign by mass popular protests (Valenzuela 2004). Some of the popular protests, like those in Ecuador in January 2000 which forced the resignation of President Jamil Mahuad, had the backing of the military. Even within the narrow confines of a Schumpeterian minimalist definition of democracy, issues such as the '(un)rule of law' (Méndez et al. 1999), i.e. the failure to enforce a legal order based on a properly working judiciary, weak mechanisms of accountability, widespread corruption, politicized states and, above all, high levels of poverty and inequality cast long shadows over the region's democratic renaissance. I deal with these issues in some detail in Chapter 5. But threats to the constitutional order and objections about the quality of democracy notwithstanding, it would be wrong to underestimate the significance of political changes in the region since the 1980s. Although Latin America had gone through previous democratic waves (Bethell and Roxborough 1992; Whitehead 1992), arguably the region's latest wave of democratization has some distinctive political characteristics that are likely to make it more long lasting than similar waves in the past.

The new democratic compact

Processes of democratization in the 1980s were characterized by strong support from both the business elite and the popular sector. This convergence was in stark contrast to the social and political polarization of the 1960s. Throughout the history of the region, when their fundamental interests were perceived to be under threat, the economic elite had shown little commitment to democracy. In the 1980s, however, processes of transition to democracy had the backing of the business elites that in previous decades had welcomed military takeovers. Business support for democratization was apparent in countries in which transition took place within a context of economic crises (Argentina, Bolivia and Uruguay), relative economic success (Brazil, Mexico) and strong economic growth (Chile), although in the case of Chile, business support for democracy was much more guarded and conditional and materialized later than in other countries.

To a certain extent, business reacted to pressures for political opening and used the transition process to defend its interests. But, with the exception of Chile, business had also become disenchanted with military rulers. The failures of the projects of economic modernization and political restructuring in Argentina and Uruguay eroded the support the military originally received from significant sectors of the business community for having restored order and eliminated the threat of radical left-wing forces. In addition to the economic crises that affected business confidence in the military regimes of Argentina, Bolivia, Uruguay and to a lesser extent Brazil, business organizations became increasingly concerned about their loss of influence with the military governments. The unpredictability and lack of legitimacy of the military regimes was an additional factor that strained relations between the military and the private sector. It became increasingly clear to the business elite that nationalism, bureaucratic empire-building and self-preservation, rather than the advance of capitalist free enterprise, were the military's guiding action principles. If the military's rabid anti-communism and their defence of the principles of 'Western and Christian civilization' could be construed as coinciding with the interests of capitalism, their nationalism brought them awkward bedfellows. An example of the unpredictability of the military was the Argentine military junta invasion of the Falklands/ Malvinas islands in 1982, which placed Argentina in conflict not only with Britain but also with the USA. The political turnaround of the Argentine military from privileged allies of the USA in the struggle against communism to new champions of anti-colonialism was manifested in a statement by Argentina's foreign minister, Nicanor Costa Méndez, to a meeting of the Non Aligned Movement on 9 June 1982 in which he claimed that the struggle for the Falklands was similar to the liberation struggles of Algeria, India, Cuba, Vietnam and the Palestinian people (Tedesco 1999: 50).

In the case of Brazil, the domestic business elite strongly supported the military coup of March 1964 and the economic changes introduced by the first military governments. Business support began to drain away in the second half of the 1970s, however, as business leaders started to question the growing role of the state in the economy and the authoritarian mode of policy-making by which policy decisions were taken by a narrow clique of technocrats and military officers without adequate consultation with business organizations. In the late 1970s, business representatives began to associate political authoritarianism with economic statism. Disaffection with the military increased in the early 1980s in parallel with the slowdown of economic growth and the rise in inflation. As the military became politically isolated and the economy deteriorated, the breakdown of trust between business and the government became more open (Selcher 1986: 79). Contacts with opposition political parties and social movements convinced business that their interests would not be threatened by democratization (Payne and Bartell 1995). During the 1984 *diretas já* campaign, which mobilized large sectors of Brazilian society into demanding direct presidential elections, prominent members of the business community joined forces with the democratic opposition in the process that led to the return to civilian government in 1985.

Business perception that a return to democracy would not mean a return to the political polarization of the 1960s and 1970s was a common factor in all processes of transition to democracy. Chile was a case in point of how during transition business sought reassurance from the opposition, while at the same time attempting to influence the policies of the future democratic administration. After the defeat of the military regime in the plebiscite of 5 October 1988 that aimed to extend Pinochet's rule, the business organization Confederación de la Producción y el Comercio (CPC, the Confederation for Production and Commerce) initiated a cycle of intense negotiations with the opposition parties and with the trade union movement to seek reassurances and win as many concessions as possible from a future democratic government. Their political interlocutors obliged by reassuring business that they had nothing to fear from them, and that a future democratic government would not undo the economic reforms of the Pinochet era. Opposition leaders publicly stated that a new democratic government would respect property rights and ensure economic stability. The electoral manifesto of the Concertación de Partidos por la Democracia (CPD) acknowledged private enterprise as a 'key productive agent', and made clear that there would be significant continuity with the economic model of the outgoing military regime (Silva, P. 1995).

The trade unions, which were repressed by the military dictatorships, also played a significant role in bringing to an end the military regimes. The popular movements' importance in processes of democratization has been obscured by accounts of democratic transitions as based on elite self-protection and behind-the-scenes manipulation. Accounts of negotiations between elite actors often fail to take into consideration, however, the ties that linked the opposition elite with popular groups (Berins Collier and Mahoney 1997; Levine 1988). Nowhere was the influence of the unions more evident than in Brazil (Stepan 1985). Of particular significance were the São Paulo car-workers' industrial actions of 1977–79. A wave of strikes in the heartland of Brazil's industry was the first mass popular challenge to the rule of the military in over a decade. The strikes were suppressed by the military, but they signalled the emergence of a new trade unionism, free from the corporatist controls imposed upon the unions since the 1930s. Workers' mobilizations placed the resurgent union movement at the head of a broad spectrum of social movements, which took advantage of the military government's policy of gradual political opening and laid the ground for the campaign for direct presidential elections in 1984 (Keck 1989). Although the demonstrators did not achieve their goal of forcing direct presidential elections, the peaceful mass protest sapped the regime's residual claims to legitimacy, galvanized the opposition, and decisively contributed to the political climate that led to the defeat of the official party's candidate in the ensuing indirect presidential elections.

In Uruguay, the process of transition to democracy brought together political parties, trade unions and social movements against the military dictatorship. In 1980, social movements joined forces with political parties in conducting the 'No' campaign in a referendum that defeated the military government's project to institutionalize and prolong their rule. In the period between the referendum and the democratic elections of November 1984, popular organizations played an increasingly active role in mobilizing against the dictatorship. Mass protests converged in November 1983 in one of the largest rallies in the history of the country, which isolated the military dictatorship and weakened the military's negotiating hand vis-à-vis the political parties (Blake 1998; Gillespie 1991; Rama 1987).

In Argentina, the unions did not play the same prominent role in ending military rule as in Brazil or Uruguay, as right-wing Peronist leaders became tainted by accusations of colluding with the military in the run-up to the 1983 election to ensure the military's impunity for human rights crimes (Barros 2002). Workers' mobilizations contributed, however, to destabilizing the military government. Although greatly weakened by repression and the shrinking of the country's industrial base, in the late 1970s and early 1980s, the country's traditionally strong Peronist-controlled unions organized strikes, go-slows and stoppages in protest at reductions in real wages as a result of the economic policies of the dictatorship. A national strike against the military government took place on 27 April 1979, and a second in July 1981, which enjoyed nearly total adherence in both the industrial and the tertiary sectors. In November

1981 there was a protest march against the dictatorship with the slogan 'Bread, Peace and Jobs', followed by a second one on 30 March 1982. Three days later, in a decision that was widely perceived as at least partly motivated by the goal of distracting attention from social protests, the military regime commenced the invasion of the Falklands/Malvinas that would lead to its downfall (Smith, W. 1989: 240; Tedesco 1999: 48–9).

Civil society, political parties, the left and the return to democracy

In the early 1980s, social movements came to embody the high hopes of the early stages of transition to democracy in Latin America. Their mobilization was important not just in terms of the movements' contribution to the ending of military rule but also because their campaigns strengthened the view that an active citizenship was an essential component of the new democratic polity. Under the umbrella term of 'civil society', these organizations encompassed a wide variety of otherwise politically and socially diverse groups that opposed the military dictatorships. Paradoxically, the condition of emergence of a more autonomous civil society developed during the years of military rule. Two separate but related developments contributed to changes in the balance of forces between the state and society, and within society itself. The first was the dismantling of the post-Second World War corporatist links between the state and social organizations. As they sought to radically reform their countries' economies and society, the military governments suppressed popular movements, particularly the trade unions, but in the process they also severed the complex links of control, co-optation and recognition that characterized the populist settlement between the state and the unions of the 1950s and 1960s. Under the new democratic governments, the unions never regained the centrality they enjoyed in the 1950s and 1960s, particularly in the relatively more industrialized countries of the region, but none the less they became significantly more autonomous than in the 'golden era' of ISI.

The second development was the closure of the public sphere under the military, and the parallel politicization of everyday relations. The banning of political activity imposed by the military meant that political parties could no longer represent social demands, which left civil society organizations as the only channels for the expression of social interests. Civil society organizations used the limited opportunities for political action allowed by the authoritarian regimes to push the boundaries of freedom of expression and social protest. Meanwhile, the scale and scope of state repression produced deep dislocations in the private life of the citizens and the disruption of social life. An unintended consequence of this state of affairs for the military rulers was the politicization of cultural activities and other forms of everyday life. Non-political organizations such as cultural associations, musical movements and even sports clubs became sites of resistance to the military dictatorships.

The dismissal of thousands of left-wing sympathizers from state agencies also contributed to the flourishing of civil society. Progressive academics and professionals expelled by the military from universities and from other public bodies formed non-governmental organizations (NGOs) to continue their work. Different from the unions and from traditional grassroots organizations, NGOs had no mass membership but they had considerable professional expertise that was used to expose the failings and shortcomings of the military governments. Often with financial and political support from solidarity groups in Europe and North America, NGOs greatly expanded in numbers during the years of military rule. They were highly effective in campaigning abroad and attracting the international solidarity that made a significant contribution to the international delegitimization of the military.

For the first time in modern Latin American history, women were at the forefront of the struggle against military repression. Their action effectively put into question the dividing line between the personal and the political, as their grief as mothers and wives of imprisoned, exiled and 'disappeared' opponents of the dictatorships became the first intensely private issue to reopen a public space hitherto closed by the military rulers to anybody but their supporters. Women's groups, such as the Mothers of Plaza de Mayo in Argentina, attracted worldwide attention to the human rights violations of the military regimes. Last but not least, the Catholic Church played a prominent role in denouncing human rights violations, in helping victims of state prosecution and in eroding the military regimes' claims to moral legitimacy, particularly in Brazil and Chile.

After the long years of military rule, some party systems were significantly altered at the time of their country's return to democracy, while other party configurations re-emerged little changed from the military interlude. A mix of continuity and change marked the case of Chile. Political parties returned to public political activity in 1988 when fourteen opposition parties joined forces in a multiparty alliance to successfully campaign against President Pinochet's attempt to prolong his rule by calling a plebiscite that would allow him to remain as president for a second eight-year term. After the defeat of the military government in the 1988 plebiscite, representatives of the opposition negotiated with the military the economic and constitutional compromises that led to the elections of 1989, which were won by the opposition alliance known as Concertación por la Democracia, comprising the Partido Demócrata Cristiano (PDC, the Christian Democratic Party), the Partido Socialista (PS, the Socialist Party), the Partido por la Democracia (PPD, the Party for Democracy) and the Partido Radical Social Demócrata (PRSD, the Radical Social Democratic Party). The Concertación represented a radical change from the country's pre-Pinochet party configuration in which a left-wing alliance of the socialist and communist parties and other smaller left-wing forces faced the Christian Democratic Party at the centre and the parties of the right. By joining the Concertación, the Chilean Socialist Party broke not only its historical alliance with the communists but moved decisively to the centre, forming with the Christian Democrats one of the two pillars of the centre-left alliance that would dominate Chilean politics over the first two decades of the new democratic era (Angell 1993).

If Chile's party system under democracy represents a mix of continuity and change, nowhere was change in the party system more evident than in Brazil. The military government sought to create a new party system by banning existing political parties and setting up a pro-governmental party, the Aliança Renovadora Nacional (ARENA) and a compliant opposition party, the Movimento Democrático Brasileiro (MDB, later renamed as the Partido do Movimento Democrático Brasileiro, PMDB). The MDB leadership, however, took advantage of the limited space for political activity left ajar by the military to evolve from a token opposition into an increasingly effective political opponent of the military government. The party became an umbrella organization that brought together opposition leaders from the left to the centre-right. Legitimized by its role in opposing the military, the PMDB emerged from the years of dictatorship as the largest party in Brazil. It played a crucial role in the negotiations for transition to democracy and dominated the first civilian administration of President José Sarney (1985–90). After Brazil's return to democracy, the party system, free from the two-party artificial straitjacket imposed by the military, started a process of fragmentation that has become one of the characteristics of the country's political system.

In Argentina, the return to democracy saw the country's two traditional parties, the Partido Justicialista (PJ, also known as Peronists) and the Unión Cívica Radical (UCR, the Radical Civic Union), re-emerge as the main political forces. The process of transition to democracy, however, produced a significant change in the historical balance of forces between the two parties. The PJ, which had been Argentina's largest political force since Perón's first electoral victory in 1949, was tainted by allegations of collusion with the outgoing military regime and was defeated for the first time in free and fair elections on 30 October 1983 by the Radicals, headed by Raúl Alfonsín. The UCR electoral triumph was seen at the time as having put an end to the hegemony of the PJ and having set the bases for a more balanced party system. The political and economic failures of the administration of President Alfonsín, however, allowed the Peronists to regain their political ascendancy with the electoral triumph of Carlos Menem in 1989, and they continued to dominate Argentinian politics in the 1990s.

In other countries of the region the return to democracy saw little change in their party systems. In Peru, the military negotiated the return to democracy directly with their historical enemy, the Alianza Popular Revolucionaria Americana (APRA, the American Popular Revolutionary Alliance), the country's oldest, most disciplined and best-organized political force (Abugattas 1987). The elections of May 1980, however, were won by former president Fernando Belaúnde Terry, as the candidate of Acción Popular, another of the country's traditional parties. In Uruguay, one of the countries with the oldest and strongest party systems in Latin America, the party system returned unchanged from the years of military rule. The electoral results of the 1984 election closely matched those of 1971, the last general election before the June 1973 military coup. As in 1971, the election was won by the traditional Partido Colorado (PC, the Colorado Party), followed by the Partido Nacional (PN, the National Party, also known as the Blancos), with the left-wing Frente Amplio (FA, the Broad Front) a distant third.

One of the goals of the military dictatorships was the political destruction of the forces of the left. In spite of the banning of left-wing political parties and the use of brutal repression against their leaders, however, the military everywhere failed in their objective. While transition to democracy was dominated by parties of the centre and the centre-right, the forces of the left and the centre-left began a long political march that would lead to electoral victories at local and national level in the 1990s and in the early twenty-first century. As mentioned above, Salvador Allende's Socialist Party was a founding member of Chile's Concertación governmental alliance, but perhaps the most important left-wing party to emerge from the years of military rule was Brazil's Partido dos Trabalhadores (PT, the Workers' Party). Officially created in February 1980 by the union leaders that led the São Paulo metalworkers' strikes of 1979, the PT received the backing of left-wing intellectuals and of progressive members of the Catholic Church, which provided logistic support throughout the country. Led by the metalworkers' leader Luiz Inácio Lula da Silva, the party's strong links with the unions and other grassroots organizations made it a central actor in the struggle against the military dictatorship. In Uruguay, the FA, which was established in 1971 only two years before the military coup of June 1973, emerged from over twenty years of military rule legitimized by the role of its militants in the struggle against the dictatorship and from its leadership moderation in the 1984 negotiations between the military and political leaders that led to elections in November of that year. Mexico, which had not suffered a military dictatorship but was under the authoritarian rule of the PRI, saw the creation in May 1989 of the centre-left Partido de la Revolución Democrática (PRD, Party of the Democratic Revolution). Founded by dissidents from the PRI and other left-wing politicians, the PRD established itself as one of the country's three main political parties, with a strong electoral presence in central and southern Mexico.

The new liberal democratic culture

Paradoxically, the years of authoritarianism brought changes in political culture that favoured liberal democratic values. Characteristic of the revalorization of principles that were part of the liberal democratic tradition but had seldom been part of the region's political practices was the new centrality attributed to human rights. During the military dictatorships human rights had first become a political issue in Latin America, and through the years of dictatorship the discourse of rights became the nodal point of the politics of resistance to authoritarianism. Demands for human rights constituted a unifying cause for both traditional and new political actors of different ideological complexions. Human rights organizations were among the most active NGOs of the period. Domestic organizations found powerful international allies in international human rights groups, such as Amnesty International, which raised international awareness about human rights crimes in Latin American and lobbied Western governments to face up to human rights violations by military governments.

As Barahona de Brito (1997: 18) points out, the need to defend basic rights, once taken for granted, fundamentally changed pre-existing attitudes towards those rights as well as towards democracy. Mainstream politicians used the question of human rights to vindicate a past political order in which human rights were formally guaranteed by the constitutions. For the left, the fact that denunciations of human rights violations contributed to the delegitimization and ultimately to the downfall of right-wing dictatorships gave an ideological twist to their view of human rights as mainly an instrument of cold war politics. The left's conception of human rights changed accordingly from a view of rights only realizable in a radically transformed socio-economic setting to the acceptance and defence of universally held rights under liberal democratic rule. 'Nunca más' (Never again), a slogan that was widely adopted by human rights movements to signify that never again would gross human rights crimes be allowed in the region, illustrates the symbolic closure effect achieved by associating human rights violations with the authoritarian past. As Manuel Antonio Garretón (1994: 222) puts it: '"Nunca más" [was] less a programme for the future than a denunciation of the past, since the future seems guaranteed by the very condition of all democracies.'

The articulation of new and old political elements that characterized the struggle for human rights during the years of military rule anticipated further changes in the political landscape in the region. Representative democracy, once denounced by the left as capitalism's best political shell, was now regarded as a goal in itself and not just as a transitional stage towards a socialist society. The return of thousands of political exiles, whose survival had been greatly assisted by international solidarity, increased domestic awareness of the cosmopolitan dimensions of democracy. As the experience of authoritarian rule deradicalized the left-wing opposition, a return to democracy no longer seemed dangerous to the economic elite. Both the left and the right had learned a historic lesson: 'Reformist, populist or socialist projects have been attempted and had failed; reactionary authoritarian projects have also been attempted and had also failed' (Whitehead 1992: 148).

More generally, in the 1980s democracy became associated with the landscape of late-twentieth-century modernity and with the promise of economic prosperity. In Chile, the experiences of the 1973 military coup and subsequent exile caused members of Allende's Socialist Party to embark upon a major rethinking of the reasons for the failure of the Unidad Popular government. This process led to a revision of their previously held economic views, and although a commitment to social justice remained part of their political programme, a new adherence to the fundamentals of a market economy was also developed (Funk 2004). As the decade progressed, the crisis of the Soviet bloc further eroded the attraction of socialism as an alternative to democratic capitalism. At the same time, the exponential growth in international communications associated with the early stages of *fin de siècle* globalization and growing awareness of global issues, such as the environment and human rights, resulted in the growth of a new international civil society with which many Latin American social activists became personally and institutionally involved.

Together, internal and external political, economic and cultural developments constituted elements of a certain narrative of modernity of which shared liberal democratic values and the broad acceptance of some form of market economy constituted a common thread. Against nationalist and 'Third Worldist' views of the region, Latin American intellectuals reasserted the region's economic, cultural and political identification with the West. The Brazilian intellectual and diplomat José Guilherme Merquior published in 1991 a passionate defence of Latin America's Western identity. He denounced the myth of the region's non-Western identity as 'a strategy of refusal dictated by resentment – a refusal of what we have long striven to become, yet allegedly always failed to achieve, namely [being] part and parcel of the modern liberal democratic universe identified with the West'. He claimed that 'Latin America is just *another West*: a poorer, darker, different, still troubled West, but West nonetheless, unmistakably, in the language, values and beliefs of its societies' (Merquior 1991: 158). A few years earlier, the French scholar Alain Rouquié had defended similar views in a book suggestively titled *Amérique Latine: Introduction à l'Extrême-Occident*. In it he argued that the similitude of values between the West and Latin America was unmistakable. He noted that the West had historically supplied Latin America with military and civil technology, religious beliefs and capital, and cultural models that became part of the region's identity (Rouquié 1987: 19).

For both Merquior and Rouquié the existence of non-Western indigenous peoples did not negate, but complemented, Latin America's Western identity. They argued that far from having an entirely separate culture and identity, the region's indigenous populations were largely Westernized in most key areas of social behaviour. As Rouquié (ibid.: 21) put it, Latin America's Western culture had smothered, absorbed and recovered pre-existing cultural and ethnic elements. Merquior (1991: 156) reminded his readers of the Zapotec Amerindian Benito Juárez, who was president of Mexico between 1858 and 1872. He noted that Juárez reportedly never spoke a word of Spanish until he was aged fourteen, and that as president he had said no to European power, and yet – Merquior points out – Juárez had said a clear yes to Western culture. Rouquié and Merquior did not ignore the fact that Amerindians had legitimate grievances against the white colonizers, but argued that their rights were not so much framed in terms of ancient, traditional, telluric roots, but were an integral part of Western discourses of rights and identity. As Alan Knight (1994: 17) puts it, candidates aspiring to govern the Mexican state of Oaxaca were now lobbying for Mixtec Indian votes in southern California.

The underside of democracy

The high hopes raised by the process of democratization in Latin America, described in the previous section, proved short lived. While there had been no return to military rule, by the mid-1990s public opinion surveys and academic writings had already begun to reflect a mood of disillusionment with the condition of democracy in the region. By 1996, 61 per cent of the population stated that they still preferred democracy as a model of government but only 27 per cent of the region's citizens were satisfied with the way democracy worked in their countries (Latino-barómetro 1996).[2] At a time during which the countries of Latin America were undergoing painful processes of economic adjustment and free market reforms, disillusionment with democracy partly reflected the social hardships and political dislocations produced by economic change. The same survey showed that unemployment was perceived as the main problem affecting the countries of the region. While the impact of economic transformations on still mainly unconsolidated democracies was central to the analyses of the problems with democracy in the region, the questions raised by the condition of democracy went beyond the social impact of economic liberalization.

In the 1990s and early 2000s, academic analyses of democracy shifted from the narrow focus of the transition literature on the conditions for the survival of democracy to broader issues concerning its quality (Altman and Pérez-Liñan 2001; Linz and Stepan 1996; Przeworski et al. 2000; Spanakos 2007). The new pessimism combined familiar themes of cultural, socio-economic and institutional obstacles to democracy in Latin America with new arguments about how free market economic reform had impacted negatively on already historically weak democracies. The result was a return to the historical pessimism about the prospects for democracy in the region that had been interrupted briefly by the optimism of transition. In contrast to the past, the new pessimism prevailed at a time in which, as noted above, there were no authoritarian reversals. But if the survival of democracy was acknowledged grudgingly, its quality was found wanting. The new mood was reflected in the qualifications attached to democracy in the region: 'democracy by default' (Whitehead 1992); 'low intensity democracy' (Gills and Rocamora 1993); 'delegative democracy' (O'Donnell 1994). Typical of the intellectual pessimism of the time was Lawrence Whitehead's (1992: 158) overview of democratization in Latin America, in which he claimed that, although some conventional liberal democratic regimes were likely to become consolidated, the dominant pattern was better understood as 'democracy by default' and in a few cases as little more than 'a façade democracy'.

What was behind the new pessimism? Arguably, transition to democracy had a double temporal and political dimension. On the one hand it was presented as a *new beginning* ('Never again!') after long years of authoritarian rule. As a new beginning, democratic transition crystallized the hopes that the new democratic wave was to be not only longer lasting, but also of a higher quality than similar waves of the past. It was expected that the *new democratic order* would be characterized by changes in the region's political culture and institutions to bring them more in line with the values and institutions of liberal democracy, among these a more active and autonomous civil society, stronger rule of law, a new culture of human rights, and revitalized party systems. On the other hand, democratization was heralded as a *return to democracy*, meaning that the countries of the region were retrieving a democratic past, troubled as this past may have been. Constitutional orders, state institutions, political parties and political leaders of the years previous to the military era regained their place in the new democratic order and brought with them some of the historical features of the region's previous democratic orders. It is in the fault line between democracy as a *new beginning* and democracy as a *return to the past* that may be found some of the clues for understanding the disenchantment with democracy.

Democracy as a new beginning was never conceived as ground-zero politics. The vindication of past democratic institutions, traditions and struggles was an important part of the new democratic imaginary. What was important was the possibility of setting up clear moral, political, social and economic dividing lines between the current democratic governments and the authoritarian past. The mode of transition to democracy, however, made these dividing lines less clear cut than hoped by campaigners for democracy. The problematic nature of a radical break with the authoritarian past became evident during the early stages of transition. It concerned what had been one of the core issues in the struggle for democracy, particularly in the countries of the Southern Cone: namely, human rights. Demands for the punishment of those responsible for human rights crimes during the years of military rule exposed the tensions between morality, justice and politics, as the new democratic governments had to balance demands for justice with the fact that the military still had considerable potential to destabilize the fledgling democratic regimes (Zalaquet 1998). Tensions generated by the conflicting logics of politics and justice translated into open conflict between the new democratic authorities and civil society, which in the past had been part of the same movement for democracy (Garretón 1996).

The governments of the region dealt with the human rights violations of the military dictatorship in different ways. Days after being sworn into office, President Raúl Alfonsín of Argentina (1983–89) commissioned an official investigation into the plight of the 'disappeared' during the years of military rule. His government also initiated criminal proceedings against the members of the military juntas, leading to the conviction of a number of former military rulers for crimes against human rights.[3] In Chile, President Patricio Aylwin (1990–94) called for an inquest but not trials, while in Brazil and Uruguay Presidents José Sarney (1985–90) and Julio María Sanguinetti (1985–90) called for neither investigations nor trials (Pion-Berlin 1994).[4] Several reasons account for the different outcomes, among these variations in the gravity of the crimes, different modes of transition to democracy, the civil–military balance of power, and the political will of those in office (Barahona de Brito 1997; Pion-Berlin

1994).[5] The overall net result was that, with the partial exception of Argentina, perpetrators of human rights abuses would enjoy impunity from justice until changes in the political climate in the late 1990s and early twenty-first century paved the way for a limited number of prosecutions in Chile and Uruguay, and for further prosecutions in Argentina.[6]

A new democratic beginning required not just the punishment of military officers responsible for crimes against human rights, but the complete subordination of the military to the civilian authorities. The history of Latin America reminds us that, even in periods of civilian rule, the armed forces frequently exercised tutelary powers over democratically elected governments. The military emerged from the transition to democracy politically weakened, and the new democratic authorities further reduced their influence in many areas (Hunter 1998). But in many countries the principle of military subordination to civilian governments was less than fully respected during the first years of democratic rule. Constraints imposed by the negotiated nature of the transition process in Brazil, Ecuador and Chile gave the armed forces considerable political influence over the first democratic administrations, while further political developments under democracy enabled the military to control internal security (Peru), obstruct judicial proceedings (Uruguay and Argentina) and appoint active officers to cabinet positions (Brazil) (Pion-Berlin 1991: 543–4).

In Chile, the armed forces retained powers that were clearly incompatible with democracy. As part of the negotiating process that led to the 1989 elections, the opposition accepted that the soon-to-be democratically elected government would be bound by the 1980 constitution, which had been drafted by members of the military government and ratified by a referendum of highly questionable legal validity. In the months before transferring power to President Patricio Aylwin, the military regime passed an organic law of the armed forces that further limited the incoming government's control over the military. Among other authoritarian constraints, the constitution curtailed the decision-making powers of future civilian governments on issues of national security through the creation of a military-dominated National Security Council. The president had no power to appoint the commanders of the three branches of the armed forces, or to remove any military commander without the permission of the Security Council; additionally, the 1978 Amnesty Law, passed by the Pinochet government, could not be annulled or overruled.

The armed forces also enjoyed budget autonomy guaranteed by 10 per cent of the income earned through copper exports (Acuña and Smulovitz 1996; Angell 1993). General Pinochet himself was allowed to remain as commander-in-chief of the army until March 1998, and a senator for life afterwards.

Politically, the reinstitution of constitutional order confronted the hopes of a better democratic order with the realities of politics as usual. As noted above, during the years of authoritarian rule social movements were at the vanguard of the struggle against the dictatorship, and were seen as the bearers of a more democratic political culture and of a more participatory form of democracy (Roberts, K. M. 1997: 138). It was generally assumed that social movements would continue to thrive under democracy, but the assumption did not match the reality of transition politics, as the high levels of social mobilization that characterized the process of transition were followed by a decline in social movements' activism (Huber et al. 1997: 331).

Several reasons account for the failure of social movements to maintain the high political profile enjoyed during the struggle against military rule. The fall of the military dictatorships deprived social movements of a common enemy that acted as a catalyst to unify their demands. After the first years of democratic rule, international solidarity organizations that had funded and supported NGOs and social movements progressively switched priorities to other areas of the world. Negotiations regarding transition to democracy were conducted between military and political elites, with little participation of social leaders. During the electoral campaigns that marked the return to democracy, political parties took centre stage and resumed their representative parliamentary role after the elections. Some social movements, particularly those active in the field of human rights, failed to adapt the confrontational tactics of the struggle against the military governments to the politics of negotiation and compromise characteristic of the new institutional environment. The refusal to compromise in their demands for punishment of all those involved in crimes against human rights made it difficult for organizations such as the Mothers of Plaza de Mayo, which had led the struggle for human rights against Argentina's military junta, to strike bargains and build up alliances, leaving the movement marginalized from the political arena (Brysk 1994; Escobar and Alvarez 1992). Other social movements were able to adapt and flourish under democracy. In Brazil, members of

93

social movements linked to the Catholic Church and activists from the 'new trades unionism'[7] shifted much of their efforts from campaigning for democratic elections to setting up the Partido dos Trabalhadores (PT, the Workers' Party). Social movements were also active in lobbying the constitutional assembly that drafted the 1988 constitution (Hochstetler 1997). But while new social movements and trade unions remained active in the new democratic environment, those who expected that civil society organizations would be at the forefront of the struggle for the radical democratization of society saw their expectations unfulfilled, thus contributing to their disillusionment with the transformative power of liberal democracy.

The return to democracy also brought conservative political and economic elites back to public life. This was particularly the case in pacted transitions (O'Donnell 1992), which allowed politicians and political parties that had supported the military dictatorships a strong political presence in the new democratic polity. A case in point is Brazil, where the military regime had allowed the continuation of limited political activity under severely restricted conditions that included the banning from political activities of most progressive opposition leaders. The arrangement favoured conservative politicians from backwater regions of the country who controlled Congress and state governments and benefited from access to patronage dispensed by the military-controlled federal state. When the country returned to democracy, local patronage networks remained in place, allowing traditional political bosses, known as *coroneis*, to maintain their electoral fiefdoms (Hagopian 1996; Kingstone and Power 2000).

In most countries of the region, the first democratic governments after the retreat of the military were controlled by parties of the centre and the centre-right. In Chile, the centre-left Concertación alliance won the presidential and parliamentarian elections, but the electoral laws imposed by the outgoing Pinochet regime gave substantial overrepresentation in Congress to the forces of the right, and made changes to the constitution impossible without support from right-wing parties. In Argentina, the centrist Unión Cívica Radical (UCR) defeated the then right-dominated Justicialists (Peronists), but the parties of the left had no significant political representation in Congress. In Uruguay, the first democratic elections were dominated by the traditional Blanco and Colorado parties, with the left-of-centre Frente Amplio a distant third. In Peru, in

1980, President Fernando Belaúnde Terry's centre-right Acción Popular defeated the populist APRA (Alianza Popular Revolucionaria Americana), and in Ecuador in 1979 another centrist alliance, Jaime Roldós Aguilera's Concertación de Fuerzas Populares (CFP), won over the right-wing candidate Sixto Durán Ballén of the Partido Social Cristiano (PSC, the Social Christian Party). Later in the democratization cycle, in Mexico President Vicente Fox's centre-right Partido Acción Nacional (PAN) ended the long years of rule by the Partido Revolucionario Institucional (PRI, the Revolutionary Institutional Party). Politics in Colombia and Venezuela, which did not experience military dictatorships in the 1970s, was also dominated by traditional political parties, in the case of Colombia by the Conservative administration of President Belisario Bentancur (1982–86) and the Liberal government of President Virgilio Barco (1986–90), and in Venezuela by the Christian Democratic government of Luis Herrera Campins (1979–84) and the Acción Democrática (AD, Democratic Action Party) administration of President Jaime Lusinchi (1984–89). One of the few left-of-centre governments of the period was that of President Hernan Siles Suazo in Bolivia (1982–85). As described in Chapter 3, however, his administration was undone by social conflicts and economic mismanagement. As a result, President Siles Suazo was forced to call an early election and hand power to his conservative successor, Víctor Paz Estenssoro, a year before the end of his constitutional term. Significantly, the 1980s drew to a close with the electoral defeat in Nicaragua of the Sandinista leader Daniel Ortega by the opposition candidate Violeta Chamorro in the presidential election of 25 February 1990.

The dominance of centre-right governments that implemented broadly similar policies of free market reforms with the support and tutelage of international financial institutions raised questions about whether democracy was effectively allowing voters to make meaningful policy choices (Weyland 2004: 144). Concerns about lack of real choice were exacerbated by the frequency with which, as noted in previous chapters, candidates opposed neoliberalism during the electoral campaigns only to implement free market reforms once in office. In analysing the gap between electoral policy commitments and actual policy decisions, Susan Stokes (1999, 2001) argues that mandate unresponsiveness reflected a sharp elite–mass conflict over economic policy: while voters pulled politicians towards economic security-oriented policies and gradualism during electoral campaigns, markets pushed them towards efficiency-oriented policies and 'big bang' reforms after taking office. Arguably, elite prefer-ences, the pressure from the IMF over highly indebted governments, and the impersonal threat of capital flights and investment strikes had more influence on governments' policy decisions than the will of the people. Impunity for the perpetrators of human rights violations, the maintenance of military prerogatives, the loss of centrality of social movements, and the political hegemony of parties of the centre and centre-right enacting policies allegedly more attuned to the will of the markets than to the will of the people raised questions about the narrow nature of democratization in Latin America.

Conclusions

In the 1980s, transition to democracy represented more than just the end of the era of military dictatorships. It provided the elements of a historical narrative that allowed the people to set up a dividing line between the democratic present and the authoritarian past. It was both a link with the past before military rule ('the return to democracy') and a promise for the future ('never again!'). The language of democracy was both *new* ('human rights', 'civil society', new constitutions) and *old* (elections, the relegalization of political parties, the return of political leaders). It brought together traditional politicians, redeemed from faults of their pre-military rule by their support for democracy, and new political and social actors: the new social movements, the returned exiles, the journalism of denunciation and resistance. It linked local struggles with international struggles for democracy and human rights. Democracy had its own epic, drawn from stories of resistance, imprisonment and exile. It was at the same time a new beginning and the retrieval of a long-lost but hardly ever existent constitutional order.

Democracy provided the Latin American people with a renewed image of their own unity (Anderson 1996). It reconstituted images of the nation with the national symbols used as celebratory emblems of democracy and of a common Latin American destiny, which saw country after coun-try becoming part of the region-wide process of democratization. The historical pessimism concerning the conditions for democracy in Latin America appeared unfounded. There were no structural conditions to democracy, or, to the extent that there were, they could be overcome by human action. Revitalized political parties and a vibrant civil society provided a better institutional framework for the flourishing of democracy than the old 'authoritarian state, weak civil society' political framework. Corporatism and populism were weakened by their failure to secure social order and economic development in the years previous to the military coups. Political learning had brought a change in political culture in which right-wing authoritarians and left-wing revolutionaries lost ground to the new politics of compromise and respect for human rights.

And yet the celebration of democracy could hardly mask the challenges facing the new democratic governments. In most countries the return to democracy coincided with the worst economic crisis since the 1930s. The authoritarian and elitist legacies of the past thwarted expectations that the new wave of democracy would mark a new political beginning in the region. Politics in the 1990s appeared to offer little real alternative to the hegemony of free market economics and centre-right politics. The high expectations of the early years of democratization gave way in the 1990s to disillusionment, if not with democracy itself, then certainly with the working of democracy in the region. Above all, the process of change associated with the introduction of free market economic reforms produced huge social, political and economic dislocations that put into question, if not necessarily the survival of democracy, at least its quality. I deal with these issues in Chapter 5.

5 | Democracy and markets: contestation and consent

Democracy, conflict and accommodation

One of the earliest and more perceptive critics of Latin America's democratic renaissance was Paul Cammack, who in the 1980s anticipated arguments that would resonate a decade later. In replying to the radical US scholars Edward Herman and James Petras's (1985: 91) contention that in South America military power had survived virtually intact, and that the new civilian authorities were little more than 'fall guys' who would take responsibility for the austerity policies of the 1980s only to give way to a new crop of military rulers, Cammack (1986) claimed that the era of military coups in Latin America was effectively over. He argued that, instead of relying on military rulers, the region's bourgeoisie had set up in place a workable system characterized by regular, competitive elections, capable of guaranteeing their class interest. He noted that there was a big difference between an ideal democracy capable of satisfying the needs of a majority of citizens, and Latin America's actually existing democracies; but, as he put it, 'the unpalatable truth may be that the new rulers of South America represent *unified and capable bourgeoisies well aware of their needs and well equipped to pursue them*' (ibid.: 125; my emphasis).

Similar views on the conservative nature of the new wave of democratization were advanced some years later by Barry Gills and Joel Rocamora (1993), as well as by Nicolas Guilhot (2005). Gills and Rocamora argued that the late-twentieth-century wave of democratization in Third World countries was little more than the product of an indirect political intervention by the USA to pre-empt more radical change. They claimed that the US government's strategy was based on promoting the electoral participation of broad popular forces, while at the same time securing continuity with the anti-reformist policies of the outgoing military regimes. Gills and Rocamora concluded that the outcome of the process was a low-intensity democracy designed to promote stability and that democracy, as understood in the West, was incompatible with societies, such as those of Latin America, characterized by extreme concentration of wealth in the hands of a tiny elite. As a result, democracy in most newly democratized countries remained confined to formal electoral participation:

> This cosmetic democratisation brings some limited change in civil and human rights and widens the legal space in which popular mobilisation for change can take place. But repression and abuses of human rights continue, usually against the familiar targets of labour, students, the left and human rights activists. (Gills and Rocamora 1992: 514)

The resilience of democracy in the 1990s did little to convince critics of the third wave of democratization of its transformative potential. Nicolas Guilhot (2005) claims that, during the Reagan administration, the promotion of democracy became a key element of the US foreign policy strategy that drew together the academic left and the policy-making right under the common ideological umbrella of the struggle against authoritarianism. He further claims that, as part of the same strategy, the World Bank shifted from an institution favouring authoritarian developmentalism to a promoter of civil society participation, democracy and decentralization. Guilhot argues that the promotion of democracy and human rights had thus changed from being part of counter-hegemonic, anti-dictatorial strategies to become 'part of the arsenal of power itself' (p. 8). He further argues that, in the last decade of the twentieth century, and particularly since September 11 2001, democracy promotion has become part of the neoconservatives' hegemonic project.

Cammack, Gills and Rocamora, and Guilhot's arguments resonate not just with the obvious democratic deficits of the processes of democratization in the region, but, more broadly, with the left's traditional critique of liberal democracy, or at least of liberal democracy as an instrument for radical economic change. Arguably, liberal democracy is rarely a conduit for radical change, as the checks and balances that are part of its institutional make-up favour compromise and incremental change at best. Although liberal democracy does not preclude challenges to the socio-economic order, there are clear limits to these challenges if democracy is to survive. The core of this argument is crystallized in Huber et al.'s (1997: 331) claim that the survival of democracy depends on a delicate balance between pressures from below and threat perception at the top. According to their argument, a stable democratic order depends on the ability of subordinate groups to fight for inclusion and on the economically dominant groups being reassured that their core interests would not be threatened by the inclusion of the popular sectors in the political order. From these premises, it could be argued that liberal democracy has a conservative bias or, in Cammack's neo-Marxist terms, it is always at roots a bourgeois democracy. Huber et al.'s argument is, however, more balanced than that encapsulated by the rather crude, but not entirely misguided, 'bourgeois democracy' characterization. The authors emphasize that, under democracy, the working and middle classes gain unprecedented capacity for self-organization and mobilization, and that their actions can effectively weaken the dominant classes' grip on power. They conclude that the real opportunity that democracy offers for the advancement of popular interests makes democracy the most favourable arena for the political engagement of the subordinate classes (ibid.: 331; Huber Stephens 1990: 167; Rueschemeyer et al. 1996: 62–3).

The argument that the survival of democracy depends on the 'right balance of class struggle' is not the sole preserve of progressive historical sociologists, such as Barrington Moore (1966), and Huber et al. As noted in the introduction in a distinctively non-Marxist work, Seymour Martin Lipset (1959) argued that both conflict and consensus are necessary for democracy. According to Lipset, extreme conflict produces violence and social disintegration, but without conflict we can have only totalitarian unanimity and political exclusion. In Lipset's view, economic development largely determines the balance between conflict and consensus. There are several interrelated reasons why development is likely to produce the 'right balance' of conflict and consensus under which democracy becomes sustainable. Lipset assumes that development is a generally benign process that generates the wealth, social conditions and cultural values conducive to liberal democracy. Socially, development lowers inequality and class polarization. It favours the growth of the middle class, and a more active and autonomous civil society. Prosperity makes distributional struggles less extreme, as the rich will offer less resistance to the redistribution of their surplus income towards the worst off. Economic development makes people less anchored to their class roots, and thus less inclined to see politics in terms of a zero-sum game between opposing social classes. Finally, economic growth also provides the state with the necessary resources to improve education and other social services, and favours cosmopolitanism as people have more opportunities to travel and become aware of cultural diversity.

Lipset's arguments have been strongly contested. The benign political nature of economic development was challenged by the dependency school (Gunder Frank 1972). The spread of bureaucratic authoritarian regimes in Latin America in the 1970s (O'Donnell 1973) gave historical support to the dependentists' intellectual pessimism concerning the possibility of democracy in developing capitalist economies.[1] But if Lipset severely underestimated the conflictive and polarizing nature of processes of development, his argument about democracy's being grounded on a balance between conflict and consensus still carries considerable weight.

How did free market reforms fit within this debate? While the free market reformation was originally formulated on narrow economic terms, the economic project of the Washington Consensus (WC) had clear political connotations. Defenders of the reforms assumed that economic modernization would allow Latin America to escape from an unstable, poorly institutionalized and economically unsuccessful past, and in the process construct consolidated, conventional liberal capitalist democracies (Whitehead 1992: 153). The strengthening of the private sector was thought to contribute to the process of democratization by limiting the discretionary power of the state and promoting the expansion of civil society (Agüero 1998: 1). Civil society organizations would become economic agents to take over the tasks that the state was not fit to perform, as well as key political actors in the democratic game.

The discourses of liberal democracy and of free markets had many terms in common, or at least terms that could be construed as part of a common politically and economically liberal outlook: impersonal market exchanges do not care for social hierarchies or privileges, and nor does democracy. Rent-seeking was another name for corruption, which free marketeers argued was caused by excessive state interventionism and by the colonization of the state by political parties. Patronage impinged on the democratic principle of equality before the law, and the substitution of arbitrary regulation for the impersonal hand of the market would reduce the power of unaccountable bureaucrats and erode the influence of patronage and clientelism. Accountability is both an economic term, meaning the proper use of economic resources, and a political term, meaning that representatives must be responsive to the demands of the represented. The rule of law protects property rights and human rights alike. More fundamentally, market-based economic development would provide the economic stability and the sustainable growth necessary for the kind of social compromises that underpin stable liberal democratic regimes.

For critics of the free market reformation, the democratizing promise of neoliberalism was always a hollow one. In the 1990s, arguments about the negative impact of free market reforms on democracy paralleled the 1970s 'dependentist' claim regarding the authoritarian nature of dependent capitalist development in providing the intellectual foundation for the new pessimism about the relations between free market capitalism and democracy in Latin America. According to its critics, neoliberal reforms had not only failed economically, but also politically in delivering the type of economic development that is a condition for a sustainable democracy. Moreover, the reforms also failed to secure the social conditions under which the dialectical balance between contestation and accommodation that characterizes 'the right kind of class struggle' is required for a sustainable liberal democracy. It is necessary to critically examine these arguments.

The weakening of contestation from below

I examine in detail the economic record of neoliberalism in Chapter 6. Suffice to recall here that, as noted in Chapter 3, in the first half of the 1990s and for a period of time that varied from country to country, the fall in inflation combined with the influx of foreign capital and the availability of credit benefited the poor, who were the main victims of inflation, and gave important sectors of the middle classes access to consumer goods and other material benefits. These developments appeared to give substance to Lipset's optimism about the benign political effects of economic development on class relations. But the gains of structural adjustment and early liberalization proved insufficient and short lived. By the end of the 1990s, low economic growth meant that the number of Latin Americans living under the poverty line was greater than at the beginning of the decade (ECLAC 2002). Income distribution, which had become more equal during the 1970s, worsened considerably in the 1980s and remained stagnant in the 1990s (Karl 2000: 150). Unemployment, underemployment and the exponential growth of the informal sector resulted in large numbers of workers and their families not having access to social security and other benefits from the formal economy.

The destruction of stable employment relations made people less tied to their class roots; but the counterpart was not social mobility that lessened class polarization, but social fragmentation that induced social anomie and political alienation. The key role that education plays, according to Lipset, in fostering a democratic culture did not materialize, as Latin America's educational levels remained below its level of economic development compared to other regions of the world (Abugattas and Paus 2007: 5). Globalization brought with it the emergence of a narrow cosmopolitan elite whose income and professional skills allowed them to enjoy lifestyles more similar to their European and American counterparts than to the societies into which they were born (Stallings 1992). For an increasing number of Latin Americans, however, the new cosmopolitanism had the bitter taste of economic migration to Europe and the USA; and for many among the poor the main global economic enterprises that they could seriously consider joining were the drugs trade and organized crime.

If the reforms of the 1990s did not produce the type of economic growth necessary for the emergence of more prosperous and equal societies, how did the socio-economic changes of the period affect the dialectic between contestation and accommodation that is of the essence within a democratic political order? In the 1960s and 1970s the economic dislocations of the ISI model led to social polarization and to the unravelling of the alliance between the state, local industrialists, organized labour and sectors of the middle class which sustained the ISI economic model. The economic failure and the political polarization that followed opened the way for the military regimes of the 1970s. Why did the economic failures and social dislocations of the free market reformation not result in a similarly authoritarian outcome in the 1990s?

A changing international environment hostile to military coups emerges as a significant factor in explaining the survival of democracy in the 1990s, but the analysis of international factors is not the concern of this chapter. Domestically, key to answering the above questions is to take on board Evelyn Huber Stephens's (1990: 167) contention that the crucial link between development and democracy lies in the effect of economic development on the structure and strength of civil society, and thus on the capacity of subordinate classes to pressure for political inclusion. In analysing the changes in Latin America's social structure in the 1990s, we find elements in common with the arguments of the 1950s and 1960s concerning how the structural heterogeneity of Latin American societies and the relative weakness of the working class negatively affected democracy in the region (Germani 1962; Prebisch 1949; Sunkel 1973; Touraine 1979; Rodríguez 1994). The new 'weakness of the working class' argument explains why, compared to the political radicalization of the late 1960s and early 1970s, the socio-economic polarization of the 1990s appeared to have generated comparatively little political radicalization. The democratic environment of the 1990s and the legacy of the human rights movement of the 1980s had considerably increased the political and, potentially, legal costs of the use of state force for mass repression. But the impersonal forces of deindustrialization, informalization and unemployment had also blunted the popular sectors' organizational and political ability to resist the forces of economic liberalization.

Kenneth Roberts (2002) claims that, while twenty years of political democratization, economic crisis and free market reforms deepened social inequalities across most of Latin America, class cleavages were eroded in the political arena. According to his argument, the political organization of the working class had been undermined not through *embourgeoisement*, as Lipset hypothesized would be the outcome of economic development, but by highly disruptive patterns of socio-economic transformation that simultaneously accentuated social inequalities and inhibited class organization from below. The class structure of Latin America in the 1990s showed a shrinking formal-sector working class and a rising informal sector of semi-employed and self-employed workers. Income inequality increased significantly for the region over the period and, with exceptions, for each individual country (Portes and Hoffman 2003: 58, 75). The politicization and mobilization of class cleavages were made more difficult by the fragmentation of labour markets, deindustrialization, privatization and public sector spending cuts that affected the large concentration of workers in the most heavily unionized sectors of the economy. The rural population witnessed a similar process of class disorganization. In his study of free market democracy in the Chilean and Mexican countryside, Marcus Kurtz (2004) argues that neoliberal reforms disaggregated and atomized the rural population, making it more difficult for the rural poor to engage in collective action and reinforcing their dependency on agrarian elites and neo-clientelistic networks.

In parallel to the shrinking of the working class and, more generally, to the erosion of formal employment, there was an expansion of the informal sector. Informality did not start in the 1980s and 1990s in Latin

America. The fact that large sections of the urban population did not have access to stable, formal jobs had already been noted by scholars in the years after the Second World War (Thorp and Bergés n.d.). The impact of the great wave of migration from the countryside to the cities of the 1940s and 1950s was captured in classic sociological works, such as Bryan Roberts's (1978) *Cities of Peasants*, which showed that, in the big metropolises of Latin America, rural migrants did not become the new industrial proletariat, as happened in Europe during the Industrial Revolution, but remained at the margins of society. Politically, these *marginal* sectors were subject to clientelist relations of representation that formed the political base of support for populist and conservative political forces alike. As noted in Chapter 1, Hernando de Soto's (1989) highly influential work *The Other Path* challenged the dominant perception of this social group as an economic and social burden to society, instead hailing them as budding entrepreneurs struggling to be liberated from the dead hand of the mercantilist state by the impersonal hand of free market deregulation. Contrary to De Soto's expectations, however, free market reforms did not lead to the shrinking of the informal sector, but rather to its further expansion, as the crisis of the 1980s and the low job creation recovery of the first half of the 1990s made it increasingly difficult for those without the right skills to compete for jobs in the modern, global-oriented formal economy. The informal sector is highly fragmented, but for the reasons outlined in Chapter 3, a large number of people working in it supported the very same centre-right political forces that were enacting the reforms that increased informality.

The political weakness of the popular sectors meant that business appeared to have little to fear about radical threats to their interests under democracy. Thus, even if we accept Lawrence Whitehead's (1992: 148) questionable assumption that democratization was a second-best outcome for both the business elite that supported authoritarianism and for the revolutionary left that had fought for a radical transformation of society, business emerged as the clear winners of the new democratic era. Having supported the return to democracy in most countries, and having seized the opportunity to influence the process according to their interests (see Chapter 3), the business elite saw their power and influence enhanced by the economic and political developments of the first decade of democratic rule.

As the private sector assumed an increasingly strategic role in investment, job creation and the generation of foreign currency, pro-market reforms increased the structural power of capital (Lindblom 1977). Politically, the collapse of the Soviet bloc, an event that was unforeseen when transition to democracy in Latin America started in the late 1970s, confirmed the failure of the only alternative to capitalism that had been tried in practice, and eliminated a source of political, ideological and material support to communist parties and other left-wing organizations. The influence of international financial institutions over domestic policy-making and the consolidation of the USA as the only global superpower added an international dimension to the domestic factors that made the region safe for private enterprise. Within this context, Herman and Petras's (1985) assumption that business would be unable to defend its interests in a competitive democracy and therefore that the business elite would need to rely again on a strong authoritarian state to protect them proved unwarranted.

As Carlos Acuña (1994) put it in relation to the politics of Argentina under Alfonsín and Menem, in a comment that could be extended to most countries of the region, the bourgeoisie found the political options offered by democracy to be better suited and less risky for their interests than an authoritarian alternative. In addition to their structural economic power, the business elite increased their leverage by using their financial and organizational resources to finance candidates, lobby parliament and generally influence governments. Addressing the question of why the late twentieth century's wave of democratization has lasted longer than previous ones, Peter Smith (2005) claims that, although other international and domestic factors have played a role, the main reason for the survival of democracy was that it had been thoroughly 'domesticated', to make it safe for the economic elite. The fears or the promises (according to one's views and interests) that democracy conveyed in earlier democratic waves had now been tempered: the left accepted capitalism and electoral processes, while the right was willing to countenance political activism provided there was no extremism (Spanakos 2007: 233).

And yet, while Latin America's business elite no longer merited its historical characterization as weak, authoritarian and protectionist, neither was it transformed into Cammack's (1986: 125) unified and capable bourgeoisie 'well aware of their needs and well equipped to pursue them'. The business sector is too diverse to act in unison except to defend itself against fundamental threats against its interests, and while generally supportive of free market reforms, significant sectors of the domestic business elite suffered from the effects of economic opening. The ability of the business elite to translate its economic power into political power, and in the process become a hegemonic group capable of shaping the policies of the new democratic governments, remained limited (Payne and Bartell 1995: 257).

The business sector certainly achieved some significant gains under democracy. Property rights, which are the most fundamental economic rights in a capitalist economy, appeared relatively more secure than in the past; and, more generally, capitalism appeared to have become the only economic game in town, at least until President Hugo Chávez proclaimed Twenty-first Century Socialism as the new economic model for Venezuelan society. But beyond these fundamental but very general gains, governments' economic competence and their ability to enforce stable economic rules, which together with property rights define businesses' fundamental interests, varied significantly from country to country and were on the whole less than secure. In the 1990s, with the exception of Chile, economic volatility affected growth and profits, and even strong pro-business governments, such as those of Carlos Menem in Argentina and Ernesto Zedillo in Mexico, were unable to protect the private sector from the adverse effects of economic crises.

Politically, impoverished societies with fragmented and politically excluded popular sectors do not pose the same kind of threat to the interests of the business elite as a well-organized and militant working class fighting for radical change. But neither did the social conditions of 1990s Latin America provide the social context for the political legitimization of the free market reformation. In a democracy, the hegemonic legitimization (Gramsci 1971) of an economic order depends on more than just a low level of threat to the interests of the economic elite. Recalling the slightly different versions of the same argument put forward by both Lipset and Huber Stephens, the lowering of the threat to the interests of the economic elite is the result not of the imposition of the naked political and economic power of an economically dominant class over the majority of the population, but of a political settlement grounded on political inclusion and economic prosperity, the achievement of which necessitates contestation from below as much as assurances from above. As noted above, for Lipset, consensus was made possible by general prosperity, the growth of the middle class, and a more affluent and educated working class, all of which softened distributional struggles. For Huber Stephens in turn, it was the mobilization of a politically strong working class that, in alliance with the middle classes, would force economically dominant social groups to accept a more inclusive political order. It is only under these conditions that we can talk of hegemony understood as a shared belief in the effectiveness and legitimacy of the system. Low economic growth, downward social mobility and the highest rates of inequality in the world hardly provided the conditions for the kind of settlement under which a market economy and liberal democracy could achieve reciprocal legitimacy.

The mediating role of political institutions

If the articulation of liberal democracy and free market reforms in the 1990s resulted in the strengthening of the structural power of capital and the political power of business and in the parallel disorganization of the popular sectors, arguably the reforms were not conducive to the promotion of the 'right balance of class struggle' essential for the flourishing of democracy. But social classes are not political actors per se, and their interests are mediated by political actors and political institutions. The state and political parties shape distributional conflicts and play a crucial role in securing democratic governability, as a democratic order is based on mechanisms of interest representation that channel, mediate and ultimately control social conflict (Haggard and Kaufman 1992b: 324). Late-twentieth-century Latin American democracy combined long-term institutional weaknesses that survived the processes of democratization of the 1980s with new ones brought about by the political impact of economic and social change. The status of political institutions can be gauged by opinion polls showing that trust in the main democratic institutions, such as political parties and Congress, was low and declining throughout the region, at 18 per cent and 24 per cent respectively, compared with trust in the Church at 71 per cent and in television at 38 per cent (Latinobarómetro 2004). In order to assess how political institutions shaped social conflict in the 1990s, it is necessary to look at how some key institutions, such as the state and political parties, impacted on the balance between conflict and accommodation that characterizes liberal democracies.

State institutions were affected by the legacy of the past as well as by the impact of economic reforms. As noted in Chapter 4, historically the Latin American state was a highly politicized machine, colonized by political parties and special interests. Extended state intervention in the economy during the ISI era politicized economic relations, making the state the dispenser of economic rents and the arbiter of distributive struggles, which ultimately undermined the state's capacity to secure sustainable development and democratic stability. In facing the reality of a bankrupted state, neoclassical political economy provided a powerful critique of state intervention. According to its arguments, the state is prone to capture by interest groups, bureaucrats and self-serving political leaders motivated only by their desire to stay in power or maximize individual gains. Actors that control the state use public office to reward those who support their holding power, and to punish those who seek to unseat them. Politicians and bureaucrats who use the state for their own individual benefits distort economic rationality, affecting economic development and general prosperity (Grindle 2001: 370).

In Latin America, the neoclassical critique of state interventionism materialized in the political critique of the populist state. As noted in Chapter 1, in the context of the economic turmoil and the crisis of social order of the 1980s, neoliberalism redefined the discursive dividing lines that framed the understanding of the period. The new political frontier lay no longer between the democratic present and the authoritarian past, but between the new economic agenda and the old model of economic development. In neoliberal discourse, the developmentalist regimes of the 1950s and 1960s, the military regimes of the 1970s (with the exception of Chile) and the democratic governments of the early 1980s equally represented a failed model of development. The institutional base of this model was a bloated and inefficient state, and its political base a rent-seeking alliance between corrupt politicians and powerful domestic actors. Advocates of free market reforms labelled this model *'populism'* (Dornbusch and Edwards 1991: 1). While economic reformers gave populism the predominantly economic meaning of a model of development characterized by protectionism, generalized controls, widespread subsidies, an inefficient public sector and disregard for basic economic equilibriums (ibid.: 1), the populist label carried with it clear political connotations. If the institutional basis of populism was a bloated and inefficient state, the new economic and political order required its radical restructuring. If populism's political basis was a rent-seeking alliance between politicians, bureaucrats and powerful domestic interests, the mechanisms that made this alliance operational needed to be dismantled. If populism had no regard for basic economic equilibriums, the political calculations that led to the neglect of rational economic policy principles needed to be replaced by a type of technocratic policy-making that would operate in favour of long-term economic stability and development.

The reform of the state was at the heart of the WC project of economic modernization. Scholars have focused on privatization as the most visible element of a strategy whose main and supposedly only objective was the shrinking of the state. Yet, while the retreat of the state from direct industrial, financial and commercial activities was high on the free market agenda of state reform, the overall agenda was far more complex than critics of neoliberalism give reformers credit for. Together with the state's retreat from certain areas of economic activity, the reform contemplated the strengthening of state autonomy to allow economic rationality to prevail over short-term political considerations. Complementing privatization, the devolution of policy implementation to private sector agents and the setting-up of new autonomous regulatory agencies was meant to depoliticize the state, lessening the opportunities for rent-seeking and state capture. Both a considerable degree of state autonomy from the economically dominant sectors and the state's political, financial and technical capacity to implement public policy are key to building an inclusive democracy, as the state plays a crucial role in mediating redistributive struggles by correcting the socio-economic inequalities generated by the market (Huber et al. 1997: 328). But the WC understood state autonomy not as autonomy from any specific social sector, less so from the economically dominant sectors, but, more radically, autonomy from politics *tout court*: politics, understood as the politics of self-interest, distorts policy choices, so that general-purpose and social welfare objectives become lost as all actors pursue narrow individual group interests (Grindle 2001: 370).

Free market reformers faced a conundrum, however. If according to public choice theory politics is by definition an activity carried out by politicians in their own self-interest, and if politicians benefit from the use of state resources for their own ends, how can the state be reformed by the same politicians who benefit from the status quo, and why would politicians agree to carry out a reform against their own self-interest? The free market reformers' solution was the substitution of public-minded technocrats for self-interested politicians, and the insulation of reforming policy-makers in a highly autonomous executive. Empowered technocrats would thus have the mind-frame, political drive and power resources to transform the state into a well-governed, economically efficient institution.

The basic flaw of the empowerment of technocrats strategy was that the reform of the state is a highly political project, and in a democracy decisions are ultimately taken by politicians and not by their technocratic advisers. Williamson (1994: 12) suggested an exogenous solution to the conundrum by introducing the hybrid category of *technopols*. According to his own definition, the technopol is a mixture of an applied economist who uses his or her professional skills to manage the economy according to normative economic principles in order to further the general good, and a politician able to persuade others to adopt the policies that he or she has judged to be necessary. But the condition of possibility of this hybrid actor is the suspension of public choice's assumption that the technopol, as in the case of any other utility-maximizing individual in a position of political authority, would take the decisions more likely to help him/her to remain in office, rather than act based on some grand version of the common good. Plausible as is the suggestion that politicians act through mixed motives that include the public good as well as self-interest and ideology, the abandonment of the assumption of the self-interested politician undermines the principles of neoclassical political economy, depriving the theory of its elegance and predictive power. Given that among the examples of technopols then in office mentioned by Williamson was the now-disgraced Mexican president Carlos Salinas de Gortari, the idealized figure of the technopol is also of dubious practical utility.

The other option available to free market reformers to conduct the reform of the state against the interests of self-serving politicians was the neopopulist alternative. The emergence in the late 1980s and early 1990s of strong personalist leaders such as Carlos Menem in Argentina, Alberto Fujimori in Peru and Fernando Collor de Mello in Brazil prompted a reassessment of the nature of populism in the region and its relation with free market economics. While, as noted above, populism was historically associated with the statist, inward-looking, post-war model of development, this was a narrow view of populism that did not account for its occurrence elsewhere and at different points in time. In common with traditional populism, the populism (or neopopulism) of the late

Five

1980s and early 1990s was the result of a crisis of representation, brought about mainly by the failure of the first generation of new democratic governments to secure economic order. Neopopulist leaders such as Carlos Menem drew on the populist tradition of the Justicialista (Peronist) party only to break with its economic content and adapt it to the realities of Argentina in the 1990s. Neopopulist politicians presented themselves as political outsiders or pseudo-outsiders fighting a failed political establishment and taking on the vested interests that benefited from a bankrupted ISI economic model: Menem and Collor de Mello as provincial leaders who challenged entrenched political elites, and Alberto Fujimori as a *'chinito'* ('Chinese', Peruvian generic for oriental), ethnically closer to Peru's *cholos* (mixed-race lower-class Peruvians) than to the white Creole elite.

Neopopulist leaders didn't wallow in nostalgia for a better yesterday, but represented a project of political and economic modernization: the *chinito* Fujimori may have presented himself as an underdog, but he was also Peruvian-Japanese, and as such evoked a technologically modern and economically successful society. Collor de Mello became known as the youthful and energetic governor of a backward state that took on his corrupt state's bureaucratic elite, which benefited from high wages and lax working conditions. He seized on the high degree of elite continuity that characterized Brazil's transition to democracy as proof that all politicians were equally corrupt betrayers of the people's interests. Menem tapped into the late-twentieth-century modern culture of celebrity by being seen mixing with his country's TV soap stars and football players. As part of his image-building, Collor engaged in glamorous pursuits, riding high-powered motorbikes and participating in other sporting enterprises that were amply reported by the main television network, TV Globo.

Both Menem's and Collor de Mello's 'private pursuits' conveyed the political attributes of leadership and decisiveness, and linked their personas to the imagery of modern popular culture. But in contrast to traditional populism's association with *dirigiste* economic policies, the new populism had strong elective affinities with free market economics. They both had in common their bases of support (an alliance between the elite and the informal-sector poor), an anti-institutional bias that mistrusted politicians and bypassed political parties and Congress to rule with the support of public opinion, and the concentration of power in the figure of the president (Panizza 2000b; Weyland 1999). Presidents

112

such as Fernando Collor de Mello in Brazil, Carlos Menem in Argentina and Alberto Fujimori in Peru epitomized the Copernican turn in the free marketeers' appreciation of the politics of populism. Having blamed historical populism for the crisis of the ISI state, they now trusted neo-populist outsiders or pseudo-outsiders with transforming the state into an institution acting according to the principles of good governance and the market economy.

If technocrats were trusted to solve the state reform conundrum because they would be guided by neoclassical normative economic principles rather than by political self-interest, neopopulist leaders were supposed to achieve the same goal because, as political outsiders, they could act with a high degree of autonomy from the vested interests of the political establishment and their rent-seeking supporters. As Kurt Weyland (2004: 150) notes, free market reform provided neopopulist presidents with useful instruments for enhancing the power and autonomy of the state: trade liberalization and labour market deregulation, which weakened trade unions and put some business sectors on the defensive. The privatization of state enterprises allowed government to save money in subsidizing loss-making public utilities, and the windfall revenue from privatization helped to lessen the political costs of structural adjustment and left funds disposable for social spending.

The neopopulist leaders of the 1990s, however, proved as unsuitable as the old populist rulers of the 1960s had proved in transforming the state into an autonomous institution capable of securing good governance and a well-functioning market economy. As could have been anticipated, neopopulist rulers did not depoliticize the state, but repoliticized it to serve their own political interests. They ran parallel agencies that bypassed traditional state structures, and used these agencies to build up their own personal networks of patronage. They set up pockets of technocratic modernization within the state, creating new agencies often with funding from international financial institutions, but the net result was the further fragmentation of the state, as modern agencies staffed by relatively highly paid technocrats coexisted with underpaid and poorly motivated bureaucrats. Privatization divested the state of inefficient and often highly corrupt public enterprises, but weak regulatory regimes allowed the constitution of new rent-seeking coalitions between the government and the new owners of private companies (see Chapter 3). The rule of law, already weak, was further debilitated by the executive's disregard both for checks and balances and for the independence of the judiciary. Ironically, neopopulist presidents who came to power as political outsiders confirmed public choice's theory that politicians control the state to further their goal of remaining in power. Neopopulist presidents did this by promoting constitutional amendments that allowed them to run for re-election, thus further increasing the personalization of politics.

A more detailed account of the transformations of the state in the 1990s requires a comparative analysis of state reforms, in addition to the study of the impact of the economic reforms in different agencies of the state. This task is beyond the scope of this chapter, and remains largely to be completed in the comparative literature. Beyond wide generalizations about the shrinking of the state, significant differences remained in state capacity from country to country, as well as in the operational capacity of different agencies within the same state. Path dependency, traditions of rule of law and financial resources accounted for significant variations in degrees of stateness (Nettl 1968). Countries with a history of a strong developmental state, such as Mexico and Brazil, maintained considerable state capacity in spite of privatizations and the retreat of the state from areas of state intervention, as did countries with a tradition of rule of law, such as Chile, Costa Rica and Uruguay; while in others, such as Bolivia and Ecuador, the state remained unable to perform the basic function of securing the political order or even securing territorial integrity.

Economic agencies, particularly central banks, gained autonomy and were able to better control macroeconomic policy. At the top of the state, particularly in the state's financial agencies, a technocratic elite liaised with private consultants and representatives of international financial institutions to create a layer of public sector managers that rotated between the state, consultancy firms and the international agencies. In a number of countries of the region, including Argentina, Bolivia, Brazil, Mexico and Uruguay, reforms of the public administration sought to depoliticize the civil service and introduce new forms of public sector management (Panizza 2004b; Panizza and Philip 2005; Barragán and Roemer 2001). But below the thin layer of modernization and the headline figures of privatization that allowed both free marketeers and their critics to talk about the shrinking of the state with opposite value judgements, large areas of the state remained unreconstructed, unaccountable and highly inefficient. Most public services remained underfunded, managed by a poorly paid and unresponsive bureaucracy. Pockets of public sector modernization were superimposed upon or bypassed traditional state agencies unable to provide basic services to the population. The result was a hybrid system of public administration that generated bureaucratic dysfunctions within the public sector, and low legitimacy outside.

The hybrid state mirrored social and economic divisions between, on the one hand, a small elite of public and private agents that adopted with various degrees of consistency and success the modus operandi and rules of the game of the globalized market economy, and, on the other hand, a majority of public and private agents that operated under largely informal sets of rules that sought to protect their political and economic interests from the encroachment of market forces and the rule of law.

The two sectors operated in parallel, but not independently from each other. Rather, in weakly institutionalized states, with no effective system of law enforcement, informal rules tended to prevail over formal ones. The interplay between formal and informal rules had implications for the 'modern' state agencies that were set up to act in accordance with the principles of the free market reformation: these agencies, such as, for instance, regulatory agencies for the newly privatized public utilities, were often set up mirroring the legal framework of regulatory agencies in developing countries. The weak rule-of-law context in which the agencies operated, however, meant that they could not regulate private companies with the same degree of legally protected autonomy enjoyed by regulatory agencies elsewhere, but remained subject to political interference whenever the interests of office-holders or of key economic actors were at stake. Under the same conditions, the contracting of private companies to undertake services previously undertaken by the state did not diminish the opportunities for corruption, but allowed new mechanisms for rent-seeking as contracts were often awarded through political influence or used to generate cash for the parties in office (Weyland 1998).

Democratic institutions do more than make social conflicts manageable; they also foster democratic conflict by giving voice to the popular sectors and allowing them to organize in order to confront vested privileges. Political parties do not have the monopoly of representation, but it is very difficult to conceive of a representative democracy without political parties. Popular parties can foster democratization by organizing and mobilizing citizens to challenge the structural power of economic interests. They also develop strong social roots and establish networks of political representation with the trade unions and other social organizations. How did the political and economic dislocations of the 1990s affect political representation, particularly party representation? An answer to this question needs to take into account several factors and, of course, changes over time and differences in national histories. The latter are particularly significant when analysing party-system institutionalization, which tends to be highly path dependent. Institutionalization is important for democracy because it brings stability and predictability to the political system. Institutionalized party systems have deeper roots in society, are ideologically more consistent and have stronger organizational structures, helping people to make better-informed electoral choices. In contrast, in inchoate party systems affiliations do not structure the vote as much as in institutionalized party systems and voters are more likely to respond to personalistic appeals than to a candidate's party affiliation (Mainwaring and Scully 1995).[2]

In their study of party systems' institutionalization in Latin America in the first half of the 1990s, Mainwaring and Scully found striking variations in the extent to which party systems were institutionalized in different Latin American countries, with Venezuela, Costa Rica, Chile, Uruguay, Colombia and, to a lesser degree, Argentina at the top of the table, and Bolivia, Ecuador, Brazil and Peru at the bottom (ibid.: 17). The relative value of this classification is made evident by the changes in institutionalization experienced by Latin American party systems in the second half of the 1990s and early 2000s, but the overall picture of the early 1990s was of weak representative institutions.

Many citizens who were able to exercise their democratic rights for the first time were not organically incorporated into democratic representative networks, while those who in the past were represented by traditional political parties or state-sponsored labour unions became disjoined from them (Hagopian 1998: 100). Dissatisfaction with political parties was also made evident by the growth in electoral volatility and the increase in electoral abstentionism, together with poor evaluation of politicians and legislatures in much of the region (ibid.: 121). If anything, the tendency towards party-system deinstitutionalization increased in the early twenty-first century, as traditional party systems collapsed in Ecuador, Bolivia and Venezuela. Even in countries that in the early 1990s appeared to have relatively well-institutionalized party systems, such as Colombia and Argentina, party-system institutionalization declined significantly in the first decade of the new century.[3]

Conclusions

A report by the United Nations Development Programme published in 2004 to assess the balance of twenty-five years since the start of the process of democratization in the region summarizes the highs and lows of democracy in Latin America by stating that, while never before had there been so many countries with democratic governments and never before had Latin American democracies been so robust, political democracy in Latin America coexisted alongside limited rule of law and serious economic and social problems. The report noted that, although democracy was the preferred system of government for a majority of the population, there was little faith in democracy's capacity to improve living conditions; public regard for political parties was at its lowest level; and the state was viewed with both expectations and distrust (UNDP 2004: 26–7).

The reasons for this state of affairs were analysed in Chapter 4 and in the body of this chapter. The debt crisis of the 1980s exacerbated social problems that in the past were the underlying causes of political instability. Democratic politics coexisted with high levels of poverty and inequality, as the structural reforms associated with the WC did not create enough jobs or generate enough economic growth to raise the living standards of the majority of the population. A politicized and inefficient state failed to address the political demands and economic grievances of large sections of the population, and political parties became increasingly detached from their social roots. Above all, the economic and political changes of the 1990s resulted in a redistribution of social and political power that was not conducive to the type of balance between contestation and accommodation that allows liberal democracy to flourish by addressing the grievances of the popular sectors without threatening the core interests of the economic elite. While business saw its fundamental interests better protected than in the past, the fragmentation and disorganization of the popular sectors made it more difficult for subordinated groups to organize themselves to fight for their interests.

If the relation between socio-economic conditions and political institutions that shapes the balance of class struggle determines the quality of democracy, this relation was on the whole not favourable for the

117

flourishing of democracy in most countries of the region. The region's high levels of socio-economic inequality appeared as the main reason for the low level of trust in public institutions. Equal treatment for all was considered by the citizens as the most important factor in determining how much trust people had in the public services. Almost half of the people interviewed by the UNDP believed that poverty was the main reason why not everybody was treated in the same way by public institutions. Survey evidence also shows that lower levels of support for democracy were associated with lower levels of education, reduced prospects for social mobility, and mistrust in democratic institutions and politicians (ibid.: 58).

As Huber et al. (1997: 336) point out, state intervention, particularly of a redistributive nature that goes against vested interests, is difficult to implement by a state apparatus characterized by fragmentation, overlapping responsibilities, non-meritocratic hiring and often corruption. Free market reforms promoted good governance to increase the efficiency of the state, but the neoclassical view of an autonomous state as a neutral entity, free from political influences and ruled from the top by technocrats and neopopulist outsiders, was not just an illusion: it did little to enhance the quality of democracy. If the consolidation of democracy depends on the ability of political institutions to process the 'right balance of class struggle', the state needs to be sufficiently autonomous from dominant economic groups to challenge their privileges, and embedded enough in society to address the demands of the popular sectors and be accountable to the citizens. Embeddedness requires that representative mechanisms be in place to channel demands and aggregate social interests. As Samuel Huntington (1968: 196) put it, in a society with no political institutions, social forces confront each other nakedly; no corps of professional leaders is recognized or accepted as the legitimate intermediary to moderate group conflict, and no agreement exists among the groups on the legitimate and authoritative method to moderate group conflict.

And yet, as will be analysed in further detail in Chapter 8, the low-intensity democracy argument was only part of a broader, more complex, picture. Shifts in power between dominant and subordinate groups are not fixed for ever in time or determined by structural changes independently of political action. For all its problems and shortcomings, it remains the case that democracy opened the possibility for the advancement of progressive alternatives to the technocratic politics of the WC. It is true, as Gills and Rocamora (1992) argue, that democracy is ultimately incompatible with societies characterized by extreme concentration of wealth in the hands of a tiny elite. But what Gills and Rocamora failed to take fully into consideration was their own observation that, even at its most superficial, democratization widens the legal space within which popular mobilization for change can take place. And while democratization in Latin America was certainly flawed, it was also more than cosmetic. It may be the case that, as O'Donnell (1994) claims, democratic accountability was mainly limited to the vertical accountability of electoral contests, but elections are still the most fundamental form of accountability in a democracy, and the succession of mainly free and fair elections gave the people a powerful instrument with which to organize and demand change.

Contrary to the prevailing view of the 1990s, popular forces remained robust in most countries of the region. For all the shortcomings of the region's legal systems for the protection of human rights, the lessening of fear of military and police brutality represented a fundamental change in the conditions under which the popular sectors could organize themselves and mobilize for their rights.[4] Business may have had its fundamental interests better protected by the political and economic changes of the 1990s, but for the economic elite it also became more difficult than in the past to resort to force in order to defend their privileges. Social movements may not have fulfilled the transformative potential hoped for at the time of transition, and unions may have suffered the effects of deindustrialization and informality, but civil society under democracy was far more diverse and robust than ever before.

The notion that the popular sectors had lost the ability to challenge free market economic reforms became less plausible as the end of the twentieth century and the beginning of the twenty-first century saw a revival in popular protests. Democratic continuity and the potentially high legal and political costs of the use of state force to repress popular protest raised the effectiveness of mass actions to protest against the status quo. In episodes that paralleled the riots that shook Venezuela in the Caracazo of February 1989, massive streets protests affected Argentina in December 2001, Bolivia between 2000 and 2003 and Ecuador in 2000 and 2005. Mass protests outside formal political institutions in these countries led not only to changes in government, but ultimately to the abandonment of free market reforms. As Eduardo Silva (2007: 3) puts it:

Demands focused on redistributive issues (social protection and services) and questioned broad private property rights by pressing for more active involvement of the state in economy and society. These demands intersected with indigenous claims for autonomy and citizen rights as well as society-wide protests against corruption in politics. Mobilizing groups included Indigenous movements, new political parties and unions, as well as newly formed organizations of the unemployed and pensioners who linked up with more traditional union movements and political parties and middle class movements. The cycles of contention in these cases also had similar outcomes. They brought down governments that unconditionally supported neoliberalism and contributed to their replacement with political leadership committed, in principle, to reforming it.

In short, the balance between contestation and accommodation that defines a democratic order was less eschewed in favour of the owners of capital than argued by critics of the quality of democracy in Latin America. As seen in the opinion polls, discontent with the working of democracy and the accumulation of grievances about the effects of market reforms did not translate into any general longing to return to authoritarian government. In contrast to the 1970s, the political repercussion of the economic dislocations of the 1990s was not the collapse of elected governments and a return to the military. Instead, different political contexts provided the bases for the alternative political scenarios that would define Latin American politics in the late twentieth century and early twenty-first century. We examine these scenarios in Chapter 8, but first it is necessary to look at the unravelling of the Washington Consensus and the emergence of the post-Washington Consensus.

6 | Paradigm lost: the unravelling of the Washington Consensus

The Miami consensus and the Tequila crisis

In a similar way to the debate that accompanied the rise of the Washington Consensus, the ideological battle that marked its unravelling in the late 1990s was fought at different levels: in academic journals and learned economic forums, in political debates and in social forums. The first presidential Summit of the Americas that took place in Miami in December 1994 represented the highest political watermark of the free market consensus. In an article reviewing the academic literature on Inter-American relations of the time, Mark Peceny (1994: 188–9) claimed that there were indications that the inter-American system was becoming a Kantian pacific union of liberal states. By that he meant that Kant's belief that the spread of republican government, liberal philosophy and international commerce would inevitably lead to greater peace and co-operation among liberal states could be transposed 200 years later to the Western hemisphere, where the spread of democracy, free trade and complex interdependence was bringing about a new era of unprecedented peace and cooperation based on shared liberal values. The summit's Declaration of Principles summarized this agreement as: the pursuing of prosperity 'through open markets, hemispheric integration, and sustainable development' (Summit of the Americas 1994). More broadly, there was a view that capitalism had triumphed in the region and that regional free trade would lock in even further the existing political commitment to the free market model. In short, because of conviction or the lack of choice, there was apparently no escape from the embrace of the free market orthodoxy as expressed in the Washington Consensus. The stark lack of alternatives was summed up by the Mexican scholar Jorge Castañeda (1994, quoted in Peceny 1994: 199):

> For any Latin American government, there are direct, often immediate and frequently dire economic consequences of pursuing a policy contrary to Washington's desires or interests ...; the price of any departure from the tenets of free-market orthodoxy is exorbitant ... The true constraint

Latin American elites – and popular movements or oppositions – must cope with today is the perspective of seeing sources of credit, investment and aid dry up and both sympathy and export markets contract if they follow policies deemed hostile, different or simply unwise. Nationalizing natural resources, emphasizing social policies or placing restrictions on foreign trade or investment no longer necessarily invite invasion or destabilization, nor are they even likely to do so. They simply entice financial scarcity and economic ostracism.

There were, of course, dissenting views. Scholars were already warning about the substantial social, economic and environmental costs of neoliberalism (Hartlyn et al. 1992). The Miami summit of Western hemisphere heads of state appeared to confirm, however, not just the mainstream academic consensus that Latin America had embraced free market economics but more importantly the political consensus that democracy, free markets and hemispheric integration were the blueprint for a better future.

And yet the apparently unstoppable onward march of the free market reformation was to be shaken by the ripple effects of Mexico's 1994 economic crisis, widely known as the 'Tequila' crisis. Brought on by the forced devaluation of the Mexican peso in December 1994, the crisis erupted just two weeks after the Miami summit and awoke the ghosts of Mexico's 1982 debt default. Investors' loss of confidence in the Mexican economy was caused as much by political as by economic factors (Springer and Molina 1995). Capital flight put the country yet again on the verge of international insolvency. As happened in 1982, there were fears that Mexico's economic ills would spread throughout the region, dragging down half a decade of political and economic stability underpinned by economic reform. As Edwin Truman (1996, cited in Lustig 1998: 178–9), the director of the Division of International Finance of the Board of Governors of the US Federal Reserve, noted:

> When the crisis erupted, investors panicked, not only investors in the Mexican stock market and in Mexico debt instruments but also investors in similar instruments issued by borrowers in other countries, especially countries in the same part of the world or perceived to be in similar circumstances.

After some weeks of delays and vacillations the USA came to Mexico's rescue on 31 January 1995 with the announcement of a US$53 billion emergency loan package, of which US$20 billion was contributed by the US Treasury through the US Exchange Stabilization Fund (ESF), supplemented by further contributions from the World Bank, the IMF and other international financial actors. The emergency assistance package produced the desired effects of calming investors' jitters, allowing Mexico to recover quickly from the crisis: after falling by 6.2 per cent in 1995, Mexico's GDP rose by 5.1 per cent in 1996 (ibid.).

The devaluation of the Mexican peso triggered capital outflows from various countries and the virtual suspension of voluntary external financing, but ultimately the regional effects of Mexico's crisis were quite limited. While Latin America's economies grew by an average of just 1 per cent in 1995, only Argentina was seriously affected by the events in Mexico, but it also recovered quickly: the Argentine economy suffered a contraction of 4.6 per cent of GDP in 1995 only to grow again by 4.4 per cent in 1996, followed by further 8 per cent growth in 1997 (IADB 1997). Moreover, neither Mexico nor Argentina substantially changed their free market economic policies as a result of the crisis. Particularly in the case of Argentina, the rapid recovery was seen as evidence of the underlying strength of the economy as a result of the liberalizing reforms introduced during the first Menem administration (1989–95). The political fallout from the crisis was also limited. In Mexico, concerns that the combination of political events that preceded the crisis, particularly the Zapatista uprising of January 1994 and the assassination of the Partido Revolucionario Institutional (PRI) presidential candidate Luis Donaldo Colosio in March the same year, and the political repercussions of the crisis itself would destabilize the country's political system proved unfounded. If anything, the birth of the North American Free Trade Agreement (NAFTA) contributed to political liberalization, as Mexico deepened the process of transition to democracy under President Ernesto Zedillo (1994–2000) (Springer and Molina 1995: 61).

Meanwhile, in Argentina the short, sharp recession of 1995 did not substantially undermine support for President Menem's free market policies, as confirmed by his re-election in the same year. The Mexican crisis, however, exposed the fragile, partial and incomplete nature of Latin America's process of free market modernization (Wiarda 1995a). Mexico was regarded as a showcase for economic reform. The government was dominated by American-trained economists who had displaced the old nationalist political elite. Under their guidance the country had emerged from several years of debt crisis to attract capital flows on a scale un-imaginable a few years earlier. Once a protectionist nation, Mexico had lowered its trade barriers and signed a free trade pact with the United States (Krugman 1995: 29–30). All these advances were now being called into question.

The Washington Consensus reassessed: the view from within

As the first major setback of economic liberalization in Latin America, the Tequila crisis produced major dislocations in the paradigm of the Washington Consensus. Doubts about Latin America's free market ex-perience were soon being expressed by mainstream economic actors. An early case in point is the 1995 Inter-American Development Bank annual report on *Economic and Social Progress in Latin America*. The report warned that, while the so-called 'Tequila effect' had all but disappeared, the crisis showed the continuing vulnerability of the economies of the region to domestically and externally generated shocks (IADB 1995: iii). Moreover, even in countries not directly affected by the crisis, disap-pointing social outcomes were undermining political support for the free market consensus. Just one year after publishing a book lauding the achievements of the free market reforms, Sebastian Edwards changed the tone of his writings about the condition of the economies of the region. In an article published in *Foreign Affairs*, he noted that although in the past few years the Latin American economies had gone through a notable transformation, economic results were disappointing and the region's social situation showed little signs of improvement. He pointed out that an average economic growth rate of 3.1 per cent between 1991 and 1996 was below the minimum rate that, according to the World Bank, was necessary to bring poverty down in the region. In the light of stagnant real wages and lack of job creation, he expressed fears that the people of Latin America, who had until recently enthusiastically supported the reform process, would not be willing to support it any more (Edwards 1997).

As the decade progressed, a number of studies looked at the economic and social impact of the reforms. Some of these studies were published by the same international financial institutions that had originally set up the reform agenda and financed its implementation. Figures for in-dicators such as economic growth, poverty and inequality were produced to support or undermine arguments about the benefits of economic liberalization, but most disagreements were not about figures. Figures, like facts, do not speak by themselves but make sense only when they are integrated in broader arguments about origins, causality and consequences. Technical arguments in turn become the building blocks for wider political narratives that seek to make sense of the past and offer a road map for the future. It is to some of these figures, arguments and narratives that we now turn our attention.

The 1997 IADB annual report *Economic and Social Progress in Latin America* was pointedly entitled 'Latin America after a decade of reforms: all pain and no gain?' Coming from an international financial institution that had been broadly supportive of the free market reforms, the title encapsulated the criticisms and doubts that were already being raised about the Washington Consensus by some mainstream economists, or rather about the assumption that free market reforms were a self-contained, technically sound, politically neutral, closed totality that contained the key to economic development. The report, published in the year the Latin American economies were about to start a new cycle of economic stagnation and declining social indicators, presented a downbeat assessment of the outcome of the reforms in the region. It is worth quoting the report's first paragraph at length to appreciate better the nature of its arguments:

Latin America's economic and social performance during the nineties has not been satisfactory. While economic growth has recovered, it has not returned to the rates of close to 5 percent that were common in the region in the sixties and seventies, and is far less than the sustained rates of over 7 percent that have been typical of Southeast Asian countries. In 1996, eight out of every 100 Latin Americans willing to work had no job; at the end of the eighties, unemployment rates had been lower, between 5 and 6 percent. Latin America is the area of the world where income distribution is worst, and the situation has not improved in the nineties. Nor has the number of poor people declined from the unprecedented level of close to 150 million that it reached at the beginning of the decade. (IADB 1997: 31)

What is notable about the above paragraph is not so much the low figures for economic growth or the high figures for poverty and unemployment but rather how the report uses these figures to interweave a set of arguments that undermine the case originally made to promote what came to be known as the Washington Consensus. Bringing these discrete arguments together is an overarching narrative about the failures of the Washington Consensus crystallized in the report's opening statement. By comparing the economic growth of the 1990s with that of the sixties and seventies, the report calls into question the free market reformers' claim that economic opening offered better prospects for economic growth than the failed Import Substitution Industrialization model that it superseded. By contrasting economic growth in Latin America with that of South-East Asia, it implicitly raised the question of what were the elements of the South-East Asia model that were missing in Latin America. Finally, by showing that unemployment and poverty were higher in the mid-1990s than at the beginning of the decade, it raised the issue of why the reforms had been largely ineffective in addressing the social legacy of the lost decade of the 1980s.

The report addresses a set of issues that framed the debate about neoliberalism in the second half of the 1990s and in the early twenty-first century. Central among these was how to define the reform agenda and how to measure the extent to which the agenda had been implemented. Also considered in the report was whether poor social and economic figures showed that the reforms had failed to achieve sustainable growth, stability and equity, or whether it was the case that they had not yet yielded the expected benefits because they had been incomplete or because not enough time had elapsed to produce the desired effects (ibid.: 31). A more complex question was the counterfactual one of what would have been the rates for growth, poverty and income distribution in the absence of the reforms. Answers to these questions were used as supporting evidence to address a more fundamental issue, namely whether the reforms were mistaken policy prescriptions or just insufficient or badly implemented policies and, if they were fundamentally wrong, what alternatives were available to put them right: a wholesale rejection of the model and its substitution by an alternative one or a more gradual combination of continuity and change.

In seeking to answer the above questions the report considers a number of different elements. Addressing the key issue of whether disappointing social and economic figures were the result of the failure to reform rather than of the reforms themselves, the report notes that the insufficient economic and social progress of Latin American countries stood in contrast with the magnitude of the changes that had taken place in economic policy (ibid.: 31).[1] Significantly, the study concludes that it was likely that macroeconomic and structural reforms, even if deepened, could not achieve the desired combination of objectives, namely greater growth in production and income, more employment opportunities, less instability in the macro environment and reduced social inequality (ibid.: 34).

The report acknowledges, however, that the reforms did bring some benefits to the region, including the correction of macroeconomic imbalances, the dismantling of practices of government intervention and the fact that markets were now able to operate more smoothly and transparently (ibid.: 33). In a counterfactual exercise the study claims that without the structural reforms of the past decade, per capita income in Latin America would have been 12 per cent lower and potential GDP growth in the future 1.9 per cent lower than the current averages. It further claims that without the reforms the joint productivity of labour and capital would have continued to fall, as it had been doing since the seventies, and investment rates would have stagnated at levels averaging less than 17 per cent of GDP (ibid.: 32). On social issues the report acknowledges that the reforms had slowed down the pace of job creation. It absolves the reforms from responsibility, however, for the increase in unemployment on the basis that while markets for goods, foreign exchange and financing were significantly liberalized, the labour market had been freed only slightly (ibid.: 32). On income distribution the study credits the reforms with halting the worsening distribution of income of the previous decade by accelerating economic growth and reactivating investment (ibid.: 33).[2]

A more detailed analysis of the reforms' achievements and failures would need to disaggregate the different aspects, distinguishing the initial period of stabilization from the broader process of structural reforms aimed at removing artificial distortions in the working of the market, such as price controls and trade privatization, deregulation and fiscal reform. It would also need to dispel some myths, such as that the 1990s was a decade of cuts in social spending when effectively social spending per person rose substantially and systematically across almost all countries in the region (ECLAC 2002; Walton 2004). The myth of the shrinking of the state would need to be balanced against the lack of evidence that neoliberal reforms produced a systematic reduction of government budgets (Cohen and Centeno 2006). It would have to take into account that the effects of the reforms on growth, stability and inequality depend crucially on other factors, including the distribution of assets, structural policies (for example, on social development and infrastructure) and political and social institutions (Walton 2004: 165). Above all, it would need to take into account that the degree to which neoliberal reforms were applied varied considerably depending on the time frame, country case and policies being considered. Finally it would have to consider that no country had implemented the full neoliberal package and that several of the most economically successful countries mixed orthodox neoliberal adjustments with heterodox government controls (Cohen and Centeno 2006; Green 1996: 110).[3]

As concerns policy issues, however, the devil is often in the detail, but in political arguments history is usually painted with a broad brush. This is why perhaps the most significant aspect of the IADB report lies not so much in the economic arguments about the balance of success and failures of the reforms per se but in the implications of these arguments for the political narrative that legitimized the Washington Consensus. In the report's own words:

> A decade ago there were clear explanations for poor economic perform-ance: Latin America was submerged in the debt crisis that had broken out in Mexico in 1982 ... The current situation is not caused by external circumstances of that nature ... Throughout the region questions are being raised about whether the reforms can modify the operation of the economy in the desired direction: greater growth in production and income, more employment opportunities, less instability in the macro environment, and reduced social inequity. (IADB 1997: 33–4)

The report's narrative contrasts the Washington Consensus sup-porters' confident explanations for the poor performance of the Latin American economies in the early 1980s with the lack of an equally con-vincing explanation for the poor performance of the economies of the region in the mid-1990s. In doing so it highlights how the Washington Consensus, as the dominant interpretative framework of the period, was unable to account for the social, political and economic dislocations resulting from policies that were implemented under its intellectual and financial influence.[4] To claim that the failures of the 1990s could not be absorbed by the discourse of the Washington Consensus is not to say that free marketeers had nothing to offer by way of explanation for these failures. On the contrary, the Washington Consensus was never a static construct frozen in the formulations of the late 1980s but an ever-evolving paradigm. The persuasive power of the original was lost, however, in the gap between promises and realities. In seeking to address these failures free market reformers incorporated an increasingly reactive and politically complex policy agenda, which lacked the intellectual confidence and self-contained elegance of the original. As such, it became increasingly vulnerable to narratives that challenged its policies and presented new policy alternatives. We will look in more detail at the changes in the Washington Consensus and the rise of alternatives to its formulations in Chapter 7, but before doing so we need to explore further its social impact in the 1990s.

The social question and the halt in economic growth

Central to the political legitimization of the reforms was the social question. A number of studies published between 1995 and 1997 assessed the condition of society in the region. The timing of these findings is particularly significant because they describe social conditions in the region after more than half a decade of economic growth and economic reforms at a time in which electoral support for reforming governments was still considerably high. The 1997 Social Progress Report of the Economic Commission for Latin America and the Caribbean (ECLAC) gave an overview of the social conditions of the region in the mid-1990s. The 1980s were a decade of plummeting social investment and steep rise in poverty. The report found that in the first half of the 1990s economic restructuring had brought significant advances in terms of macroeconomic stability, international linkages and regional integration. Social improvements were also noticeable, particularly where there had been sustained economic recovery. Between 1990 and 1994 – the golden years of free market modernization – poverty declined in nine out of twelve countries and increased in only one. On average, the incidence of poverty declined from 41 per cent to 39 per cent of all households during the first half of the 1990s, but the decline was not enough to offset the increase in poverty in the 1980s (from 35 per cent to 41 per cent). In absolute terms, the number of people living in poverty in Latin America in 1996 – 210 million – was higher than ever before. Indigence remained stubbornly high: 18 per cent of families were living in extreme poverty, compared with 16 per cent in 1980. With almost no change in the distribution of income in the first half of the 1990s Latin American countries relied almost exclusively on economic growth and on the reduction in inflation as the tools to overcome poverty. At an annual average of 3 per cent between 1990 and 1996, however, economic growth was well short of the 5 per cent annual rate that ECLAC estimated necessary for the region to catch up with the developed world. Moreover, growth was grounded on shaky foundations, as many countries had achieved macroeconomic stability by relying on large current-account deficits financed with volatile capital, which tends to produce short cycles of growth followed by economic contractions in which the number of people living in poverty is likely to increase disproportionately (ECLAC 1997: 1–2).

Economic restructuring produced new winners and losers. The historically large income disparities of the region were exacerbated by the increasingly wide productivity gap between relatively few technologically advanced companies at the vanguard of the modernization process and a majority of less advanced firms that failed to keep pace with the increase in productivity brought about by technological change. Key to the lack of significant social progress in the region was the condition of the labour market. Economic growth was not only sluggish but it created few jobs and most of the jobs that it created were in the informal sector. Eighty-four out of every hundred new jobs created between 1990 and 1995 were in the informal sector, which employed 56 per cent of all people at work in the region. As productivity in the informal sector is lower than in the formal one, average labour productivity remained basically flat over the period. Low job creation and low productivity translated to low wage levels and high wage differentials. Average wage levels in 1995 were still below those in 1980, but average figures reflected the counteracting tendencies of large wage gains among those employed in the more dynamic and technologically advanced sectors of the economy, and stagnant or declining wage levels in more traditional activities. The real minimum wage in 1995 in thirteen out of seventeen countries was lower than in 1980, and the gap between earnings of professional and technical workers and workers in low-productivity sectors grew by between 40 per cent and 60 per cent between 1990 and 1994 (ibid.: 3).

Economic inequality exacerbated deeply rooted social divisions. Latin Americans of indigenous and African descent, female-headed households and children were overrepresented among the poor, reflecting their lower education, higher unemployment rates and high presence in low-wage sectors, such as agriculture. In the case of people of indigenous descent, other factors such as geographical isolation, language barriers, racial discrimination and political exclusion further exacerbated their social exclusion. Racial discrimination also affected black Latin Americans. In the early 1990s Brazilians of African descent were 60 per cent less likely than whites to complete secondary education and 90 per cent less likely to have a university degree. Their median earnings were only 58 per cent of white earnings, and blacks were almost twice as likely to live in poverty as whites (Andrews 1992; Helwege 1995).

Inequality was a major contributory factor to the lack of progress in alleviating poverty. In the 1980s Latin America was the most inequitable region in the world, and it remained so in the 1990s. Inequality is a problem deeply grounded in Latin American history, culture and institutions (Glade 1996). Rooted in patterns of land ownership during the colonial era, it crystallized in the twentieth century as large disparities in the ownership of economic assets and human capital. Not even the supposedly more socially progressive policies of Import Substitution Industrialization of the 1950s and 1960s were able significantly to bring down the region's historically high level of inequality, as neither the gains of economic growth nor social security benefits reached the poorest sectors of the population. Inequality worsened during the years of high inflation and economic recession in the 1980s, compounded by the impact of the adjustment processes of the end of the decade and the early 1990s. The impact of the free market reforms on inequality was indirect rather than direct, as economic liberalization and the wider process of globalization exacerbated inequality by increasing wage differentials between skilled and unskilled workers (Berry 1997; Ocampo 1998; Robbins 1996).[5]

Poverty, exclusion and high socio-economic inequality combined with other social trends, such as the rise of the drug economy and mass migration, exacerbated the dislocations resulting from economic change on the region's social fabric. An increase in travel and communication exposed the people of the region to a symbolically close but materially distant world of luxury consumer goods and affluent lifestyles. The contrast between new patterns of conspicuous consumption in the developed world and among the region's socio-economic elite and the hardships of the majority of the population increased feelings of relative, as well as of absolute, deprivation. Young people were particularly exposed to media messages about consumer goods and lifestyles that became symbols of social success inaccessible to the majority of them. As the ECLAC (1997: 4) report put it, whole sectors of society saw their expectations frustrated, particularly the urban youth, whose educational levels were greater than those of their parents but whose unemployment rates were higher. For some of these youths the only avenue open to them to participate in the world of globalized consumption was to engage in drug trafficking and other forms of organized crime. An explosion in social violence associated with common crime became one of the region's top social concerns and led to the polarization of urban spaces into secured and non-secured territories. The rich surrounded themselves with walls, gates and private security forces, insulating themselves from wider society and ring-fencing the spatial concentration of affluence (Massey et al. 2006: 26).

The year 1997 marked the last one of the cycle of economic growth in Latin America that started around 1990, when the economies of the region started to recover from the crisis of the 1980s. The trigger for the new downturn was the East Asian financial crisis that started in Thailand with the collapse of the Thai baht in the summer of 1997 and gripped much of Asia, raising fears of worldwide financial contagion. The financial turbulence that arose in Asia was heightened by the Russian Federation's moratorium on its public debt and currency devaluation in August 1998. This led to a deepening of the crisis in 1999, which left a trail of financial instability in its wake (ECLAC 2001a: 12). Global financial turmoil particularly affected Brazil in 1998 and, while in the run-up to the 1998 election President Fernando Enrique Cardoso was able to resist pressures on the country's currency, the real, he was forced to devalue it shortly after the inauguration of his second term in office in January 1999.

The region-wide effects of the new financial crisis were more severe than those of the 1994–95 Tequila crisis. Investors' loss of confidence in emerging markets brought to a halt the inflow of capital that had fuelled Latin America's economic growth between 1990 and 1997. Between 1998 and 2003 capital outflow ushered in a new half-decade of economic volatility, slow economic growth, high unemployment and unchanging (or, in many cases, rising) poverty in the region (ECLAC 2002: 13). The downturn drained political support for the expanded labour and institutional reform agenda promoted by the organic intellectuals of the Washington Consensus as a complement to the minimalist agenda of structural adjustment, liberalization and privatization of the early 1990s (Naím 2000; Margheritis and Pereira 2007; Pastor and Wise 1999). While there was a marked slowdown in the forward march of the free market reforms, however, the changing economic circumstances did not mean that popular support for free market modernization disappeared overnight. Rather, a more complex process of continuity and change began to shape the politics of the region. As noted in Chapter 3, moderate reformers such as Fernando Henrique Cardoso in Brazil (1998), Fernando de la Rúa in Argentina (1999), Alejandro Toledo in Peru (2001) and Vicente Fox in Mexico (2000) won elections in that period. In Uruguay, Jorge Batlle, a long-standing advocate of free market economics, won the presidency in 1999. In Bolivia, Gonzálo Sánchez de Losada, the architect of the free market reforms of the late 1980s and early 1990s, won a second term in office in 2002, and in Chile the Concertación alliance won the presidential election for the third consecutive time in 2000 on the back of economic policies that made the country the most open economy in the region. But the political tide was already changing and would change even more, as new political and economic developments further eroded the political and intellectual status of the Washington Consensus.

The case of Argentina

The case of Argentina is particularly relevant, because the political and economic developments of the period between President Menem's re-election in 1995 and the economic collapse of 2001/02 are illustrative of many of the broader issues that are explored in this chapter. To say that what happened in Argentina had broader regional implications is not to ignore the strong domestic elements of the case. Rather, it is to argue that the events in Argentina illuminate wider points about the failures of the Washington Consensus and the emergence of a post-Washington Consensus.

The Alianza por el Trabajo la Justicia y la Educación (better known as 'the Alianza'), which governed Argentina between 1999 and 2001, was a centre-left coalition between the centrist Unión Cívica Radical (UCR) and the left-of-centre Frente por un País Solidario (FREPASO), set up in 1994 by dissident Peronists and a number of small left-wing parties and political activists. The Alianza was launched in August 1997 as the main opposition to the government of President Menem in the context of a deteriorating social and economic background. At all times during its

133

period in opposition, however, the Alianza reaffirmed its commitment to some of the key principles of the government's economic policies: convertibility (the one-to-one parity between the peso and the US dollar); privatizations; economic opening and fiscal equilibriums. Rather than changing the economic model, Alianza leaders promised to address the country's social deficit, fight corruption and strengthen public institutions and the rule of law (Novaro and Palermo 1998: 185).

It was in the context of an economic recession that Fernando de la Rúa assumed office on 10 December 1999. If the newly elected Alianza government's explicit agenda was to introduce corrections to the existing model, its implicit goal was to regain investors' confidence in the Argentine economy in order to attract the investment necessary to bring the economy out of recession (Novaro 2002). Instead of the government's hoped-for virtuous circle of fiscal adjustment, investment and growth, the Argentine economy entered a vicious one of deepening recession, falling fiscal revenue, runs on bank deposits, spiralling financial costs and capital flight. When in December 2001 the IMF announced that it was withholding the disbursement of the latest tranche of an emergency loan agreed in August because of the government's failure to meet agreed fiscal targets, economic and political collapse became inevitable. A haemorrhage of bank deposit withdrawals and a run against the peso followed the end of the IMF's financial support. Riots, looting and at times violent street demonstrations followed, with around two dozen persons shot dead by the police (Levitsky 2005). After an unsuccessful attempt at declaring a state of emergency, and with the opposition Justicialista (Peronist) party refusing to join a government of national unity, President de la Rúa resigned on 20 December 2001. Following de la Rúa's resignation, Adolfo Rodríguez Saá, the new president elected by Congress to finish de la Rúa's term, announced that Argentina was defaulting on its sovereign debt. The announcement was received with a standing ovation in Congress. In early January 2002 the government abandoned the convertibility plan that had been the cornerstone of the country's economic order since 1991. It was the start of Argentina's worst recession since the 1930s, as the economy shrank by almost 11 per cent in 2002 (ECLAC 2007b).

In the 1990s Argentina was paraded by the IMF as the showcase for free market reforms, but by the turn of the century the country was effectively bankrupted. What were the wider implications of the collapse of the Argentine economy for the Washington Consensus? As noted above, some of the key issues that led to the collapse of the Argentine economy were specific to the country's political and economic policies. This was particularly the case with convertibility, which went against the Washington Consensus preference for competitive exchange rates but, after some initial misgivings, was eventually accepted and effectively endorsed by the IMF. The success of convertibility in securing economic stability became a political constraint on any policy initiative that could be perceived as threatening its permanence. Political weaknesses and internal divisions within the Alianza and President de la Rúa's lack of leadership also played a significant role in the events that led to the crisis, as they drained away power and authority from the government at a time that required decisive leadership.

As suggested above, the Alianza government failed fully to take into account the extent to which the economic situation had deteriorated at the time in which it was elected to office. Why, given that so many indicators showed the need for radical changes in economic policy, didn't the government take more decisive action to implement the necessary changes? Part of the answer lies in the ambiguous legacy of the 1990s. President Menem's economic reforms (crucially including the fixing of the exchange rate) had tamed inflation, stabilized the currency and sparked a short-lived economic boom. They had also given the middle classes access to credit and imported consumer goods that were out of reach of most Argentinians before the reforms. The underside of the reforms in terms of increasing income differentials and high unemployment did not escape the notice of large sections of the population. But many Argentinians thought that these were either temporary costs in the onward march to becoming a fully developed nation or a price worth paying for the transformation of the country.

In February 2001, after more than two years of economic recession and barely eleven months before the collapse of convertibility, the leading Argentine newspaper *Clarín* published a review of the economic policies of the past decade. Its opening paragraph captured the ambiguous mood of the time:

Since the 1990s there has been no need any more to wait twenty-five years to have a telephone line. There was also no need to travel abroad to buy an imported perfume or to buy the best cognac or a camera. It also became unnecessary to buy dollars to prevent inflation devouring our savings or even our salaries. We became *globalized*. We opened ourselves to the world. We forgot about hyperinflation. Since the 1990s, however, we have fallen into debt, the rich became richer and the poor poorer, and we have lived under the sword of unemployment. It is said that in the 1990s Argentina entered a path of [economic] transformation and take-off. But falling social indicators suggest that, paradoxically, Argentina's take-off had a reverse gear. (*Clarin*, 4 February 2001, p. 3, my translation)

The ambiguous legacy of Menemismo weighed heavily in the Alianza's approach to the chronicle of a crisis foretold that characterized its time in office. If most Argentinians wanted change, they wanted a change that would not put into danger the gains of the 1990s. In backing convertibility, de la Rúa sought to align his electoral campaign with the preferences of both the citizens and the markets. Even those within his administration who favoured a more radical economic adjustment, such as economy minister Machinea, were reading the economic context through the narrative of the political and economic failures of the administration of President Alfonsín (1984–89), of which Machinea had been a member, and of President Menem's subsequent successful restoration of economic order.[6] The events of the late 1980s became part of the hegemonic narrative of the 1990s, which contrasted Menem's success with Alfonsín's failures, and its legacy weighed heavily on the Alianza government's policy decisions. The fear of history repeating itself made it unthinkable for the Alianza to make a radical break with Menem's version of the free market model in spite of its already obvious dislocations. Ironically, owing to the government's policy mistakes and vacillations, history did repeat itself and, as happened to President Alfonsín in 1989, President de la Rúa was forced to leave office prematurely in 2001. It would take the traumatic events of December 2001 and early 2002 to give new resonance to early critiques of the policies of Menemismo and allow the emergence of new discourses that became part of the narratives of the post-Washington Consensus.

The blame game

A key issue for the symbolic and political break with the economic policies of the 1990s that characterized the administration of Néstor Kirchner (2003–07) was the role of the IMF during that decade. As noted above, in the 1990s Argentina was regarded by the IMF as a success story of free market economic reforms in the region. During the 1990s the country maintained close relations with the IMF and received considerable financial assistance from the Fund and the World Bank. The high status of the government of President Menem in the eyes of the IMF was made apparent when the Argentinian president was invited to address the IMF's Annual Meeting in October 1998. Thus, the 2001/02 crisis put the Fund in the awkward position of trying to explain why Argentina's success story had turned into an economic nightmare. As Daseking and colleagues (2004: 1) put it:

> The events of the crisis, which imposed major hardships on the people of Argentina, are all the more troubling in the light of the country's strong past performance. Less than five years earlier, Argentina had been widely hailed as a model of successful economic reform: inflation, which had reached hyperinflationary levels during the 1980s, was in the low single digits, output growth was impressive, and the economy had successfully weathered the Tequila crisis of the mid-1990s.

There is a vast academic literature on the causes of Argentina's economic crisis and on the role of the IMF in it. Some economists believe that the crisis was the result of fiscal factors, particularly of insufficient fiscal tightening in the middle of the 1990s (Mussa 2002). Others emphasize the role of the exchange rate policy, arguing that the fixed exchange rate made it impossible to achieve competitiveness by traditional currency devaluation (Feldstein 2002; Perry and Servén 2003). A third group of scholars claim that the crisis stemmed from a combination of external factors, among these the sudden reverse of capital flows to Latin America in the late 1990s, economic constraints derived from the extensive dollarization of the economy, and political factors, notably insufficient political support and resolve to take the necessary measures to face the crisis (Daseking et al. 2004). The main issue for the purpose of understanding the impact of the crisis on the Washington Consensus is, however, the ideological battle between the Argentine government and the Fund over the role played by the IMF in the events leading to the Argentinian crisis. The polemic encapsulates the competing narratives that marked the end of the Washington Consensus and the emergence of the post-Washington Consensus.

In 2004, the IMF's Independent Evaluation Office (IEO) published a review of the Fund's relationship with Argentina between 1991 and 2002. The report does not regard the problems of Argentina as representative of a wider failure of free market economics in the region but rather as specific to the country's economic policies and political situation, arguing that the Argentine situation was so unique as to make previous experience inapplicable. It attributes responsibility for the crisis, however, to both the Fund and the Argentine government. It acknowledges that the IMF erred in the pre-crisis period by supporting the country's weak policies for too long, even after it had become evident in the late 1990s that the political ability to deliver the necessary fiscal discipline and structural reforms was lacking. According to the report, however, the balance of guilt rested clearly on the Argentine authorities. It concludes that 'the crisis resulted from the failure of Argentine policy makers to take necessary corrective measures sufficiently early, particularly in the consistency of fiscal policy with their choice of exchange rate regime' (IMF 2004: 3).

The report shows that the Argentine government had considerable leverage in its dealings with the Fund. It shows that on a number of occasions the IMF reacted to the Argentine government policy initiatives and endorsed them retroactively. For instance, this was the case with the convertibility plan, which was initially greeted with scepticism by the IMF but was subsequently endorsed with enthusiasm.[7] The gap between free market rhetoric and reality also worked in favour of the Argentine authorities. Throughout the 1990s the Fund presented Argentina as a model of successful structural reforms. The report claims, however, that while the Argentine authorities shared with the IMF the view that a number of reforms (fiscal reform, social security reform, labour market reform and financial sector reform) were crucial for the medium-term viability of the country's economic programme, only limited progress was made in implementing the reform agenda. The report remarks that little progress was made in later years and that the earlier reforms were even reversed in some cases (ibid.: 4).

The report gives an insight into the dialectic between conditionality and ownership in the setting of the economic agenda and the competing rationalities of the Fund's decision-making process. It shows that far from being guided purely by considerations of technocratic rationality, the Fund often took decisions for political reasons. Staff advice was frequently overruled by management or by the board. Conditionality appeared as highly ineffective and vulnerable to political pressures.

Although Argentina missed agreed fiscal deficit targets every year between 1994 and 2001, the IMF granted the Argentine governments repeated waivers and maintained financial assistance. Structural conditionality (i.e. conditions related to the implementation of structural reforms) was kept to a minimum. When staff expressed reservations over the weak structural content of successive agreements, the IMF management and the Executive Board overruled staff and approved the Argentine government's economic programmes (ibid.: 4).[8]

The report also addresses the issue of ownership, which, as noted above, was a crucial element in relation to the adoption of IMF-sponsored free market reforms. In a recommendation that exposes the paradoxical and self-contradictory nature of ownership, the report notes that emphasis on country ownership in IMF-supported programmes can lead to an undesirable outcome, if ownership means misguided or excessively weak policies. It recommends that the IMF 'should be prepared not to support strongly owned policies if it judges they are inadequate to generate a desired outcome' (ibid.: 6).

The reply of the then Argentine minister for the economy, Roberto Lavagna, to the IEO's document, dated July 2004, centres on the Argentine case but includes broader criticisms of the IMF's support for free market reforms in the region. Mr Lavagna points out that 'while the full-fledged program of privatizations, deregulations, trade and financial liberalization, and fiscal and social security reforms contributed to give Argentina the image of a stellar performer', the structural reforms implemented in Argentina during the 1990s suffered from a number of weaknesses that were wilfully ignored by the Fund for ideological reasons (ibid.: 115). Among these weaknesses Mr Lavagna highlights the flagship privatization process, which was carried out in 'a rather non-transparent manner' and in which 'monopolistic market structures were allowed to remain, coupled with a blatantly inadequate regulatory framework' (ibid.: 116). The minister argues that in spite of its flawed nature, the structural reforms implemented in Argentina during the 1990s, and very particularly the privatization of all its public services, was in line with the so-called 'Washington Consensus recommendations', and Argentina's policy was heralded by the Fund as an example to be followed for ideological reasons. He also claims that ideology rather than evidence was behind the Fund's belief that all structural reforms would necessarily lead to increased growth, and highlights the Fund's insistence on labour market reforms as yet another instance of the said ideological bias (ibid.: 116).

In addressing the report's recommendation on ownership, Mr Lavagna acknowledges that Argentina's ownership of policies under the programme was for the most part unquestionable. He argues, however, that the IMF's approach to ownership in Argentina was highly inconsistent.[9] On a more general note, Mr Lavagna argues that where ownership is clearly present, the authorities should be given the benefit of the doubt since they are the ones who know all the facts impinging on a given issue and they are the ones who risk their own political future if they take the wrong decisions. He believes that the acceptability of the Fund's policy advice should be gained, *inter alia*, by presenting it as one alternative among others, and not as the only reasonable one (ibid.: 117).

Finally, Mr Lavagna raises questions about the transparency of the IMF's decision-making process, particularly regarding 'the practice by certain prominent shareholders of bypassing the Board' as to the agenda that such shareholders might be advancing (ibid.: 119). It is in this regard that Mr Lavagna raises a scarcely veiled accusation that the Fund's decision in September 2001 to lend further resources to Argentina while earmarking some of the resources for debt restructuring was meant to 'facilitate the exit from Argentine exposure of the sophisticated investors that still remained rather than to actually support the Argentine program'. In other words, by providing the means to facilitate an easily predictable capital flight the Fund was acting on behalf of private investors rather than discharging its duty to support the Argentine economy (ibid.: 117–18). Mr Lavagna concludes by pointing out that while indeed neither the Fund nor Argentina benefited from the misguided policies that led to the 2001 crisis, the difference was that Argentina was the debtor and was forced to pay not only for its own errors but also for those of the Fund, while the Fund remained the creditor for a debt for which Argentina was not solely responsible (ibid.: 119).

Conclusions

The 1990s were the decade in which the Washington Consensus became hegemonic in Latin America. The ability of the Washington Consensus to establish itself as the dominant interpretative framework of Latin America's economic development was, however, disrupted very early by social processes and economic events that became increasingly difficult to be accounted for by its own discourse. Even when relatively more successful, in the early and mid-1990s, the Washington Consensus over-promised and under-delivered on economic growth, poverty and inequality. As the decade progressed, a succession of financial crises (Mexico 1994/95, Argentina 1995, Brazil 1999, Argentina 2001/02) exposed the fragile underbelly of the free market reforms. If the Mexican crisis represented the first major setback for the neoliberal reformation, Argentina's 2001/02 economic collapse had much wider implications, as it raised fundamental questions about the reforms themselves, about the relationship between politics and economics in processes of economic reform, and about the competence, transparency and motivations of the IMF's interventions in the country. Crucial among these is the evidence that economic policies are strongly dependent on political contexts that affect not only the range of policy options available to governments but also influence how governments interpret the economic situation.

The failure of Argentina's free market reformation was far more effective in undermining political support for free market economics in the country than left-wing critics of the Washington Consensus had ever been (Healey and Seman 2002). And yet, as has been repeatedly noted in this book, crises do not have predetermined outcomes but rather outcomes contingent on the narratives that best make sense of the crises and offer an alternative for the future: the Mexican, Brazilian and Argentinian crises all had different politically mediated outcomes. The succession of crises in the region's largest economies at the turn of the century's new 'lost half-decade' for development made it politically increasingly difficult, however, for the organic intellectuals of the Washington Consensus to explain the failures of its policies by reference to the legacies of the past, incomplete reforms or ad hoc policy mistakes. Instead, the dislocated narrative of the Washington Consensus opened economic policy-making to alternative interpretative frameworks that in different degrees adopted, adapted and rejected the reforms of the 1990s and articulated them to different political visions. It is to these new alternatives that we turn in the next chapter.

7 | The opening of a paradigm: growth, equity and democracy

The term 'Washington Consensus' (WC) was coined by an individual, John Williamson, and even has a birthdate (see Chapter 1). No such attributions should be made to the denomination 'post-Washington Consensus'. The problems of attribution are partly a product of the ambiguous meaning intrinsic to any corpus of ideas that is preceded by the prefix 'post', which implies both continuity and change or, to put it in slightly different terms, something new that none the less incorporates significant elements of the old. 'Post' also denotes something that is ill defined, unfinished and in a state of flux. In this case, the ambiguous nature of the post-Washington Consensus is compounded by the changing nature of what is meant by 'to succeed', as under the appearance of a highly codified and prescriptive policy agenda – Williamson's decalogue – there was a surplus of meaning in the WC that left the so-called 'consensus' open to interpretation, contestation and redefinition by friends and critics alike.

This chapter maps the international financial institutions' (IFIs) revision of the WC and the intellectual grounds of the post-Washington Consensus (PWC). It looks at the redefinitions, reinterpretations and contestations of the WC, and examines the emergence of a set of alternatives that sought to create distance with the original while incorporating substantial elements of continuity into the new policy agenda. Some of the changes to the agenda were driven by the same IFIs that had been the originators, systematizers and propagandists of the original. Arguably, by promoting a new development agenda – the so-called second-generation reforms – the World Bank (WB) and the International Monetary Fund (IMF) sought to add new elements to the WC without changing its basic premises. The process led, however, to an attempt to design an agenda more sensitive to the failures and shortcomings of the original and more open to alternative policy formulations.

Other changes have been advanced by regional development agencies, such as the Economic Commission for Latin America and the Caribbean (ECLAC) and the Inter-American Development Bank (IADB), which, while accepting the need to reform the old Import Substitution Industrialization

(ISI) model, were always critical of the dogmatic assumptions and narrow approach to development of the WC. The provisional end result has been a significant narrowing of the differences between the WC and what for want of a better name can be said to be its mainstream critics among development economists and regional development agencies.

A changing paradigm

The revision of the premises of the WC is a natural occurrence in the life of a paradigm. In his analysis of the structure of scientific revolutions, Thomas Kuhn (1962) argues that the development of science can be understood as a succession of more or less enduring paradigms punctuated by periodic 'revolutions' during which the ascendant paradigm is challenged and ultimately replaced. Peter Hall (1993) extended Kuhn's ideas to the policy-making arena, arguing that policy is made within the context of a 'policy paradigm'. As such, it comes to define a range of legitimate policy techniques, mechanisms and instruments, thereby defining the very targets and goals of policy itself. A successful paradigm comes to circumscribe the realm of the politically feasible, practical and desirable (Hay 2001: 197).

Paradigms, however, change through time. In studying the rise of the neoliberal paradigm, Colin Hay differentiates between periods of 'normal' policy-making and change, during which the paradigm remains largely unchallenged and in which change is largely incremental and evolutionary, and periods of 'exceptional' policy-making, during which the very parameters that previously circumscribed policy options are cast asunder and replaced, and in which the realm of the politically possible, feasible and desirable is correspondingly reconfigured. He argues that, in normal times, the process of policy evolution tends to be characterized by successive stages or iterations of strategic learning within the broad parameters of an evolving paradigm. Within this process, policy failures are dealt with by a process of iterative (as opposed to fundamental) policy modifications within the parameters defined by the existing policy paradigm. In a highly politicized policy-making climate, however, an accumulation of perceived policy-making failures, contradictions and steering problems may give rise to a profusion of 'crisis narratives' from politicians and public intellectuals. This may take the identification and definition of the problem out of the hands of the (domestic or international) civil servants and the state elite and into the political arena (ibid.: 201–2).

Changes in the WC's diagnosis, agenda, policy and rhetoric closely mirrored Hay's paradigm-evolution cycle. These changes were a way of dealing with the anomalies and dislocations of the free market reforms. Among the anomalies were the high transition costs of free market reforms, disappointing economic growth, increasing economic volatility, and persistently high levels of poverty and inequality. The succession of crises of the 1990s that affected Asia, Russia and Latin America, and particularly some of the poster nations for free market reforms in Latin America, such as Mexico and Argentina, forced the IFIs to revise the premises of the free market development model in order to account for its failures.

The new thinking also reflected changes in the most pressing development problems facing Latin American nations in a post-stabilization environment, such as increasing financial volatility and stagnant economic growth, as well as the development successes of Asian countries, such as China and India, that, while based on foreign trade and investment, were far from mirroring the orthodoxy of the WC. Last but not least, changes in the IFIs' intellectual outlook followed the ebbing of the political hegemony of free market economics in the developed world, marked by the end of the administrations of Ronald Reagan in the USA and Margaret Thatcher in the UK, and the emergence of the Third Way political discourse (Giddens 1998) emanating from the Clinton administration in the USA and from a number of social democratic governments in Europe, particularly the New Labour government in Britain.

As a result of this conjunction of events, the neoliberal sense of certainty of the late 1980s gave way in the second half of the 1990s to a more open, less dogmatic discourse on development. The following excerpt from the World Bank's *World Development Report* (WDR) 1999/2000, *Entering the 21st Century*, captures the change in mood:

> As with many subjects, a deeper understanding of development involves a recognition that sweeping beliefs are often incomplete, that layers of complexity are buried not far beneath the surface, and that wisdom is often contingent on the conditions of time and place. In recent decades both experience and intellectual insight have pushed development thinking away from debates over the role of states and markets, and the search for a single overarching policy prescription. (World Bank 1999b: 2)

As was noted in Chapter 1, the Washington Consensus had a double grounding. The first, which we may call its intellectual roots, was based on changes in development thinking that crystallized in the claim that the WC's policy prescriptions embodied 'the common core of wisdom embraced by all serious economists of the time' (Williamson 1994: 18). The second, closely related to the first, which we may call its political roots, was based on the technical, financial and political capital of what this book has labelled the WC's organic intellectuals: the Washington-based IFIs, particularly the WB and the IMF, which allowed these organizations to define the development process in Latin America in the 1990s in terms of their own visions of development. IFIs continued to play a significant role in framing the region's development agenda in the late twentieth century and early twenty-first century.[1]

The intellectual roots of the PWC

While the Washington Consensus was under intellectual attack from its inception from, among others, traditional developmentalist and structural economists, by the mid-1990s its policies began to be subject to systematic criticism from more mainstream economists. Prominent among these was Joseph Stiglitz, whose arguments carried the special weight of coming from the then chief economist and senior vice-president of the World Bank. His 1998 Wider Annual Lecture, entitled 'More instruments and broader goals: moving towards the post-Washington Consensus', marked a seminal moment in the transition from the Washington Consensus to the post-Washington Consensus. As the lecture's title implies, Stiglitz's arguments were 'post-Washington Consensus' rather than 'anti-Washington Consensus', in that although he argues that some of the policies of the WC were 'sometimes misguided', his main claim was that the policies were incomplete rather than utterly wrong (Stiglitz 2001: 17).

As he would further elaborate in subsequent writings, Stiglitz's criticisms were directed at what he referred to as 'free market fundamentalists' rather than at the market economy itself. Stiglitz historicized the Washington Consensus in the context of the experience of Latin American countries in the 1980s and re-examined its economic prescriptions in the light of the economic developments of the 1990s in Latin America and elsewhere. Integral to his analysis was the Asian crisis of 1997 to 1998, whose recent occurrence at the time of his lecture served as background to his theoretical reflections. He argued that the narrow set of policies stressed by the Washington Consensus (macroeconomic stability, liberalized trade and privatization) may have been reasonable means for addressing the particular set of problems confronting the Latin American economies in the 1980s, but these policies might not necessarily be the only, or even the central, elements of an economic programme aimed at addressing other sets of problems in different circumstances (Stiglitz 2002, 2005).

Stiglitz also questioned some of the key policies of the Washington Consensus, such as the paramount importance assigned to controlling inflation, achieving budgetary and current-account equilibriums, financial liberalization and privatization. His criticisms, however, were carefully nuanced. He acknowledged that high inflation is socially and economically costly but questioned whether relatively low-level inflation is a fundamental obstacle to development. He agreed that large budget deficits are deleterious to economic performance but argued that there are no simple formulas for determining the optimum level of the budget and current-account deficits. He also agreed that privatization is important but argued that there are critical issues about both the sequencing and the scope of privatization and claims that fostering competition is more important than ownership in promoting economic efficiency. He argued that while the Washington Consensus promoted liberalization as a solution to poorly functioning financial systems, the key should not be liberalization or deregulation but the construction of an adequate regulatory framework to ensure its proper working. Against the promotion by the Washington Consensus of a minimalist, non-interventionist state he argued that the government and the private sector are much more intimately entwined than assumed by the free marketeers. As he put it, the choice should not be *whether* the state should be involved in the economy but *how* it gets involved (Stiglitz 2001).

It could seem like an exaggeration to assign too much importance to a public lecture delivered by a technocrat in front of an elite audience of fellow technocrats and academics. Many of Stiglitz's criticisms of the policies of the Washington Consensus were not particularly new. Coming from someone who was chief economist of one of the leading institutions of the Washington Consensus (the World Bank), however, Stiglitz's attack on the dogmas of the free market orthodoxy had the resonance of a Lutheran protestation. If not a turbulent priest, critics of the Washington Consensus had found their own *technopol* (Chapter 5).

Moreover, the development goals set up by the lecture (a new role for the state, improving health and education, maintaining a healthy environment and promoting economic development that is both equitable and democratic) would mark the agenda of the post-Washington Consensus in the early twenty-first century.

Some left-wing critics argued that Stiglitz's prescriptions for economic development, which he further elaborated in other works (see Stiglitz 2002, 2005), did not represent a fundamental break with the WC. In a review of Meir and Stiglitz's (2001) book *Frontiers of Development Economics: The Future in Perspective*, Paul Cammack (2001: 661–2) claims that the authors' approach remains neoliberal:

> Economic growth comes from investment and productivity gains; inflation should be low, labour markets flexible, and fiscal, monetary and exchange rate policy prudent; trade should be liberalized; and property rights should be secured and enforced. The prescription is for an *active* neo-liberal state [...] The approach is progressive only in the specific sense that it promotes self-reproducing capitalism in the developing world, rather than just forced access for capital and goods from the USA and other advanced capitalist countries.

As is the case with so many aspects of the polemic about the Washington Consensus, Cammack's arguments beg the question of what is understood by neoliberalism and whether a discrete economic policy can be defined as neoliberal independently of its articulation within a wider economic policy framework. The pitfalls of policy qualification are evident in Cammack's listing of alleged neoliberal policies. Some of the policies that he considers as part of the neoliberal dogma, such as the belief that economic growth comes from investment and productivity gains, are shared by a wide section of economists, from free marketeers to socialists. And few would disagree that prudent fiscal, monetary and exchange-rate policies are a good thing, although, as noted by Stiglitz himself, there could be significant disagreements about the meaning of 'prudence'. By claiming that the only progressive aspects of Stiglitz and colleagues' development strategy is that it promotes 'self-reproducing capitalism', Cammack appears to equate neoliberalism with capitalism itself.

The World Bank's and the International Monetary Fund's new approaches to development

As happened with the WC, IFIs, particularly the WB and the IMF, also played a crucial role in setting the agenda of the PWC. The new, expanded development agenda included policies that were at the heart of the WC, particularly regarding labour flexibilization and trade opening reforms. Its novelty element was what has come to be known as 'second generation reforms' (Naím 1994). These are complex reforms aimed at strengthening the institutions that provide the foundations for market-oriented growth, and at tackling Latin America's social deficit. Central to the institution-building agenda was also 'bringing the state back in' to the development process (Navia and Velasco 2003).

The WB's and the IMF's views on the development process underwent parallel processes of revision and reformulation. In dealing with a more uncertain intellectual and political environment, the WB's and, to a lesser extent, the IMF's agendas evolved from the promotion of a model of development based on a narrow range of economic policy instruments centred on economic growth through market liberalization to a more integral approach that sought to articulate the social, institutional and political dimensions of development to its economic core. This approach, as exemplified by the WB's so-called Comprehensive Development Framework (CDF) (Wolfensohn 1999), also entailed moving away from top-down technocratic policy-making typical of the WC and opening the policy-making process to wider political participation.

The WB's new approach to development discovered the importance of institutions in the working of markets, rediscovered the role of the state in economic development, promoted a pro-poor agenda, acknowledged the importance of equity for sustainable development, and took on board the importance of ensuring broad political participation in processes of economic reform. In parallel to the revision of its policies, the IFIs adopted a new rhetoric that incorporated a number of signifiers that were traditionally part of progressive political discourses on democracy and development, such as 'consultation', 'ownership', 'empowerment', 'pro-poor', 'participation' and 'equitable development'.

Changes in the WB's framing of economic development are reflected in the Bank's annual *World Development Reports* (WDRs) of the late 1990s and early 2000s. In the revised economic thinking of the WB, markets continued to be key institutions for economic development, and macroeconomic stability an essential prerequisite for economic growth, but the Bank sought to limit the primacy of the markets by introducing other elements into the development process, such as 'institutions', 'the state', 'participation' and 'equity', in order to take on board charges of market fundamentalism. In drawing on what the Bank calls the 'critical lessons' from fifty years of development experience, the WB's WDR 1999/2000, *Entering the 21st Century*, is notable for emphasizing that markets alone are not capable of achieving sustainable development or eliminating poverty. In what became one of the Bank's mantras of the PWC, the report emphasizes that 'institutions matter', and that sustainable development should be rooted in processes that are 'socially inclusive and responsive to changing circumstances'. The report also concedes that growth alone does not trickle down, and therefore development must address human needs directly (World Bank 1999b: 1–2).

On one of the key issues in the debate about development, namely the role of the state, there was a shift in the thinking of the Bank from a highly prescriptive, narrow agenda, in which the main purpose of the state was to set up the rules for markets to prosper, towards a broader, although still limited, role. The shift was partly the result of changes in the nature of the ideological opponent of the Bank's development discourse. In the 1980s, the Bank's main ideological battle was fought against statist development strategies, a struggle in which state intervention had to be exorcized from the agenda. Primary attention was given to policies aimed at the removal of macroeconomic and microeconomic rigidities, on the grounds that removing distortions would be good for growth and that this would in turn lead to poverty reduction. There was also a belief that many distortions were themselves the consequence of rent-seeking by a relatively well-off state-dependent elite, and thus that the removal of distortions would be inequality-reducing (Kanbur and Vines 2000).

The WB's new thinking on development shows a distinctive change in emphasis and a less significant one in substance on the role of the state, the institution-making machine par excellence. As the 1987 WDR put it, other than establishing clear rules of the game, providing infrastructure, transport, health and education and welfare for the poor, the state should intervene *sparingly and carefully* (World Bank 1987: 60). Ten years later, the WDR *The State in a Changing World* (World Bank 1997) was devoted to the role and effectiveness of the state. It was the first report to make a systematic attempt to show that an effective – not minimal – state was vital for economic development (World Bank 2008b). The report addresses the failures of market-led development and acknowledges that past WB documents had significantly underestimated the role of the state in the successful development economies of South-East Asia. Consequently, the dividing line between market-led and state-led development was now drawn in a more subtle way. The WDR argues that both models of development (i.e. market-led and state-led) share a belief in the centrality of the state for economic and social development, but while developmentalists believe that development should be state-provided, the market-friendly approach sees the state role as 'a partner, catalyst and facilitator' of development (World Bank 1997: 1–2).

According to the WB, the main difference concerning the role of the state is that the 1980s' concern with limiting its role has in the late 1990s been replaced by the PWC's emphasis on effective state action.[2] States and markets are now seen as complementary rather than in a relation of mutual antagonism (ibid.: 4). In another move designed to distance itself from the perceived dogmatism of the free market agenda of the late 1980s and early 1990s, the 1997 WDR argues that the range of differences among states is too big to allow for a one-size-fits-all recipe for an effective state, and claims that reducing or diluting the role of the state cannot be the ultimate aim of the reforms. Instead, the report emphasizes the importance of matching the state's role to its capabilities by reinvigorating public institutions: 'Enhancing the efficiency rather than reducing the size of the state is now the Bank's main goal' (ibid.: 2–3).

The Bank's repositioning of the state allowed the organization to move from its traditional view of the state as a technocratic rule-making machine at the service of the markets to considering the state as part of a wider political and social agenda. In the Bank's view, the main role for the state remains to put in place the appropriate institutional foundations for markets, but now public policies should also ensure that the benefits of market growth are shared, that growth contributes to reducing poverty and inequality, and that people are protected against material and personal insecurity (ibid.: 4). In order to achieve these goals, the WDR argues that the state should be brought closer to the people by bringing the voice of the poor and marginalized groups of society into the policy-making process. Treading carefully in the political arena, given the limitations imposed by its charter on political involvement, the report notes that the best-established mechanism for giving citizens a voice is the ballot box, although it points out that other mechanisms, such as decentralization and the participation of civil society organizations in policy-making councils, are needed to ensure that the concerns of minorities and the poor are reflected in public policies (ibid.: 10).[3]

The WB's thinking on poverty followed a similar pattern to that on the role of the state. In the 1980s, the Bank considered structural adjustment and market-led economic growth to be the primary means for reducing poverty. Adjustment programmes aiming at bringing down inflation were seen as highly beneficial for low-income groups, and export-oriented growth was considered to be the best way of promoting the productive use of labour, which is the poor's most abundant asset. Openness and liberalization would lead to growth that would in turn lead to poverty reduction. Targeted monetary transfers and safety nets were added to the agenda in the early 1990s to compensate for the social cost of transition to market-led development (Gilbert et al. 2000; World Bank 1990: 3).

Ten years later, the WB's *World Development Report 2000/2001, Attacking Social Poverty*, argues that there is a two-way relation between poverty, growth and development: while the focus of the WB's argument in the 1980s was on the positive impact of economic growth on poverty and inequality, there was now a recognition that severe poverty and inequality have a negative effect on economic growth. The WB's new discourse on poverty also articulates the para-political language of voice, power and representation with its traditionally technocratic approach to policy reduction: 'The strategy of this report recognizes that poverty is more than inadequate income or human development – it is also vulnerability and a lack of voice, power and representation ... The way to deal with this complexity is through empowerment and participation – local, national and international' (World Bank 2000: 12). The 'empowerment of the poor' rhetoric brings together discourses of democracy and good governance: empowerment requires 'having transparent institutions, with democratic and participatory mechanisms for making decisions and monitoring their implementation, backed up by legal systems that foster economic growth and promote legal equity' (ibid.: 9).[4]

The orthodox neoliberal view that the alleviation of poverty matters more than the promotion of equality is further challenged in the WB's new social thinking. In the 1980s, issues of inequality were sidelined in the strategy of reducing poverty through economic growth. When equity was taken into consideration, it was assumed that, when markets worked well, greater equity would come naturally. The WB's 2006 *World Development Report* not only makes equity central to the Bank's anti-poverty agenda, but claims that equity has both an intrinsic and an economic value, as greater equity can, over the long term, contribute to faster economic growth (World Bank 2006: 4, 9, 17). The WB's equity agenda does not, however, encourage redistributive struggles. For the Bank, equity enhancement is about the distribution of assets, economic opportunities and political voice, rather than lessening income inequality. In its view, inequality is the result of political factors and imperfect markets rather than the negative distributional impact of markets. According to the Bank's social thinking, impaired institutional development and market imperfections generate the wrong incentives for a more equitable society. Rent-seeking is regarded as the main explanation for inequality, as the Bank argues that patterns of domination persist because economic and social differences are reinforced by the overt and covert use of (state) power. By accepting that trade liberalization can be associated with higher inequality, however, and that privatization can, under certain circumstances, lead to further inequity, the report at least includes a qualified acknowledgement of the negative impact of market reforms on equity (ibid.: 14).

If the WB's intellectual and political journey of the late 1990s and early 2000s led to claims that it could come to be regarded as a truly progressive organization (Pender 2001: 405), a similar claim has seldom been made regarding the IMF. In parallel with the WB, however, the IMF has incorporated into the macroeconomic stability and structural reform agenda questions of governance, institutions and poverty. The Fund has also revised conditionality lending and placed a strong emphasis on consensus-building and policy ownership. The IMF has, however, been altogether far less open than the WB in acknowledging the shortcomings and limitations of market liberalization as a strategy for economic development, and has maintained a narrower view of the development process. Differences between the two institutions are partly the result of their different mandates, which in the case of the Fund comprises maintaining the stability of the global financial system rather than promoting economic development or ending world poverty. It has also been suggested that the IMF's governance structure, which includes a large role for central bank governors, who typically are neither representative of the population as a whole nor, increasingly, directly accountable to the electorate, has contributed to the IMF's reluctance to own up to the significant failures of its programmes of assistance (Stiglitz 2000).

The IMF, however, has not been oblivious to what its staff papers call the 'disappointments' of the 1990s in Latin America. A paper written by the Fund's senior western hemisphere (WH) staff summarizes the failures of the development process of the 1990s:

> Since the latter part of the decade [the 1990s], per capita income has increased very little, thereby extending for another decade the stagnation of the 1980s ... Overall, no clear trend emerged toward reducing the region's high poverty rates and income inequalities. As a result, the gap in living standards with North America has grown over the past decade, and Latin America has continued to fall behind fast-growing economies in Asia. (Singh et al. 2005: 107)

In making a balance of a decade of stabilization and reform, however, the document argues that the economic and social failures of Latin America in the 1990s were the result of incomplete, uneven and inconsistent market reforms rather than of the policies themselves: limited trade openness, high ratios of foreign debt and debt-servicing payments and macroeconomic imbalances are explanatory variables for what in the foreword to the WH staff's document the Fund's former acting managing director, Anne Krueger, describes as 'a decade of disappointment' (ibid.: ix).

In the IMF's thinking, behind the failed policies of the 1990s was the fact that more progress was made with measures that had low up-front costs, such as privatization, relative to reforms that promised long-term benefits, such as improving macroeconomic and labour market institutions, and strengthening legal and judicial systems. Waning support for the reforms was the fault of insufficient emphasis being placed on ensuring that the benefits of the reforms were broadly shared (ibid.: 107–8). In the view of senior IMF managers, responsibility for this state of affairs lies fundamentally with the countries' politicians, who, in the punchy phrase of Anne Krueger, 'meant well, tried little, failed much' (Krueger 2004). The consequences of governments' failure to reform were economies that were far from being modern market economies. Krueger (ibid.) approvingly cites former Mexican minister of finance Francisco Gil Díaz's claim that:

The policies that we have undertaken are not even a pale imitation of what market economics ought to be, if we understand market economics as the necessary institutional framework for a sound economy to operate and flourish. What has been implemented throughout our continent is a grotesque caricature of market economics.

As noted above, in the late 1990s the WB became increasingly aware that it was now operating in a far less secure, less confident and far more complex environment than the simpler institution of the past (Marshall 2008). The Bank also accepted that the development process was infused with uncertainty, and that the contingencies of time and place made it unwise to promote overarching policy prescriptions. No such self-doubts emerge from the view of senior IMF staff. Criticizing politicians who use the uncertainty of policy outcomes as a reason to minimize reforms, Krueger argues that uncertainty should not be an obstacle against governments to seizing the opportunity to confront difficult issues because, as she puts it, 'we do know what works, and what doesn't' (Krueger 2004).

The Fund concedes, however, that repeated adjustment programmes undermined popular support for reforms, and that the benefits of global integration benefited mainly those in the upper income brackets, while the costs were borne by the less wealthy majority (Singh et al. 2005: 107). The IMF's recommendations for righting the wrongs of the 1990s consist of a long list of market-liberalizing reforms mixed with a good governance and institutional reform agenda.[5] In common with the Bank's rediscovering of the state and renewed emphasis on fighting poverty, the Fund's reform package also incorporates 'an improved and more strategic role for the state'. In its new, market-friendly incarnation, the state should promote good governance, ensure the rule of law, fight corruption, set up transparent regulatory systems, improve the business climate, secure property rights and promote social stability by targeting social spending, improving land access and encouraging job creation in the formal sector (Camdessus 1998; Singh 2004; Singh et al. 2005).[6]

New wine in old bottles?

To what extent can changes in the thinking of the WB and the IMF be regarded as part of a new, emerging paradigm in development thinking, or just as part of the natural evolution of the WC? It is hard to imagine a fairer and more prosperous Latin America without better public institutions, a more efficient state and a concerted strategy to lower poverty and improve equity, as promoted by the WB (Navia and Velasco 2003). In the words of a critic of the PWC, Ben Fine, in the new thinking of the WB, the virtues of the market and its opposition to the state are replaced by a balance between the two: the perfection of the market gives way to emphasis on informationally led market imperfections that need to be corrected, and there is a more rounded understanding of the interaction between market and non-market institutions. These changes make the WB's new vision of development less dogmatic and more intellectually sophisticated than that of the old WC (Fine 2001: 10). And yet, as Fine notes, the new consensus, if it can be called such, is still an inchoate current of thought, possessing none of the prescriptive and profoundly misleading sharpness of the Washington Consensus (ibid.: xiii).

An illustration of the ambiguous nature of the new PWC agenda is the emphasis on the importance of institution-building and the rule of law for economic development. The concept of institutions, understood as the humanly devised constraints that structure human interaction (North 1993), is extremely broad and includes several different aspects of society, from the stock exchange to the family. The rule of law is of the essence of formal institutions, as it is the ultimate mechanism by which the rules that structure human interaction can be formally enforced. The rule of law can be interpreted in a broader or narrower sense, however, and the way in which it is interpreted has significant political and policy implications. Economists regularly use two different definitions of the rule of law: a 'thick one' and a 'thin one' (Trebilcock and Daniels 2008). According to the 'thick' meaning of the concept, the rule of law is inseparable from the institutional forms of liberal democracy, including strong representative institutions, political accountability and the full gamut of legally protected civil and political rights. In contrast, 'thin' definitions of the rule of law are closer to the technocratic concept of good governance that puts the emphasis on institutions as market-creating and regulating devices. The key institutions for the thin version of the rule of law are not democracy and freedom, but property rights and the efficient administration of justice to enforce contracts (Economist 2008).[7]

The relation between the rule of law, institutions and economic development is not linear or easy to establish. The two conceptions of the rule of law have different implications for the understanding of the relations between institutions and economic development, and, as will be shown below, different international development agencies have understood it in different ways within the common framework of the PWC. Starting with the narrow definition of institutions, the rule of law may be a good thing in itself, but, as the case of China appears to suggest, there is no conclusive evidence that the rule of law is a precondition for economic development. Dani Rodrik (2007: 188–90) argues that, in the short run, large-scale institutional reform is rarely necessary to accelerate growth, but in the long run institutions play a crucial role in sustaining economic growth. Even in the long run, however, the causal relation between institutions and growth has not been clearly determined. There is a clear long-term correlation between institutional strength and economic development, but such links do not reveal enough about causation: i.e. whether economic growth helps the rule of law, or vice versa. Strong institutions could be the outcome of economic development and not a condition for it, as historical evidence suggests that today's developed nations achieved significant levels of economic development with much lower institutional standards than those of today's developing countries at a comparable stage of development (Chang 2005: 119).

The above considerations are not meant to deny but to qualify the relevance of institutions for economic growth. Institutions are deeply embedded in society and difficult to change. It took the developed countries a long time to develop sound institutions in the earlier days of development. Demands that developing nations should adopt global institutional standards as a condition for development may thus be unrealistic (ibid.). Accordingly, a shopping list of institutional reforms applicable to all countries is arguably neither useful nor politically feasible. An alternative development strategy may be to assume that institutional functions do not map into unique institutional forms, and that effective institutional outcomes do not map into unique institutional designs. The policy implication of these assumptions would be to prioritize the institutional reforms that better suit the country's history and context in order to achieve the best development effects (Rodrik 2007: 189–92).

Whether we adopt a thin or a thick definition of the rule of law, the PWC's reform agenda also has significant political implications. While seeking to be more participatory and ultimately more democratic, the agenda is also more interventionist. The IFIs' so-called comprehensive approach to development pushes the agencies to intervene in areas such as political institutions, democracy and public governance, in which these organizations may have neither the mandate nor the expertise to interfere. Taken to the extreme, the drive for the adoption of institutional standards becomes open to accusations of neo-imperialism, for not only is intervention justified on the basis of market imperfections, but also the success of such interventions is attached to non-economic factors (Chang 2005: 112; Fine 2001: 15). Moreover, the shift from 'quick fixes', 'stroke-of-the-pen' reforms (market liberalization) to 'deep fixes' and 'country ownership' (institutional change) makes even more evident the political nature of the policy-making process and thus more necessary the shift from the coercive element of hegemony, represented by the use of conditionality, to an emphasis on the construction of consensus, as successful policies need not only the backing of the government, but also broad popular support to be effectively implemented (Hoff and Stiglitz 2002).

The shift from shallow to deep intervention raises questions about the nature of policy ownership and the limits to political participation in the policy-making process. Ownership is an elusive concept, hard to define and to pin down. Implicitly, it refers to a situation in which the policy content of the programme is similar to what the country itself would have chosen in the absence of IMF involvement. This is because the country – or, rather, the government and all those involved in the policy-making process – agrees with the IMF on both the objectives of the economic programme and the means to achieve them. In such a situation, the country 'owns' the programme in the sense that it is committed to the spirit of the programme, rather than just to complying with the letter. But one of the problems with seeking programme ownership through wider participation around a large reform agenda is that the larger the number of policy objectives included in the programme, the less likely it is that the country's stakeholders and the Fund will reach a consensus on the programme's goals and instruments (Khan and Sharma 2001: 14–15). Questions have also been raised concerning the extent to which reforms financed by the IFIs are effectively driven by the priorities established by recipient countries. There are indications that a number of reforms that are at the heart of the second-generation reform agenda, such as civil service reform, are mostly driven by supply rather than by demand. As Yasuhiko Matsuda, a WB public sector specialist in the Poverty Reduction and Economic Management Unit of the Latin American and the Caribbean Region, puts it:

It is the Bank's policy to work specifically with governments. In most countries, civil service reform – narrowly defined – is not a priority for anyone. If you ask people what they want, they will point to better health services, greater access to water etc. and the experts will argue that to get that you need more efficient government machinery; that is the civil service bit. (Matsuda 2000)

Differences in the reform agenda content and priorities are not limited to those between the WB and IMF's technocrats on the one side and the representatives of national governments on the other, but are also internal to the agencies' staff. For instance, in the case of the WB's programmes of civil service reform, there have been tensions between the Bank's market liberalization and institution-building agendas. Within the Bank, there is still the view that institutional reform is under-theorized and soft compared with the hard discipline of economics that dominates the Bank's thinking (Shepherd 2000; Nissenbaum 2000). As a WB public sector specialist puts it: 'The economics group within the Bank sees government as a burden. Because of our location here in the US there is a bizarre anti-public sector discourse. The notion of a benevolent government is absent' (Manning 2000).[8]

In spite of their internal and external differences, the WB and the IMF adopted a predominantly thin version of institutions and the rule of law. In contrast, ECLAC and the IADB, the two foremost development agencies in Latin America, openly adopted a thick version of institutions and the rule of law that explicitly linked economic and democratic institution-building. An account of how the new framing of development has led to a substantial convergence in outlook between multilateral and regional development agencies can be produced by comparing the WB's views on development to those of ECLAC and the IADB.

The reframing of development: ECLAC and the IADB

ECLAC's economic thinking has changed substantially since Raúl Prebsich's (1949) advocacy of Import Substitution Industrialization (ISI) as a strategy for development. In the 1980s and 1990s, ECLAC was broadly in favour of economic liberalization, but it always advanced a more structuralist and interventionist agenda than those of the WB and the IMF. In the early twenty-first century, ECLAC's *Equity, Development and Citizenship* report (ECLAC 2001b), published with the goal of providing a comprehensive view of the institution's thinking on development, notes the need to build on the achievements of the free market reforms of the 1990s in reducing fiscal deficits and inflation, strengthening linkages with the global economy, increasing the role of the private sector and making the state more efficient. ECLAC rejects the idea, however, that there is a single or universal solution for the problems of development, in addition to the notion that macroeconomic adjustment, free market liberalization, institution-building and equity enhancement can be seen as sequences in a linear and universal change process implicit in the narrative of first- (liberalization), second- (institutionalization) and third- (equity-enhancing) generation reforms (ibid.: 10).[9]

In contrast to the WC, ECLAC's neo-structuralist approach to development emphasizes the negative impact of high levels of socio-economic inequality and of structural heterogeneity – i.e. the considerable differences in productivity between large firms, medium-sized firms and small formal businesses and informal microenterprises – on economic development. It traces back the origins of these problems to the region's history and institutions, in particular to high concentration of assets, low levels of education, low rates of technical progress and an export structure characterized by low levels of value added to natural resources, but argues that inequalities and structural heterogeneity were exacerbated by the specific characteristics of the development process of the 1990s.[10] Well before the WB's and the IMF's new prioritization of the reduction of poverty and inequality, ECLAC promoted what it calls *an integral concept of development*. At the core of this concept is an emphasis on the extent to which inequality negatively affects investment and innovation, and on the goal of constructing more equitable societies. ECLAC's so-called integral concept of development is close to Sen's (1999) notion of development as freedom, as for ECLAC the goal of development should be 'to create a social and human climate of greater security and mutual trust, consolidate a democratic system that provides for greater participation, enhance the well-being of those who have less access to the benefits of modern society and protect and improve the natural habitat' (ibid.: 23).

To promote integral development, ECLAC combines a thick concept of institutional reform with a more activist role for the state. Institutional reforms should not just be aimed at making markets work more efficiently, but should have the goal of making human rights and equity the ethical frame of reference for economic development. According to ECLAC, this goal could be achieved by taking advantage of the democratic advances of the 1990s to promote citizens' participation in public decision-making, as well as promoting the advancement of economic, social and cultural rights (ibid.: 20). To achieve these goals, the state should play a crucial role in ensuring greater equality of opportunities, the integration of excluded groups into the growth process, the reduction of structural heterogeneity, the promotion of a more knowledge-intensive productive structure, and the provision of incentives for innovation through WTO-compatible industrial policies.[11]

While ECLAC's role is limited to providing intellectual outputs to the development process, the IADB has played an active role in financing it. Founded in 1959 as the first regional development bank, the IADB remained marginal to the needs of the region during the 1980s, even when the debt crisis cut off capital flows to Latin America. In the 1990s, the Bank started to play a more significant role in financing market reforms, with particular attention paid to addressing social constraints to economic development (Scheman 1997). As shown in Chapter 6, however, by the mid-1990s the Bank was already critical about the economic achievements and social costs of the free market reforms. By the late 1990s, the Bank increasingly distanced itself from the orthodoxy of the WC. As an IADB internal strategy document puts it:

The current state in the development debate is one in which old ortho-doxies of the 'Washington Consensus' are being re-examined, the impor-tance of reducing poverty and inequality are being moved to the centre of the agenda, along with the critical importance of good policy and good governance. There is also widespread agreement that macroeconomic growth alone cannot be sustained with macroeconomic policies alone. (IADB 1999b: 10)

ECLAC's and the IADB's development strategies for the twenty-first cen-tury incorporate a comprehensive approach to development that includes as its main goals sustainable economic growth, poverty reduction and the promotion of social equity (IADB 2002). In common, ECLAC and the IADB assign a high priority to institutional reform and to the building of state capabilities. While the WB maintains a fundamentally technocratic approach to matters of governance, the state and institution-building, however, the IADB and ECLAC adopt a 'thick' concept of institutions that defines the modernization of the state as a political process of reform for strengthening democratic governance and explicitly links democracy and development under the argument that sustainable and equitable development requires a democratic, modern and efficient state (ibid.: 6).

The IADB views economic reform as fundamentally a political process that cannot be separated from issues of democracy. This view crystallizes in the Bank's *Economic and Social Progress in Latin America* 2006 report, 'The politics of policies' (IADB 2005). The report issues the now standard PWC generic warning against universal policy recipes that are supposed to work independently of time and place, and the more specific argument that the processes by which policies are discussed, approved and implemented have an important impact on the quality of public policies. It distances itself farther from the WC by questioning the wisdom of an approach based exclusively on a single model of technically correct policies, such as across-the-board privatizations or unrestricted international trade, and notes that the most successful countries in the region, such as Brazil, Chile and Mexico, have combined orthodox and heterodox economic policies, while countries that in the past followed more orthodox policies, such as Argentina and Bolivia, suffered grave political and economic crises (ibid.: 256). The document places heavy emphasis on the institutional aspects of development. It warns that processes of institutional reform are generally incremental and slow, and need to take advantage of windows of opportunity and available resources (and restrictions) rather than relying on ideal models (ibid.: 258). Politics and institutions are inseparable, and institution-building requires not just incentives, but also time and leadership. Moreover, as the IADB points out, institutions are not just technical devices, but political and cultural expressions. Legitimacy, as much as technical correctness, determines the success of economic policies. Thus, the IADB concludes, the policy-making processes in a democracy must incorporate the dual requirements of representativeness and effectiveness (ibid.: 256–8). The changing of the development agenda, however, particularly the adoption of a thick version of the rule of law that incorporates issues of democracy, has significant political implications that merit further analysis.

The politics of the new development agenda

A rather overlooked common assumption of the WC and the PWC is the belief that, in the development process, liberal democracy and markets reinforce each other in a non-problematic way. This belief is grounded on the fact that all advanced economies are liberal democracies, and on the discrediting of theories that argue that authoritarianism fosters higher economic development (Przeworski et al. 2000; Weyland 2004). What the PWC fails to take into consideration, however, is the implications of its own insights concerning the context-dependent nature of the development process. If this is indeed the case, it means that the successful articulation between markets and liberal democracy is dependent also on the political context in which development takes place, and cannot be derived for all cases from highly abstract principles, such as the shared importance of the rule of law for both development and democracy. Historically, in Latin America most societies have not been particularly economically or politically liberal, and attempts to articulate the two together in a project of democratization and economic development are fraught with difficulties. Arguably, the relation between democracy and markets depends on the specific characteristics of each country – that is, on the country's history, social structure, external linkages, institutions and political dynamics. More generally, as suggested in Chapter 5, it depends on how the process of development affects the balance between consensus and conflict ('the balance of class struggle') that allows democracy to flourish, and how this balance is mediated by the country's political and economic institutions.

In this light, the PWC's faith in political participation and institution-building as the glue that binds together market-led development and liberal democracy should, at least, be qualified. The PWC's institution-building, participatory development strategy fails to take sufficiently into account two closely related questions. The first is that, while the weaknesses of political institutions in Latin America have long historical roots (Philip 2003), institutional weaknesses were exacerbated by the social and economic dislocations of the 1990s. Free market reforms in the context of already weakly institutionalized countries further undermined relations of political representation, restructured relations between the state and society, and fragmented social actors, thus contributing to institutional crises in relatively new and fragile democracies, as shown by the forced resignation or impeachment of constitutionally elected presidents in Argentina, Bolivia, Brazil, Ecuador, Peru and Venezuela in the late 1990s and early 2000s. The second question concerns the extent to which an active civil society, which the PWC regards as a condition for a more inclusive development process, has fuelled movements of resistance rather than of adaptation to market reforms. As Eduardo Silva (2007: 23–4) puts it:

> The evidence suggests neoliberalism produces the very conditions that caused mass mobilization and cycles of contention: extensive economic exclusion coupled with political exclusion, the latter largely driven by the need to keep redistributive economic policies and economic planning off the national policy agenda ... The dominant literature's faith in institutional design to contain mounting social tension and conflict against neoliberal reforms overlooks the fact that institutions are social constructions that crystallize relations of domination and subordination in society. Therefore, it misses the fact that the inequalities generated by the very institutions they advocate fuel the grievances that sustained mass mobilization, and that these cycles of contention constitute organized, politically significant pressure to reform neoliberal capitalism and liberal democracy.

Within a context in which civil society organizations have been at the forefront of the struggle against policies such as privatization and economic opening in many Latin American countries, the PWC's belief that opening up the policy-making process to wider participation would result in a more consensual process of reform underestimates the conflictive nature of the political process and its potential for exacerbating antagonism as much as for fostering consensus. Moreover, in the context of weak representative institutions, participation can lead to new forms of domination and exclusion, depending on how participation is defined and organized and who is entitled to participate at which level of the policy-making process. Last but not least, the borderline between civil and uncivil society and between institutional and extra-institutional forms of political participation is a dangerous political territory, not always leading to practices of communicative rationality.

Conclusions

The above overview of the new development agenda shows the extent and limits of the PWC's differences with the orthodoxies of the WC. In its different versions, the PWC is a more comprehensive, context-sensitive and politically aware model of development. While the WC was narrowly economicist in its conception of development, the PWC seeks to bring into consideration its economic *and* social dimensions, and to rediscover the importance of politics, institutions and the state. Perhaps the best summary of the new orthodoxy, which refuses to recognize itself as such, is given by the executive secretary of the ECLAC, José Luis Machinea:

> [W]e are witnessing the emergence of a new consensus on growth. The basic precept of this consensus is that policy outcomes depend on the context in which policy measures are applied and, therefore, vary from country to country. Hence, the lessons learned from other countries' experiences do not translate into an uncritical transposition of other countries' policy initiatives or institutional arrangements to the region. Experiences cannot be copied without taking into account of history, social structure, external settings, political dynamics, and institutions, i.e. the specific characteristics of each country ... while it is possible to find a set of principles that are common to all successful growth strategies, there are many different ways these principles can be applied, depending on the characteristics of each country. (Machinea and Kacef 2007: 9)

Notwithstanding differences in approach to policy-making highlighted by Machinea and Kacef, there is significant common ground between the WC and the PWC on the higher-order economic principles of a successful strategy for economic development. While the inchoate nature of the PWC makes a prescriptive enumeration of its principles problematic, these would generally include the importance of economic stability; the reliance on market forces and integration into the world economy as the engines of growth; the importance of the protection of property rights and the enforcement of contracts to encourage entrepreneurship and diminish transaction costs; the need for prudential regulation to avoid financial volatility; the importance of economic diversification to minimize commodity dependency; and, last but not least, the relevance of policies aimed at increasing social cohesion and political stability.

It would be difficult to argue that these principles depart in any significant way from the orthodoxies of the WC, but the real difference may lie in Dani Rodrik's argument that general principles can and should be operationalized in diverse ways in order to take into account differences in history, context, priorities and resources (Rodrik 2007: 87–8). There are, however, significant differences as well as common ground between the WC and the PWC regarding the relation between policy-making, democracy and markets. In contrast to the WC's top-down, technocratic and elitist view of the policy-making process, the PWC favours a more socially inclusive and participatory form of policy-making. As noted above, in the more progressive versions of the PWC this approach includes a 'thick' conception of the rule of law that incorporates human rights and democratic principles into the development agenda.

For radical critics of the WC, the main flaw of the revised agenda of the PWC is that it does not amount to a fundamental change in the underlying approach to economic development. As noted above, in most versions of the PWC the framing of the development process is still grounded in the primacy of markets with added institutional and social dimensions. The PWC approach to macroeconomic policy remains orthodox on fiscal and monetary matters. It continues to favour free trade and privatization despite evidence that the benefits of trade liberalization are more questionable than claimed by its supporters and that privatization – done wrongly – may lead to higher prices of utilities (Fine 2001; Stiglitz 2005). While the World Bank's rediscovery of the state amounts to the recognition that 'rolling back the state' is not enough to produce economic growth, the Bank's ideal state is still a fairly minimalist one, based on a state that is highly effective in carrying out market-friendly reforms and policies (Bøås and McNeill 2003). While there is an acknowledgement that the original WC agenda did not give enough attention to questions of poverty, equity and the environment, there is yet no full recognition of the extent to which liberalizing reforms, such as trade and labour market reforms, have contributed to worsen income distribution (Berry 1997).

For its critics, the PWC's change of rhetoric is part of a conscious strategy for co-opting critics of the WC and defusing antagonism to the market economy. The logic of participation, institution-building and poverty reduction strategies is still one of constructing a social order required for the constitution of a free market economic order (Motta 2006). In other words, the strategy aims to include people in '*the* system' rather than *changing the system*. The new rhetoric of 'participation', 'empowerment' and 'poverty reduction' could be seen as part of a strategy for neutralizing and depoliticizing once-potent political terms, and turning them into an apoliticized form that everyone can agree with (Cornwall and Brock 2005: 1043). As Ben Fine (2001: 16, 12) puts it, the PWC, 'on its own, marginally less narrow principles, is seeking not only to set the agenda, but also to incorporate dissidence in its own reductionist form';

and '[e]ducation, good governance, policy ownership and democracy are all about doing what the World Bank/IMF would do but also appearing to do it by yourself and willingly'.

And yet, critics of the PWC in their different ideological shades run the proverbial risk of throwing the baby out with the bathwater. The new thinking on economic development constitutes a powerful critique of some of the key assumptions of neoclassical theory, such as its blindness to market failures, its disregard for institutions, history and distribution, and its lack of attention to the policies needed to propel developing countries out of a self-perpetuating cycle of poverty (Hoff and Stiglitz 2002). The incorporation of politico-institutional and social concerns into the original model does not signify that the Washington institutions have 'moved to the left' in any significant meaning of the term. The employment by the IFIs of the rhetorical and linguistic devices of their critics, however, and their mimicking of the concerns of those who previously attacked them, means that the ideological foundations of the debate have shifted towards a political terrain in which the left should feel naturally at home (Buckingham 2004). The PWC has adopted a new agenda about the value of democracy for economic development, the strengthening of state institutions, the need for strategic state intervention, the importance of investment in health and education, and a higher priority for social justice and the fight against poverty (Panizza 2005b). When compared with the agenda of the 1980s and 1990s centred on the failures of state interventionism and the need for structural adjustment, the shift is not trivial.

In short, the PWC is an arena of contestation as well as of consensus. The WB and the IMF have sought to articulate the new agenda about participation, social justice and the integration of the excluded to the continuous primacy of markets as the drivers of economic development, but different political views coexist with broadly similar policy proposals within international financial agencies and in the broader world of economic and political debate. Despite the apparent ideological blandness of today's development consensus, different actors invest key terms such as 'poverty reduction', 'empowerment' and 'participation' with a range of different meanings (Cornwall and Brock 2005: 1046–7). As essentially contested concepts (Connolly 1983), they can be rearticulated to alternative visions of development and political projects. These terms have a multiplicity of contingent, situational and relational meanings, which will continue to be contested as they are put to use. It is within this context that the rise of the left in Latin America and the relations between left-of-centre governments and the PWC ought to be understood. We shall explore these relations in Chapters 8 and 10.

8 | The rise of the left

A change in Latin America's political landscape?

As was seen in Chapter 5, throughout the 1990s it was commonly assumed that a weakened popular sector could offer little resistance to the hegemony of the WC and that confronted with a powerful alliance of centre-right parties and free market economic forces the political left had become a marginal political force throughout the region. How much has changed in the twenty-first century, and what are the causes behind this unexpected change? In order to answer these questions this chapter critically explores the so-called turn to the left in Latin America within the context of the achievements and failures of the parallel process of democratization and economic reforms that have been the subject of previous chapters.

The electoral victories of left-of-centre (LOC) presidential candidates have been the events most commonly associated with the resurgence of the left in the region. After a decade – the 1990s – in which Latin America's political landscape was dominated by governments of the centre and the centre-right, the political tide began to turn with the triumph of Hugo Chávez in Venezuela in 1998. As noted in the book's Introduction, Chávez's victory was followed between 1998 and 2008 by the triumphs of other presidential candidates representing different shades of the left, including, crucially, Luiz Inácio Lula da Silva in Brazil in 2002, Ricardo Lagos and Michelle Bachelet in Chile in 2000 and 2006 respectively, Nestor Kirchner and Cristina Fernández de Kirchner in Argentina in 2003 and 2007 respectively, Tabaré Vázquez in Uruguay in 2004, Evo Morales in Bolivia in 2005, Daniel Ortega in Nicaragua and Rafael Correa in Ecuador, both in 2006, Alvaro Colom in Guatemala in 2007, Fernando Lugo in Paraguay in 2008 and Mauricio Funes in El Salvador in 2009. Furthermore, two of the most emblematic leaders of the region's left turn, Presidents Chávez and Lula, were re-elected in 2006.

The long list of presidents that are considered to be LOC is not enough to determine whether the region has actually turned to the left. Without a definition of what is meant by 'the left' and what qualifies a government as being 'of the left', *ad hominem* classifications may be misleading.

Arguably, some of the recently elected LOC presidents may have won not because of their left-wing ideas but because they represented the opposition to unpopular incumbents. Moreover, politicians' careers are characterized by ideological journeys across the political spectrum, as shown by the change in President Lula da Silva's image from a firebrand leftist former unionist in the 1980s and early 1990s to a moderate reformer in the twenty-first century, and by the transformation of Peru's Alan García from an 'irresponsible populist' in his first term as president in the 1980s into a champion of economic orthodoxy in his second one in the 2000s.

Furthermore, the political inclinations of a country's president do not necessarily define his or her government's politics. Governments do not always enjoy parliamentary majorities or achieve them by putting together broad political coalitions, which have obvious implications for their ability to effect radical change. Latin America's LOC presidents have often gained office as heads of minority governments or of highly heterogeneous coalitions that include political forces that are not of the left. In Brazil, President Lula's two administrations (2003–06; 2007–10) have relied on broad parliamentary coalitions of parties ranging from the radical left to the traditional right in order to secure a broadly based but brittle majority in Congress. A similarly broad coalition headed by the centrist Partido Liberal Radical Auténtico (Authentic Liberal Radical Party) supported the election of President Lugo in Paraguay, and in Nicaragua the Frente Sandinista de Liberación (FSLN) controls only about 40 per cent of seats in Congress.

If we move from presidents and parties to citizens there is no evidence that the people of Latin America have significantly shifted to the left. Surveys of the polling organization Latinobarómetro between 1996 and 2007 show little variation in the citizens' self-identification in the left–right scale, with the average voter located just slightly right of centre.[1] In Bolivia and Venezuela, the countries with arguably the more radical left-wing administrations in South America, electors placed themselves almost exactly within the Latin American centrist average (Latinobarómetro 2007: 75).[2] Latinobarómetro's figures confirm the findings of a similar survey carried out in 2006 by the Latin American Public Opinion Project (LAPOP) of Vanderbilt University, which concludes that even as the region puts more 'leftists' into presidential palaces the median voter remains slightly right of centre (Seligson 2007: 86–7).

Public opinion surveys offer useful snapshots of political preferences but do not by themselves provide straight answers to complex questions. That Latin American politics in the early twenty-first century has changed the region's political landscape of the previous decade is beyond dispute, but the nature and scope of this change are less simple than just 'a turn to the left'. A better understanding of the political changes of the first decade of the twenty-first century depends on the definition of what is understood by 'left', on how we trace the dividing lines both between left and right and within the left, and on the assessment of whether the LOC governments have delivered on their promises of change.

The social democratic, populist and grassroots lefts

Political classifications are by definition arbitrary and open to debate, and the concepts of left and right are more contested than most. To be of the left has been related to ideological affiliations such as Marxism and socialism (Chilcote 1993), political principles such as equality and justice (Bobbio 1994), political forces such as the social democratic and communist movements (Angell 1996) and policy choices, such as a preference for state intervention and redistribution over market forces and private property (Rabotnikof 2004). The left has also been historically associated with the subordinate classes, particularly but not exclusively with the working class. As a result it is assumed to be predisposed towards challenging the prevailing system, in a struggle between the 'haves' and 'have nots' (Burton 2008; Miliband 1989).

While ideology, values, history, policies and social roots are valid elements of any definition of the left, these elements cannot be taken as abstract criteria that define the left irrespective of time and history. Classifications have to be made in the light of the historical context in which political forces operate, as the left is also defined by what it opposes, namely the right (Castañeda 1993: 18–19). Two corollaries follow from these initial observations: first, left-wing politics are largely defined by the relations of antagonism and differences they establish with other political forces of both the right and the left and on the contested interpretation of their core values and practices; second, there is not one left but many, as the forces of the left differ according to how they articulate the constitutive elements of their identities (values, history, practices, etc.) and what kind of tensions they are willing to accept among them (Arditi 2008).

The above criteria can be taken as the basis for a broad, descriptive definition of the left which, following Cleary (2006: 36), is understood here as:

> A political movement with historical antecedents in communist and socialist political parties, grassroots social movements, populist social organizations, or other political forces that traditionally have had anti-systemic, revolutionary or transformative objectives. The mobilizational form and the degree of radicalism may vary across countries. But in all cases the Left shares (at least rhetorically, and usually substantively) a concern with redistribution and social justice, and it finds mass support among segments of the population that are severely disadvantaged under the current socioeconomic order.

The characterization of the left in Latin America has to be considered in the light of the criteria and caveats applied to the above definition of the left. Writing about the Latin American left in the early 1990s, Steve Ellner (1993: 15) argued that the main divide between the left and the centre is set 'between those who advocate far-reaching structural change [...] and those who are mainly concerned with policy reforms', a claim that appears to rule out the reformist left. He further claimed that because of the (then) fading out of radical populism in much of Latin America the left was no longer divided between its pro-socialist and pro-populist wings, which, if the claim is to be accepted, would make traditional socialist and communist forces and their successors the only true representatives of the left. Similarly, surveying the Latin American left in the 1990s, Alan Angell (1996) lists among the forces of the left the traditional communist and socialist parties and leaves out of his classification the populist parties that, as he put it, in the past adopted, used and discarded socialist ideas and have had far more electoral success than the orthodox left.

More than a decade later it is clear that Ellner and Angell's lack of regard for the reformist left and for radical populism as part of the contemporary left in Latin America is unsustainable on both theoretical and political grounds. A social democratic, reformist tradition has always been part of the left in Latin America (Vellinga 1993), and while Marxist and other radical left political groups have traditionally spent as much time denouncing social democratic reformism as a betrayal of the true interests of the working class as fighting the right, these ideological battles within the left carry less political weight in a post-Marxist, post-socialist era. More worthy of consideration than intra-left accreditation struggles, however, are arguments that question the possibility of social democratic politics in developing countries, particularly in the era of global capitalism. Typical of this argument is the following quote from K. M. Roberts (1998: 276):

> Historically, social democracy has been grounded in conditions that are not present in contemporary Latin America and are highly unlikely to develop under an increasingly transnational neoliberal model of capitalist development – namely centralized and densely organized labour movements that have close political ties to socialist parties, ample fiscal resources to sustain universal norms of social citizenship, and domestic power balances that spawn institutionalized forms of class compromise in which democratic checks are placed on the privileges and functioning of capital.

Roberts's arguments need to be addressed both theoretically and empirically. Theoretically, the elucidation of whether social democratic politics are possible in contemporary Latin America requires the previous characterization of the main political features of social democracy. As with the broader definition of the left, social democracy can be characterized in terms of self-identification, values, practices and socio-political foundations (Leggett 2007). In terms of self-identification, the Latin American section of the Socialist International, an umbrella organization that groups social democratic parties worldwide, was set up in 1955, and in 2008 some twenty-five parties were full members of the organization across the region.[3] While self-identification is an important criterion for establishing collective identities it cannot, however, be accepted as the ultimate answer to the question about the viability of social democracy in Latin America. In Latin America as elsewhere, some political parties that have never defined themselves formally as social democratic have pursued policies that are closely associated with social democratic values and policies while parties that are formally members of the Socialist International have arguably little in common with these policies and values.

The limitations of self-identification in defining political practices raise the question as to what the values and practices that define social democracy may be. Answering this question is particularly problematic as there are no sacred canons of social democratic thought, as the works of Marx and Lenin were for the communist parties. Hay (1999: 56–7) lists as social democratic values economic redistribution, democratic control of the markets through state intervention and the guarantee of citizens' welfare throughout their lives. To these should be added the acceptance of liberal democracy as the preferred model of political organization, together with the promotion of some mechanisms of substantive democracy that incorporate social rights and mechanisms for political consultation and participation (Huber et al. 1997). To implement these values social democratic governments have traditionally used a number of political strategies that include tripartite corporate agreements between the state, the unions and business, an activist state that promotes both economic redistribution and economic growth, and a preference for universalist welfare policies that promote equality and protect citizens from the uncertainties of economic cycles. Underpinning values and strategies are political institutions grounded on a capable state and strong political parties with organic roots in the popular sectors, particularly in the industrial working class.

The impact of globalization on the traditional socio-economic bases of social democracy has led to claims that it has become more difficult, if not totally impossible, to promote social democratic policies even in the developed world. These claims, however, have been shown to be at least exaggerated by the resilience of social democracy in its European core and, as will be shown below, by its recent growth in Latin America and elsewhere in the developing world (Sandbrook et al. 2007). Globalization, however, has forced social democracy to adapt and change. One of the most visible ways in which adaptation took place has been through the rise of Third Way politics as a project to modernize social democracy (Giddens 1998). Alternatively presented as 'beyond left and right' and as an alternative to both neoliberalism and old-style social democracy, Third Way social democracy has effectively articulated elements of the neoliberal agenda, such as the primacy of the markets in consumer-oriented societies, the importance of fiscal prudence and the retreat of the state from the direct provision of goods and services, to traditional social democratic concerns about poverty and equality (albeit redefined as equality of opportunities rather than outcomes) and the importance of high-quality public services. Politically, Third Way social democracy has sought to loosen social democracy's working-class roots in order to appeal to wider social sectors, redefining voters in terms of their social aspirations rather than their class membership. In government Third Way administrations have introduced some forms of participatory democratic practices that coexist uneasily with a predominantly managerial and technocratic ethos that has sought to combine economic efficiency with the enhanced provision of public services (Burton 2008; Huber et al. 1997; Przeworski 1991).

Different versions of social democracy are not new within a political tradition that has been historically characterized by high doses of pragmatism and the ability to adapt to changing environments. What best characterizes Latin American social democracy in the early twenty-first century and differentiates it from early versions of social democracy is the changing context in which parties that are broadly aligned with social democratic politics and policies have gained political ascendancy in recent years. Politically, these parties have gained office during the longest period of democratic continuity in Latin America's history. Socially, they are rooted in more fragmented societies in which collective popular identities are more precarious than in the past and traditional links between the state and society have been radically redefined by the free market reformation. Economically, social democratic forces are in office at a time in which the Latin American economies are more market oriented than ever in the past but also at a time in which a backlash against the Washington Consensus (WC) and the post-Washington Consensus (PWC) has sought to bring the state back in to address both economic and social issues (see Chapter 6). Within this context, social democratic governments in Latin America have sought to institutionalize the tensions between conflict and accommodation that, as argued in Chapter 5, characterize a liberal democratic order by balancing the need to address the social deficits of the WC with reassuring those who benefited from the free market reforms that their fundamental interests would not be substantially affected.

In the early twenty-first century populism of a national popular variation has re-emerged as a powerful political force in the region. Theoretically, the inclusion of populism within the broad field of left-wing politics depends on how we define both populism and its relation with the left. The concept of populism is highly contested, but whatever definition of populism one chooses to adopt, it is clear that populism is not necessarily of the left. Moreover, the controversy surrounding the meaning of populism is compounded by the fact that while self-identification is one of the elements that allows us to characterize a certain political actor as belonging to the social-democratic left, the same criterion is not applicable to populism, as no contemporary political leader calls him/herself 'populist' in the way they call themselves 'socialists', 'social democrats' or 'liberals'.[4] Politically, populism has been characterized by a strong, personalist leadership, a direct appeal to the people, unmediated by political institutions, and by the preference for majoritarian rather than pluralist forms of democracy (Roberts, K. M. 1995; Weyland 1999). A contentious and normatively highly charged concept, populism by its very nature is defined by its anti-status quo appeal to the disenfranchised and the never-enfranchised, who do not feel represented by existing institutions (Panizza 2000b, 179). The anti-status quo element of populism makes it a typical occurrence at times of crises of representation in societies deeply polarized on socio-economic, religious, ethnic or regional grounds, in which important sections of the population regard themselves as oppressed or discriminated against by the economic order or the political elite (Panizza 2005a). It often includes a nationalist appeal, as the 'people' and the 'nation' become one and the same in their common cause against internal (corrupt politicians, the economic elite, a dominant ethnic group) and external (imperialist nations, international organizations, multinational corporations, etc.) enemies (De Ipola and Portantiero 1989).

The association of populism with political movements of both the left and right is understandable because, in contrast to socialism or liberalism, populism is not an ideology but a form of political identification that has been articulated in discourses of both the left and the right. Given that 'the people' and their 'oppressors' are discursive constructs rather than sociological categories, right-wing populism can construct 'the people' as the white European working class threatened by the influx of Third World immigrants, or, in its left-wing version, as the inhabitants of the barrios of Caracas oppressed by the Venezuelan oligarchy and the Venezuelan people threatened by US imperialism, as interpellated by Hugo Chávez's discourse in Venezuela.

Twenty-first-century radical populism in Latin America has its roots in the so-called national-popular populist tradition that was hegemonic in many countries of the region in the 1940s and 1950s. During this period populist movements and parties appealed to social sectors that had no voice in the oligarchical political order of the time and offered these groups both symbolic recognition and material benefits. But while rooted in the mid-twentieth century's national popular tradition, the twenty-first century's populism in Latin America is not just a return to the past. The latest wave of Latin American populism is linked to popular backlashes against the social and economic dislocations of the WC in the context of weakly institutionalized and exclusionary democracies. Economic nationalism and an appeal to the sovereign people against a discredited and unrepresentative political system are part of the twenty-first century's populism as it was in the 1940s and 1950s. Twenty-first-century national-popular populism has emerged, however, in a context in which political, social and economic changes have forced a radical reformulation in the ways in which the nation and the people are conceived by modern-day national-popular discourse.

Historically, national-popular populism was regarded as a barrier to the advancement of the left in Latin America (ibid.). Socialist and communist parties denounced national-popular movements, such as Argentina's Peronism and Brazil's Varguismo, as bourgeois-led class alliances that sought to co-opt and subordinate the true interests of the working class to those of the national bourgeoisie and blunted the left's struggle for radical change by controlling the workers through a mixture of repression and top-down social benefits (Ianni 1975). In the early twenty-first century neither working-class vanguardism nor the promise of socialism is a significant part of the political imaginary of the left, and the left's weakening of its class and socialist affiliations has blurred the historical dividing line between the national-popular and socialist left traditions. As Schamis (2006: 21) rightly points out, while progressive politics in Latin America will inevitably draw from the historical legacies of socialism and populism, the dividing line between the two traditions has far less importance today than it had fifty years ago, when socialism and populism each put forward different visions of the future that could capture the imagination of vast sectors of society. Paradoxically, for reasons that will become clear below, while the formerly radical left has drifted towards centrist social democracy, populism has embraced the left's promise of radical change and even, as in the case of Hugo Chávez's Venezuela, adopted its socialist banner.

While social democracy and the twenty-first century's national-popular populism have become established categories for the analysis of the divisions within the Latin American left, there is a third tradition that has been overlooked in the classifications, namely the grassroots left. The term means here both a political ideology that promotes the direct participation of social organizations in political decision-making and the social movements associated with this ideology. The Latin American grassroots left has its origins in the *basista* movement of the 1970s. It partly occupied the vacuum left by the banning of institutional political activity and the prosecution of the parties of the left by the military dictatorships of the 1970s, but it also represented a reaction against the bureaucratic, top-down politics of the communist parties and other forces of the left at the time. It became particularly strong in Brazil, where it took the form of grassroots church groups, the so-called Comunidades Eclesiásticas de Base (CEBs), neighbourhood associations and the 'new trade unionism' of the state of São Paulo, which set up the Partido dos Trabalhadores (PT) (Cavarozzi 1993; Stepan 1985, 1988).

Social movements are not necessarily of the left but both socialist and national-popular populist political forces have a long history of association with the trade unions and other popular organizations (Eckstein 1989; Lievesley 1999). The grassroots left's relation with the social democratic and (national-popular) populist traditions is informed by the historical and political contexts in which they interact. In contrast to social democratic and national-popular political forces, grassroots organizations are not holders of state power and do not usually participate in elections (although Bolivia can be regarded as a partial exception to this rule). Grassroots left movements, however, relate to the other traditions of the left in at least three important ways: first, grassroots organizations have helped to set up some of the most successful LOC parties in contemporary Latin America. This is the case with the Movimiento al Socialismo (MAS) in Bolivia and of the PT in Brazil; second, social movements constitute the organized base of support of LOC governments, and they also constrain their political autonomy (Panizza 2008); third, while social movements have very different political complexions and ideological leanings, some radical social movements claim to be repositories of the left's utopian ideals and seek to act as vanguards for the development of alternative political practices (Motta 2006).[5]

The distinction between the three traditions is a useful heuristic device that allows us better to understand the rise of the left in Latin America and master its diversity, but the political and ideological influence of different traditions does not always allow for a clear characterization of historically situated actors in terms of one specific tradition. Identities change through time and actors incorporate elements of the different traditions into their political practices. For instance, Hugo Chávez draws on both the socialist and national-popular populist traditions to construct the political imaginary of his Bolivarian revolution, and President Lula da Silva of Brazil uses social democratic, populist and grassroots elements in his political appeals. Moreover, actors' identities and practices cannot be defined outside the political context in which they operate and, as discussed below, it is the political and institutional contexts in which actors interact, as much as the actors' political identities and strategies, which make social democracy, populism or grassroots politics the dominant form of LOC politics in a given country. While the predominance of different traditions of the left in specific countries is explored in some detail below, it is first necessary to explore the common roots of Latin America's left turn.

The rise of the left

As seen in Chapter 5, in the early 1990s the left appeared to be waning throughout the region. During the same period, national-popular populism was a byword for economic chaos and democratic deficits, and civil society organizations had lost the political centrality they enjoyed in the 1980s. Writing shortly after the collapse of the Socialist bloc at a time of ascendancy of conservative, pro-business governments throughout Latin America, Jorge Castañeda claimed that although the left remained influential in the grassroots movement and at the intellectual level the political left was, in his own words, 'on the run and on the ropes' (Castañeda 1993: 3). He argued that while the original causes that gave birth to the left in the region – poverty, injustice, gaping social disparities and overwhelming social violence – were as compelling as ever, with the exception of Cuba, the left had failed in its efforts 'to take power, make revolution, and change the world' (ibid.: 4).

What accounts for the remarkable transformation in the political fortunes of the left in the relatively short time between Castañeda's downbeat assessment of its political condition and the proliferation of LOC governments in the 2000s? Castañeda (2006a: 30) himself offers a clue when he notes that the combination of inequality and democracy tends to cause a movement to the left everywhere. Given that both democracy and inequality coexist in Latin America, it makes sense that Latin

America's social deficit motivates citizens to vote for the type of policies that, as he put it, they hope will make them less poor. Latin America was already a highly unequal region in the 1980s, however, when the current wave of democratization swept away military dictatorships throughout the region, and at that time the left was not generally perceived as the best option to solve the region's social and economic problems. While there is no question that social conditions have been an important factor in the rise of the left, there are three other factors that have to be taken into account to explain the left's political revival.

The first has to do with processes of political accumulation and de-accumulation under democracy. For all its many weaknesses, in the early twenty-first century democracy has become effectively the only legitimate political game in Latin America, as most countries are experiencing the longest uninterrupted period of democratically elected governments in their history. Undemocratic actors, such as the military, who blocked the advances of the left in the past, now have diminished political influence. The end of the cold war has rendered obsolete the rationale for the US administration's support for right-wing dictators. The economic elites have also lost most of their motives and ability to subvert democracy, as conservative groups are generally less fearful that electoral defeat will lead to radical, social, economic and political change at their expense (Mainwaring and Scully 1995: 466), although this may not be entirely the case in Venezuela and Bolivia. The ability to act in a democratic environment represents a major change for the parties of the left that were proscribed and prosecuted by undemocratic governments throughout long periods of Latin American history.

In the 1980s and early 1990s left-wing parties were weakened by a combination of the legacy of prosecution during the years of military dictatorships and the decline of their popular bases of support as a result of economic restructuring. Also, in the 1980s left-wing and national-popular populist parties such as Bolivia's Unión Democrática y Popular (UDP) and Peru's APRA became discredited because of their failures in office (see Chapter 1), but while the political crisis of the left in the late 1980s and early 1990s was real it was less than terminal. Democratic continuity helped the left to regroup and develop and also prompted the forces of the left to change and adapt. Several factors contributed to the left's survival and subsequent revival in the late 1990s. In spite of the loss of ideological certainties brought by the collapse of the Soviet bloc and the fading of Marxism as the dominant ideology of the left, the left retained a significant chunk of the symbolic capital it had gained in the past, particularly during years of struggle against the military dictatorships, and was able to retain a considerable number of experienced and dedicated political cadres, a core social base of support and historical links with social movements.

Claims that political parties are weak in Latin America (see Chapter 5) obscure the fact that, as noted in Chapter 4, even at the time of maximum political weakness of traditional socialist and communist parties, new LOC parties, such as the PT in Brazil, the Frente Amplio (FA) in Uruguay and the PRD in Mexico, flourished and were able to gather considerable political and organizational strength, as well as popular support (Branford and Kucinski 2003; Bruhn 1997; Buquet 2008). Political movements of the left, such as the Movimiento al Socialismo (MAS) in Bolivia, became some of the best-organized political forces in their countries (Harten 2008). Access to parliament gave the parties of the left an important political arena to project their image and the opportunity to mix radical opposition to centre-right governments with more subtle games of parliamentary alliances and compromises. In the 1990s LOC parties gained office at state and municipal level in a number of countries, including, among others, Mexico City, the Federal District in Mexico, Buenos Aires, the federal capital in Argentina, Bogotá in Colombia, several states and hundred of municipalities in Brazil, and the capital, Montevideo, in Uruguay. Governing states and municipalities allowed the parties of the left and centre-left to confront their own myths, accumulate administrative experience and test alternative policies at local level (Chávez and Franklin 2004; Panizza 2005b).

Democracy has also helped to strengthen civil society, including old and new social movements associated with the left. As noted in Chapter 5, civil society organizations ebbed and flowed during the years of transition to democracy, but they retained a significant political presence throughout the 1990s (Feinberg et al. 2006; Stahler-Sholk et al. 2008). Social resistance to economic liberalization intensified in the late 1990s and early twenty-first century, as successful social movements were able to cut across popular identities and interests and spawn new forms of collective action (Roberts, K. M. 2008; Silva, E. 2007). In Brazil, the Movimento dos Trabalhadores Rurais Sem Terra (MST, the landless rural workers' movement) emerged in the 1980s to campaign for agrarian reform and has since become one of the largest and most influential social movements in the whole of South America (Branford 2002; Wolford 2006). Political decentralization in the 1990s favoured the growth of social movements organized on a local base. Furthermore, in the process of resisting neoliberalism the grassroots left incorporated in its ideology and practices new cultural, ideological and organizational elements from the anti-globalization movement, which has a significant presence in Latin America. Known originally as the Forum of Porto Alegre and now as the World Social Forum (WSF), it gathers together a variegated number of social movements under the slogan 'another world is possible' and has become an important forum for the exchange of experiences and coordination of activities (Teivainen 2002). Resistance to free market reforms has led to the emergence of new social movements, such as the *piqueteros* in Argentina, which organize unemployed people from poor neighbourhoods, demanding jobs and funding for community-based projects (López Levy 2003). Perhaps the most politically influential new social movements in Latin America, particularly in the Andean region, are those linked to the resurgent ethnic nationalism of indigenous peoples in countries such as Ecuador, Peru and, particularly, Bolivia, where they have been a major influence in the rise of the Movimiento al Socialismo (MAS) party, led by the now president Evo Morales (Becker 2008; Sieder 2005; Van Cott 2005).

The electoral triumphs of LOC parties were preceded by almost two decades of hegemony of the parties of the right and centre-right. If the 1990s was a decade of resistance, adaptation and political accumulation for the forces of the left, in contrast the parties of the right and the centre-right went through a gradual process of loss of political capital and erosion of their bases of support. As discussed in more detail in Chapter 5, in the early 1990s centre-right parties enjoyed considerable electoral success by cobbling together an alliance between business and low-income voters grounded in the free market reforms' success in bringing down inflation, attracting foreign direct investment and promoting economic openings. When low inflation was discounted by the electorate, however, and the free market reforms failed to create enough jobs and economic growth, support for the parties of the centre-right narrowed down to the relatively small sectors of the population that had the economic and human capital necessary to benefit from the reforms. During the same period, social and economic changes affected the right's traditional bases of support, particularly in rural areas and in the shanty towns that surround most Latin American cities. Control of the state gave parties of the centre-right access to important patronage resources, but changes in the role of the state, including privatization and structural adjustment, limited the resources for the type of mass popular clientelism that characterized the ISI period. Instead, the spoils of the colonization of the state were shared between a relatively limited number of political cadres and well-connected businessmen and monopolized by political parties that colonized the state but did not reach out enough to their popular bases with jobs and other material benefits.

The second factor that contributed to the rise of the left has to do with the government–opposition cleavage (Luna 2007). I have already discussed the economic shortcomings and social deficits of the WC in previous chapters. Defenders of the free market reforms argue that rather than being the fault of neoliberal reforms, failures of social and economic development in the region are the product of incomplete and badly implemented reforms. They cite Chile as an example of a successful economy run on free market principles. They may have a point. Different countries implemented the reforms to different degrees and at a different pace, and aggregate figures mask significant differences in economic performance. Nevertheless, as argued in Chapter 6, for the majority of the Latin American people, the legacy of a decade and a half of free market reforms has been one of disappointment.

In the 1990s in many countries of the region parties of the left and the centre-left were the main opposition to market reforms. When elections take place in the context of poor economic performance incumbents tend to be punished regardless of their political orientation. It is surely not a coincidence that the rise of the left coincided with the 'lost half-decade' of negative per head growth and rising poverty of 1998–2002. As most incumbents were from the right and centre-right, dissatisfaction with the status quo opened a window of opportunity for left-wing and, more generally, anti-establishment candidates. In that sense, the electoral victories of LOC political candidates had as much to do with popular demands for change as with the specific content of the change package on offer. The gap between the promises and delivery of free market reforms provided LOC candidates with a compelling narrative about the failures of neoliberalism and the WC. In the electoral campaigns LOC candidates rallied against neoliberalism and its domestic and international political champions, the traditional parties of the centre-right, the USA and the IMF. The opening paragraph of Ollanta Humala's 2006 electoral manifesto for the presidential election in Peru is illustrative of this narrative, which attributes to neoliberalism social ills that were evident well before the free market reformation, even if they were exacerbated by the reforms: 'The facts are irrefutable and the reality, whoever it grieves, is stubborn: the systematic application of neoliberalism, the Washington Consensus model in our country has meant a social fracture without precedent in Peruvian life [my translation].'[6]

Evo Morales's condemnation of neoliberalism is equally forthright: 'Neoliberalism is the reproduction of savage and inhuman capitalism that continues to allow for the concentration of capital in few hands, and which does not provide solutions for the majorities of the world [my translation].'[7] The supposedly more moderate FA of Uruguay attacked neoliberalism in broadly similar terms:

> The structural inheritance of neoliberalism has left our country with hundreds of thousands of countrymen in a situation of poverty, inequality, emigration, unemployment, wealth concentration and social disintegration, annulling the possibilities for the full exercise of citizenship and discrediting the importance of ethical values. (Frente Amplio 2003; my translation)

While anti-neoliberal rhetoric was common to all LOC candidates, the extent to which a vote against the government represented a mandate for radical change varied considerably across the region. Surveys show that the role of ideology in defining electoral preferences differs significantly from country to country. In some cases, voters (and thus viable candidates) cluster heavily in the centre while in other countries vast ideological chasms separate voters, who in turn align behind candidates spanning the left–right spectrum (Seligson 2007: 86–7), but the logic of electoral participation forced LOC parties to reach beyond their narrow historical constituency and, as noted above, among those who voted for LOC parties there were a significant number of citizens who did not identify themselves as left-wingers.

Electorally successful LOC parties appealed to broad, heterogeneous constituencies to attract disenchanted but not necessarily radical voters (Luna 2007). Elections also prompted LOC parties to seek political alliances with parties of the centre-right. These alliances were no longer defined in terms of class alliances hegemonized by vanguard Marxist parties claiming to represent the working class in the way of the communist-led popular fronts of the 1930s and 1940s. Instead, highly pragmatic alliances with parties of the centre and the centre-right that were shaped by electoral calculations as much as by ideological affinities became a common feature of many LOC parties' electoral strategies throughout the region (Panizza 2005b). Cases in point include the ruling Concertación in Chile and the broad multiparty coalitions that backed Luiz Inácio Lula da Silva's presidential bids in 2002 and 2006. In Uruguay in 2004 the Frente Amplio expanded its electoral appeal by incorporating the Christian Democrats in the already broad coalition of radical and moderate left-wing groups, and in Paraguay the twelve-party electoral coalition that backed Fernando Lugo's presidential candidacy comprised parties with very broad political definitions.

The balance of class support for LOC parties and presidential candidates varied considerably from country to country and even between different elections in the same country. Recent elections in Peru, Bolivia, Argentina, Venezuela, Mexico and Brazil showed significant social, ethnic and regional voter polarization, with the majority of the poor, members of ethnically subordinated groups and inhabitants from the more economically backward regions of their countries voting for LOC candidates, and the middle classes mostly supporting candidates of the right and the centre-right (Latinobarómetro 2007). As will be explored in more depth in Chapter 9, social polarization does not, however, always equate to politico-ideological polarization. The two went together in the elections in Bolivia, Ecuador, Peru and Venezuela, countries in which there were significant politico-ideological differences between the forces of the left and their adversaries on issues such as the role of the state, attitudes towards foreign investment, the control of natural resources, economic integration and constitutional order. In contrast, programmatic differences were not particularly significant in the case of Brazil, where, in spite of the class divide in the support for President Lula and for the opposition in the 2002 and 2006 elections (Hunter and Power 2007), there was little political polarization in terms of the policy proposals of the main presidential candidates contesting the election (Tavolaro and Tavolaro 2007).[8]

The third factor that contributed to the rise of the left has to do with the relation between politics and institutions. Elections in Latin America have been free and fair almost everywhere, but political institutions have remained weak and unstable (see Chapter 4). As seen in Chapter 5, corruption and lack of accountability have discredited political parties and state institutions, and discredited political institutions favour the rise of anti-systemic candidates. Latin America has a long tradition of popular support for political outsiders, which some scholars have associated with the politics of presidentialism (Linz 1994) and others with the region's populist tradition (Roberts, K. M. 2007). Anti-status quo leaders have been of very different political orientations. In the late 1980s and early 1990s Carlos Menem, Alberto Fujimori and Fernando Collor de Mello were political outsiders or pseudo-outsiders from the right; more recently, Hugo Chávez, Evo Morales and Rafael Correa won elections as anti-establishment candidates from the left. The ideological differences between the anti-establishment candidates of the early 1990s and those of the early twenty-first century reflect the changes in the political and economic environments in which these candidates contested elections, with those of the early 1990s opposing a political order unable to secure economic stability and those of the late 1990s and early 2000s campaigning against a political establishment identified with the failures of neoliberalism.

If processes of political accumulation and deaccumulation under democracy, government–opposition cleavage and support for anti-systemic candidates help to explain the electoral victories of LOC candidates and parties, a number of different factors contribute to a better understanding of the internal differences within the left. In the next section I look at how different forms of political representation relate to the three traditions of the left and how this relationship has shaped differences within the left.

Democracy, representation and varieties of the left

Classifications are more or less helpful rather than true or false and, normative biases and problems of definition aside, the distinction between the social democratic and national-popular populist left overlooks significant internal differences within forces of the left that are usually ascribed to the same tradition. For instance, one of the constitutive characteristics of populism is personalist leadership, but there are significant differences in the leadership style and capabilities of Hugo Chávez, Evo Morales and Rafael Correa, all of whom have been regarded as populists by some scholars (Castañeda 2006b: 59).[9] In the case of social democracy, strong links with the trade unions and other social movements have been considered an important feature of social democratic parties and governments. Relations between governments, parties and social movements are, however, very different in Chile, Brazil and Uruguay, the three countries in the region whose governments are usually considered closer to social democracy, and in Bolivia the MAS has strong roots in the country's popular movements. Moreover, a simple dichotomic division between social democrats and populists makes it difficult to categorize governments that do not easily fit in one of the extremes.

A way of exploring internal differences within LOC forces representing different traditions as well as among forces belonging to the same LOC tradition is to consider the contexts of political representation within which these forces operate. In modern democratic societies popular sovereignty is exercised through complex forms of political representation, which are mediated by political parties, political leaders and politicized social actors. For the purpose of this classification, what defines each form of political representation is who the main representative actors are and the margins of autonomy that representatives enjoy in relation to the represented. Party-dominated forms of political representation are characteristic of institutionalized political systems (Mainwaring and Scully 1995) in which political parties, parliaments and the state are the privileged locus of political activity. Although open to the influence of interest groups and social actors, party political representation is based on a clear distinction between political and social actors based on the principle that political parties are the only actors capable of aggregating social demands and transforming them into political projects with the aim of winning office and governing a country (Hagopian 1998; Sartori 1976). In this classification the status of political parties cannot be divorced from the strength of other political institutions, such as parliaments and the state, and from the overall level of institutionalization of the political system, as distinct from that of an individual party.

Personalist forms of political representation have been traditionally mistrusted by liberal democratic purists as a threat to rational political deliberation and to the checks and balances that define a liberal democratic regime. Personalist leadership, however, is part of the democratic tradition and, if anything, it has become more of a feature in a modern politics dominated by the mass media and weaker ideological differences. Personalist representation privileges leadership as a key element in political action and vindicates political will as decisive for taking political decisions (Gardner 1966; Laclau 2005b: 63). Personalist leaders often emerge at times in which significant sectors of the population do not feel represented by political parties. Particularly at times of crisis, leaders can enjoy significant autonomy over institutional forms of political representation and draw on emotional and affective elements to create strong relations of charismatic identification between the leader and the people (Weber 1991).

Social forms of political representation have been part of the democratic tradition since the time of de Tocqueville (Waisman 2006). In modern times the politicization of social relations has blurred the public–private divide and thus the distinction between social and political actors. Politicized social actors argue that political actors should have a strictly limited margin of autonomy in relation to their represented and that representatives should act more as spokespersons of the social actors whom they represent than as autonomous actors. Social representation emphasizes civil society as the privileged arena for transparent, democratic deliberation and it considers that the common good can only be truly constructed by the direct participation of social actors in decision-making through horizontal processes of deliberation (Santos 2005). Politicized social movements have also developed a rich variety of participatory practices that challenge the representative monopoly of political parties at national and local level, as well as being key actors in global politics. While some grassroots movements participate in institutional arenas of consultation and decision-making, others view the state and political parties with suspicion, and in some cases regard them as institutions that reproduce the elitist politics of neoliberalism (Motta 2006: 900–901).

Party, personalist and social forms of political representation are present in different combinations in all modern democracies. Social democratic governments are more likely to emerge in the context of highly institutionalized political systems in which there is also a relatively capable state and strong and active social movements. In these political environments social democratic forces tend to rely on the social democratic party as the main channel for political representation and in parliament as the natural locus for political activity. In contrast with centre-right political parties, however, social democratic parties tend to combine party representation and parliamentary activity with strong representative links with the unions and other social actors and use state intervention to mitigate the impact of the market on social inequality. It could be argued that attributing to social democratic forces strong relations with social movements is an anachronistic and Eurocentric view of social democracy, and that in its lighter 'Third Way' incarnation social democratic parties have no such links, or at least these links are much less relevant. As argued below, however, the precise nature and intensity of these links are important to distinguish between varieties of contemporary social democracy not only in Europe but also in Latin America.

In contrast with social democracy, populism privileges personalist forms of political representation and defines democracy in majoritarian rather than institutional terms. This is not to say that all personalist forms of political representation are necessarily populist or that populism is a purely personalist relation of representation, but that personalist representation unmediated by institutions is constitutive of populism: in common with populism, personalism tends to thrive in contexts of crises of representation that weaken institutional forms of political representation. As noted above, populism mistrusts traditional parties as divisive of the people and denounces established political institutions as illegitimate or representative of a narrow and self-serving elite. As populism privileges a direct relationship between the leader and the people, the relationship between the populist leader and the citizens becomes the nodal point of a process of identification that constitutes the symbolic unity of otherwise fragmented popular identities (Laclau 2005b: 99).

Social forms of political representation can coexist with both highly institutionalized political systems and with weakly institutionalized ones. Among the former, social representation can assume corporatist and pluralist forms. Corporatism and pluralism share a number of elements, among them the importance of interest-group representation and the interpenetration of public and private decision-making arenas.[10] Yet pluralism differs from corporatism in that pluralist representation is less hierarchical, more diffuse and more competitive than corporatism (Schmitter 1974: 96–7).[11] Societal forms of political representation are also present in weakly institutionalized societies in which political participation grows more rapidly than the political institutions that channel representation. The gap between politicized social actors and the public institutions' ability to mediate these demands leads to the displacement of political struggles outside formal political institutions. The result is what Samuel Huntington (1968: 79–80) has characterized as 'mass praetorianism' – that is, the proliferation of unmediated direct action by highly mobilized social actors that can lead to institutional breakdown. The social mobilizations that led to the fall of Presidents Sánchez de Losada and Mesa in Bolivia in 2003 and 2005 respectively, and of Presidents Jamil Mahuad and Lucio Gutiérrez in Ecuador in 2000 and 2005 respectively, are cases in point.

LOC forces have gained office in political contexts in which certain forms of political representation predominate over others: in Brazil, Chile and Uruguay strong political institutions (parties, parliament and the state) mean that well-organized LOC parties – the PT in Brazil, the PS and the PPD in Chile, and the FA in Uruguay – have been the main agents in the ascendancy of the left. In contrast, in Bolivia the left has historically had strong roots in the country's social movements, while in Venezuela and Ecuador the leadership of Hugo Chávez and Rafael Correa has been decisive in their countries' shift to the left. Meanwhile, in Argentina the return of national-popular populism under Néstor Kirchner and Cristina Fernandez de Kirchner has coincided with the deinstitutionalization of the country's party system and the reassertion of the hegemony of the Justicialista (Peronist) party over a weak and divided opposition.

This classification is, however, a rather simplistic way of taking into account the relations between the forces of the left and their countries' representative institutions. In order to understand better internal differences within the left it is necessary to look at how different forms of political representation combine in different countries. The FA in Uruguay combines strong party representation with an equally strong social representation, as the country's powerful union movement, the Plenario Intersindical de Trabajadores–Convención Nacional de Trabajadores (PIT–CNT), exercises a significant influence over the ruling FA and constrains the political autonomy of the government. In contrast, Chile's Concertación links with the union movement are looser and weaker than those between the FA and the PIT–CNT. As a result, the Concertación government enjoys a significant margin of autonomy from social forms of political representation (Luna 2007). The case of Brazil shows the importance of a dynamic analysis of relations of representation. The PT was founded by union leaders and has deep roots in the country's social movements, combining party and social representation. The personal leadership of Luiz Inácio Lula da Silva was a significant factor in the growth of the party, but his leadership was framed within the party's structures and set in the broader context of Brazil's political system in which the presidency and Congress are the key political institutions. Since taking office in 2003, however, the PT has distanced itself from its social bases in the unions and other movements and has concentrated its activities on the game of political and parliamentary alliances. Although the PT maintains fluid links with social movements, union leaders occupy important positions in the federal administration and social participation is still important at municipal level, its politics have been characterized more by parliamentary alliances cemented in patronage and machine politics than by organic forms of political participation by social actors (Baiocchi and Checa 2007; Flynn 2005; Zucco 2008). Furthermore, as shown by the outcome of the corruption scandals of 2005 and 2006, the personal leadership of President Lula da Silva has gained considerable autonomy from the PT, as the direct links between the president and the people became a major factor in the 2006 electoral campaign that led to his re-election (Zucco 2008).

If we take into consideration country variations in political representation it is possible to make some relevant distinctions between the region's social democratic administrations. Given the presence of both strong party and social forms of political representation, the FA administration in Uruguay is the closest to a typical social democratic government, *at least when political representation is taken into account.* Meanwhile Chile's Concertación, regarded as an early model of social democracy government in Latin America, may instead be considered as more of a Third Way social democracy or even a social liberal government, given the high margins of autonomy that the coalition government enjoys from its historical allies in the unions and social movements. The case of Brazil combines the three forms of political representation, as the PT is still a party with roots in civil society and President Lula exercises his political leadership with an important margin of autonomy from other representative institutions. President Lula's personal leadership is framed, however, in a political environment in which the formal and informal institutional checks and balances of Brazilian politics make its leadership very different from that in which populist leadership typically emerges. Moreover, the relative importance of each form of political representation has changed through time, with social forms of representation losing relative ground to party and personalist representation.

As could be expected, all national-popular, populist governments are characterized by high degrees of personalist representation, but if we take into consideration the governments headed by Chávez, Morales and Correa in Venezuela, Bolivia and Ecuador respectively, they all have representational links of a very different nature with their countries' social actors. In Bolivia, social actors have become increasingly active in the early twenty-first century, while the traditional parties, MNR, MIR and Acción Democrática Nacionalista (ADN), have effectively lost their legitimacy (Crabtree 2005; Cyr 2006; Sanjinés 2004). Highly politicized social movements acting outside formal institutions, particularly but not only the coca growers, are closely linked with the MAS party to the extent that in order to differentiate MAS from traditional parties the coca growers call it 'a political instrument' (of the rural *sindicatos*) rather than a political party (Harten 2008). Although close to the government, social movements in Bolivia are not controlled by the Morales administration, as they maintain a high capacity for autonomous mobilization to both support and challenge the government (Mayorga 2008).

Under the presidency of Hugo Chávez, Venezuela has also been characterized by high levels of social mobilization (Levine 2006). The importance assigned to participatory politics by the Bolivarian revolution is reflected in the preamble of the Bolivarian Republic of Venezuela's constitution, which defines the country's political regime as 'democratic, participatory and self-reliant' (Constitution of the Boliviarian Republic of Venezuela 1999). The extent to which legal dispositions have translated into autonomous participative institutions is, however, a matter of contention. Arguably, social representation in Venezuela combines some highly autonomous organizations, particularly groups that had a record of social activism before Chávez came to office, with others that are highly dependent on state patronage and act as conveyor belts for the decisions of the government (Hansen and Hawkins 2006). Moreover, in contrast to Morales, who started his political career as the leader of a grassroots social movement, Chávez came to politics as a rebel military officer, and his strong personalist leadership is not nearly as constrained or influenced by the country's social movements as the MAS administration in Bolivia (Ellner and Hellinger 2003; Ellner and Tinker Salas 2007; McCoy and Myers 2004).

Ecuador is perhaps the country in which personal leadership is the most important form of political representation among the LOC governments of South America. Political representation in Ecuador has historically been characterized by the institutional weakness of its party system (Mainwaring and Scully 1995: 20) and by the low legitimacy of political parties. The country also has a strong tradition of populism (de la Torre 1997). In the late 1990s and early 2000s new social movements associated with ethnic groups and other social sectors became increasingly politicized. Social mobilizations reflected and at the same time contributed to the loss of legitimacy of political institutions crystallized in the impeachment of one president and the resignation of another two under pressure from street protesters between 1997 and 2005 (Mainwaring et al. 2006). Social movements in Ecuador, however, lack the centrality and organizational strengths of similar movements in Bolivia, and groups representing indigenous people that had a strong influence on the mobilizations that led to the resignation of President Jamil Mahuad in January 2000 have seen their political influence decline in the second half of the 2000s. The rise to office of Rafael Correa in the 2006 election in which his ad hoc party Alianza PAIS did not present candidates for Congress has given Correa's mandate a strong personalist element (Ramírez Gallegos 2008). Although Correa's electoral campaign was supported by a number of social organizations, the Ecuadorean president has no organic links with the country's social movements comparable with the links that both Morales and Chávez have developed in their own different ways. Given the fragmentation of power characteristic of Ecuador's political system it is, however, unlikely that Correa could concentrate power in the executive to the same extent as Hugo Chávez in Venezuela.

Finally, the case of Argentina exemplifies the changing dynamics of political representation. In the 1990s, under the leadership of Carlos Menem, the Justicialista (Peronist) party loosened its historical link with organized labour and replaced it with clientelistic networks associated with the provincial governments' political machines (Levitsky 2003). At the same time, the party system was becoming increasingly institutionalized, with the Peronists as the dominant party and the Radicals and Frepaso providing a strong opposition. The forward march of political institutionalization of the late 1990s came to an abrupt halt following the economic crisis of 2001/02 and the forced resignation of President de la Rua (see Chapter 6) (Levitsky and Murillo 2005; Malekzadeh 2006).

TABLE 8.1 Forms of political representation

Country	Form of political representation		
	Party	Social	Personalist
Argentina	Medium	Medium	High
Bolivia	Low	High	High
Brazil	High	Medium-low	Medium
Chile	High	Low	Low
Ecuador	Low	Medium	High
Uruguay	High	High	Low
Venezuela	Low	Low-medium	High

After winning the presidency in 2003 with just over 20 per cent of the popular vote,[12] Néstor Kirchner built up a strong personal leadership and concentrated financial and political resources in the executive to the extent that a once weak president was allowed to dominate Argentina's politics. At the same time, Kirchner re-established links with sectors of the Peronist trade union movement and co-opted the *piquetero* movement, which had emerged as an autonomous social movement representing informal workers by the early 2000s (Grugel and Riggirozzi 2007: 99). The combination of the discrediting of the political parties as a result of the events of 2001/02 and Kirchner's strategy of co-opting opposition governors and social movements has further weakened the opposition parties, reinforcing the Peronists' neo-corporatist hegemony in Argentina.

The differential articulation of forms of political representation highlights important differences among governments commonly associated with the national-popular populist tradition. In all four cases considered above, personal leadership and weak or discredited political parties combined to provide the framework for populist politics. Chávez, Morales, Correa and Kirchner have, however, exercised their leadership in very different ways and, personalities aside, the differences can be attributed to the relations between leaders, parties and their bases of support, which allow for different margins of autonomy.

Table 8.1 shows how LOC governments in South America can be classified in relation to the respective weight of different forms of political representation in each country.

Conclusions

This chapter has examined definitions of the left, its conditions of emergence and its internal differences. It has argued that the failures and achievements of the parallel processes of democratization and free market reforms in the 1990s provided the conditions for the rise of political forces of the left that a few years earlier were considered a spent force in the region. It is within the political framework of democratic continuity that the dynamics between conflict and accommodation that define a democratic order changed the region's political landscape. To return to the arguments presented in Chapter 5, democratic continuity provided a more fertile ground for the accumulation of forces by the left than allowed for by the 'new pessimism' of the 1990s about the condition of democracy in the region. Social movements, political leaders and political parties of the left politicized and articulated deep-seated social grievances and unmet economic demands to become an effective opposition to ruling centre-right parties and challenge the technocratic free market development consensus of the 1990s.

Political mobilization progressively shifted the 'balance of class struggle' – that is, the balance between pressures from popular sectors for further political and economic inclusion and elites' interest in preserving the status quo – towards the forces of the left that represented change. Resistance to the free market reformation found a variety of political outlets in different national contexts, ranging from grassroots protests to top-down populist mobilization and institutionalized forms of partisan and electoral representation (Roberts, K. M. 2008: 336). Modalities of opposition to the status quo and the institutional settings that mediated political conflict are crucial for understanding the rise of the left as well as its internal differences. Free market reforms increased socio-economic inequalities but dissatisfaction with the status quo was not the same as support for radical change; nor did it imply a common vision about the direction and intensity of change.

The socio-economic changes of the 1990s increased social fragmentation, making more difficult the creation of unified popular actors. The case of Brazil, one of the socio-economically more unequal and fragmented societies in the world with a highly federal political structure that adds to political fragmentation and shows low levels of political polarization, illustrates the point. Radical, national-popular, populist forces gained office in socially polarized societies in which political institutions were weak or fell into disrepute. Leaders such as Hugo Chávez and Evo Morales articulated heterogeneous demands and partially divergent interests into popular identities based on their common opposition to the existing economic and political order. Denunciations of the evils of neoliberalism were a crucial part of the common antagonism that held together popular identities, but political factors were also constitutive of the dividing line. These leaders, as well as Ecuador's Rafael Correa, emerged in societies in which alienation from institutional forms of political representation made more difficult the institutionalization of conflict and compromise characteristic of liberal democracy. Yet it would be wrong to perceive the rise of personalist leaders as the inevitable by-product of a crisis of representation without taking into account the active role played by these leaders in unifying the popular sectors by denouncing the elitist and illegitimate nature of the political order and presenting themselves as an alternative to the status quo. The result was an increase in political polarization that has made it difficult to reconcile elite interests with popular demands.

In contrast, LOC social democratic forces are more influential in political systems with strongly institutionalized political parties, checks and balances between the different powers of the state and less politically polarized societies. Institutional settings prompted LOC leaders to fight elections on the centre ground and to make pragmatic alliances with parties of the centre. While the political identity of national-popular populist forces is based on relations of antagonism between the people and the status quo, the political identity of social democratic forces is based on their differential insertion into a political order in which institutional mediations and a plurality of arenas of contestation tend to favour political compromise and gradual inclusion. Lower levels of political polarization may be indicative of significant country differences in terms of the path dependency of institutional settings, the lasting benefits of economic stability, the impact of cycles of economic growth and the complex balance of winners and losers from the free market reforms in each society.

This chapter has also argued that there are significant internal differences within the social democratic and national-popular populist forces that can be linked to the relations between leaders, parties and the social movements that constitute their bases of support. The leverage that social movements have over leaders and parties constrains the margins of autonomy of populist and social democratic governments alike to define the balance between conflict and accommodation in processing change. Looking at the relations between leaders, parties and grassroots organizations has the further advantage of giving a more nuanced perspective to the rather simplistic dichotomization of the left into populists and social democrats and of presenting populist leaders as acting in a political vacuum. The analysis of the differences between the left and their adversaries of the right and the centre-right as well as between the forces of the left cannot be limited to their conditions of emergence and institutional setting, but must also take into consideration the extent to which LOC governments have been able to change the polities and societies they were mandated to govern. Chapters 9 and 10 address political and economic change under LOC governments.

9 | Left governments and the deepening of democracy

The left has traditionally viewed itself as the political force best positioned to channel demands for radical democracy and economic justice (Kirby 2003). This chapter examines the extent to which the politics and policies of left-of-centre (LOC) governments are making progress in bringing about change to a more democratic order, as promised by LOC parties and candidates when in opposition. Any assessment of the democratic condition of LOC governments in the region is fraught with difficulties. Meaningful change is a long-term process, and most of these governments have been in office for just a few years. Differences among LOC forces analysed in the previous chapter mean that they have divergent visions with regard to both the means and the ends of democratic change. The political achievements and failures of any government cannot be assessed independently of the external and domestic constraints in which governments operate. Nevertheless, the spread and variety of LOC governments currently in office in Latin America provides a rich natural laboratory within which to examine some of the fundamental issues of the left's relations with democracy. The cases of Venezuela and Brazil are used here to illustrate wider points about LOC governments and democracy.

Democratizing democracy

Arguably, changing attitudes towards democracy shown by both the left and the right and the shift from the zero-sum polarized politics of the 1970s to the politics of moderation and compromise of the 1980s greatly contributed to the democratic transformation of Latin America during the last decades of the twentieth century (Mainwaring and Pérez-Liñán 2005). Twenty years later, when the current wave of LOC governments came to office, the region, with the exception of Cuba, was ruled by liberal democracies. As noted in previous chapters, however, it is not necessary to be a left-winger to be critical of the condition of democracy in the region. While genuine democratization has taken place, countervailing tendencies are apparent, including, among others: the continued weakness of political parties; a politicized state; the persistence of clientelism, corruption and repression; high levels of crime and insecurity; and the marginalization and victimization of subaltern groups (Gray 2007: 212).

How have the forces of the left addressed the condition of democracy in the region? The reality of Latin American democracies at the turn of the century presents the left with complex dilemmas associated with both the sustainability and the quality of democracy. These issues are linked to one of this book's core arguments: democracy is grounded in a balance between conflict and accommodation that creates the political space for the popular sectors to advance their rights, while avoiding the extreme polarization that has led to democratic breakdowns in the past. Arguably, conflict and accommodation have opposite effects on the sustainability of democracy and on its quality: a sustainable democracy requires limited levels of threat to the interests of the political and economic elites, but this is secured at the cost of weakening the ability of the popular forces to press for more egalitarian and inclusive polities, which are the essence of democracy. As seen in Chapter 5, according to some scholars in the 1990s, the survival of democracy in Latin America was achieved precisely because free market reforms tilted the balance of class power against the subordinated classes, thus limiting their ability to press for their political and economic demands (Huber et al. 1997; Weyland 2004).

The ascendancy of the left in the region indicates that the popular sectors had a greater ability to challenge the hegemony of the free market reformation than assumed by many scholars (Roberts, K. M. 2002, 2008; Silva, E. 2007). The empowerment of the popular sectors, however, itself a product of democratization, has come in some countries at the cost of increasing polarization and political instability. Mass forms of political protest, whether in the form of street demonstrations, disturbances, road blockages or the occupation of public buildings and public spaces, have led to political turmoil and to the collapse of constitutionally elected governments in a number of countries.

In Latin America, street politics has always been the means by which more vulnerable social groups can get their voices heard by those in power, given that formal channels have failed to address their grievances (Eckstein 1989: 20; López-Maya 2002: 213). As James Dunkerley (1984: 251) puts it, in an analysis concerning Bolivia which can be extended to a number of other countries in the region, constitutionalism is weak not because it is nascent, a stage to be achieved, but because it has never represented an adequate means of control for the ruling class or a historic source of liberty for the masses. Democratic rights, Dunkerley argues, have been obtained in practice by collective action, and within the orbit of direct, popular democracy rather than that of parliamentary politics.

Different forms of mass protest by the popular sectors tend to increase at junctures where larger societal changes, such as free market reforms, generate political volatility and dealignments, and open new possibilities for collective action (Levine 2002: 256). Their intensification indicates that social conflict can no longer be contained through the institutional means used in the past for solving them (López-Maya 2002). While disruptive protest may be one of the main sources of influence of subordinate groups aiming to open the political game, however (Levine 2002: 256; Piven and Cloward 1998: 367), its spread and intensity raise legitimate questions about the impact of mass protests on democratic governability.

In Bolivia, mass mobilization ended a period of broad political consensus that had seen the longest period of democratic stability in the country's history. In Ecuador, the political activation of the indigenous movement represented an important democratic advancement; however, the indigenous leadership's willingness, in January 2000, to sanction an alliance with the military to dissolve a democratically elected government comprised a clear transgression of the democratic threshold (Carrión 2007; Zamosc 2007). Against a background of deep-rooted popular discontent, combined with a revival of social protest, the coming-to-office of LOC governments in countries with weak or discredited representative institutions, such as Bolivia, Ecuador and Venezuela, had the potential to further increase conflict as these governments sought to fulfil their commitments to political change and economic redistribution.

In contrast, the LOC parties of Brazil, Chile and Uruguay, respectively the Partido dos Trabalhadores (PT, the Workers' Party), the Partido Socialista (PS, the Socialist Party) and the Frente Amplio (FA, the Broad Front), have gained power in countries with lower levels of political conflict by moving from radical origins to the centre-left. They have done so at different times, to different extents and at a different pace, which can be accounted for by each of their histories and circumstances. There are, however, some common political elements and reciprocal influences that account for this shift, among these the legacy of the struggles against dictatorships, institutional constraints, electoral calculations and political learning. Democratic continuity has shaped the political terrain in which these parties operate. Among the formal rules of the game, electoral institutions have exerted a major influence in the three parties' political strategies. The lessons of past electoral defeats and the need to appeal to new 'emergent constituencies' (Luna 2004: 200), as well as to their traditional constituencies of the organized working class and public sector workers, have together constituted a major factor in explaining both the PT's and the FA's shift to the political centre. Political moderation was required not only by the strategy of appealing to moderate voters, but also by the need to build electoral alliances with parties of the political centre, which became governing coalitions after the elections. To the electoral incentives must be added political learning, as a factor leading to the social democratization of the parties of the left. Crucial in the case of Chile were the lessons drawn by the PS's leadership from the failures of the government of Salvador Allende. In the perception of the leadership of the PS, political polarization and economic mismanagement were major contributing factors to the fall of the Allende government (Funk 2004). But the politics of consensus has its own risks for the left: it can blunt the message of change that brought left parties to government in the first place, and can create new crises of representation.

As is always the case in the analysis of Latin America, there are significant differences in the LOC governments' strategies to address issues of conflict, polarization, inclusion, representation and accommodation. As Kenneth Roberts (2008: 329) points out, where new leftist governments have taken office, dramatic differences exist in the levels of social mobilization and party-system institutionalization, as well as the policy orientations of their leaders. A comparison between the politics of the left-wing administration of President Hugo Chávez in Venezuela and those of Lula da Silva in Brazil will help to analyse these differences.

Chávez's Venezuela: the politics of polarization

It is not necessary to fully accept Carl Schmitt's (1996) definition of politics as based on the distinction between friend and enemy to agree that, if conflict is at the essence of democracy, polarization is constitutive of the political. Political antagonisms define political frontiers, constitute identities and shape political interests. In the previous chapter, it was noted how recent elections in Peru, Bolivia, Venezuela and Brazil showed significant social, ethnic and regional voters' polarization. As suggested in the same chapter, however, social polarization per se does not equate with political polarization. Political antagonism is always the result of a political operation mediated by a political system's institutional settings.

Hugo Chávez's Venezuela is illustrative of the relations between social and political polarization. The 2006 presidential election showed a high level of both political and social polarization between President Chávez, who was seeking re-election, on the one hand, and the opposition on the other, with the majority of the middle and upper classes voting for the opposition candidate, Manuel Rosales, and the popular sectors supporting President Chávez's quest for re-election (López-Maya and Lander 2006). In contrast, Chávez's first electoral victory in 1998 showed a much lower degree of social polarization, as he gained the support of a broader constituency that included voters from different social classes, including significant number of voters from the upper classes (Álvarez 2006). Moreover, Venezuelan society was socially polarized well before Chávez's electoral victory, without social polarization translating into political polarization.

What accounts for the political polarization of Venezuela under Chávez? Chávez's 1998 electoral victory was the culmination of a crisis of representation in Venezuela, in which the country's traditional parties, Acción Democrática (AD) and Copei, had become political machines beholden to special interests and prone to factionalism and immobilism. As Michael Coppedge (2005: 308–9) puts it, 'parties monopolized nominations and choices on the ballots, controlled legislators tightly, penetrated most civil society organizations and politicized them along party lines, and centralized authority in a small circle at the top'. He further argues (ibid.: 311) that there was a strong moral element in the citizens' rejection of the country's *partidocracia* ('partyarchy'), as the parties were blamed for the corruption and waste that, in the view of a majority of Venezuelans, were the main cause of the country's economic decline in the 1980s and 1990s, while generalized impunity ensured that those responsible for corruption were seldom brought to justice.

A crisis of representation does not, however, automatically translate into political polarization. Political fragmentation, rather than polarization, is the natural result of such crises. It expresses itself in the form of citizens' alienation from politics, loss of civic trust, electoral volatility and, under certain circumstances, an increase in extra-institutional forms of political protest and explosions of popular anger. All the elements of a crisis of representation were present in Venezuela during the late 1980s and the 1990s, but it required Chávez's political intervention to unify and give voice to different grievances, articulating them in the political antagonism between himself, as an outsider representing change, and the country's traditional parties, representing the status quo, that defined the 1998 election.

After starting his government as a moderate 'Third Way' reformer, Chávez radicalized his positions and progressively expanded the political dividing line between himself and his enemies with attacks against neoliberalism and US imperialism that, together with the *partidocracia*, the political opposition and the economic oligarchy, came to represent not just his political enemies but the enemies of the Venezuelan people. In Chávez's discourse, the reconstitution of the sovereignty of the Venezuelan people required a radical break with the failed neoliberalism and the oligarchical democracy of the past.[1] The so-called 'Bolivarian Revolution' embodied this rupture. The new social order promoted by Chávez entailed a new political system that devolved to the people the sovereign power that had been appropriated by traditional political parties, a new economic system to end the inequities not just of neoliberalism but also of capitalism (the so-called 'twenty-first-century socialism'), and a leader with both the charisma to unify the people and the political vision to lead them to a more democratic and equitable social order. The means by which Chávez has sought to implement his radical project for the transformation of Venezuelan society is as important as its goals for understanding the nature and limits of the political antagonisms that define his politics. Over the years, Chávez has combined mass mobilizations and the promotion of grassroots organizations with personalistic leadership and the setting-up of new political institutions in a way that reflects the tensions and contradictions between polarization and institutionalization, as well as between bottom-up and top-down politics (Ellner 2007b), that characterize the country's new political order.

At the heart of Chávez's project is the belief that an organized and mobilized populace, rather than political parties, best represents the sovereign people. Implicit in this idea regarding the exercise of popular sovereignty, however, are two different notions of civil society, and ultimately of the people.[2] One is the notion of the people as the *crowds in the streets* confronting their enemies, supporting their leader and campaigning for their demands. This notion has strong historical roots in Latin America's history of popular mobilizations, and its ideological roots exist in the populist tradition.[3] In common with the politics of mass protest elsewhere in Latin America, mass collective action in Venezuela has come to represent more than just a vehicle for expressing demands to become part of political struggles for the legitimization and delegitimization of political power. The choreography of mobilizations and counter-mobilizations by the left and the right characteristic of Chávez's Venezuela crystallizes political antagonisms and seeks to validate claims to represent civil society, a term that has become highly contested between pro- and anti-Chávez forces, with both groups claiming to speak in its name and denying legitimacy and authenticity to the other (Levine 2006).

There are political as well as ideological considerations in Chávez's appeal to the mobilized people in the streets. Originally without a political party of his own, Chávez needed to mobilize the people if he was to succeed in defeating the *partidocracia* and their allies. As an anti-party, anti-establishment candidate, he appealed to the marginalized sectors of society rather than to popular organizations, such as the unions and other social movements under the control of the 'partyarchy'. While Chávez's control of the state has since given him significant financial and political resources with which to confront his adversaries, mass mobilizations by both Chávez and his opponents have remained crucial weapons of political confrontation between the two opposing camps, particularly at times when political tensions have reached critical levels: this was the case, for instance, in the failed military coup of April 2002, the recall plebiscite of August 2004 and the plebiscite for the constitutional reform to allow his indefinite re-election in December 2007.

There is, however, another form of rapport between the government and civil society in Chávez's Venezuela that is closer to the grassroots left's political tradition of bottom-up politics as discussed in Chapter 8. This relationship entails a notion of civil society as grassroots associations participating in policy-making forums, taking political decisions at local level, politicizing everyday life and developing new forms of political activism. Participation in social movements is meant not only to satisfy immediate demands, but also to express claims to citizenship and equal status among the poorest sectors of the population apart from established, conventional structures of representation (Ellner 2007b; Levine 2006: 173).

The government of President Chávez has actively promoted the organization of its grassroots supporters at both political and economic levels. Among the main political organizations set up by Chávez are the *Círculos Bolivarianos* (Bolivarian Circles), created during his first presidency, and the *Consejos Comunales* (Communal Councils), set up during his second. The latter are meant to oversee and undertake activities ranging from public works to health programmes at the neighbourhood level, promote direct participation and involvement in community projects, and take actions for the regularization of land titles. The Chávez government has also financed and promoted a wide range of social and economic enterprises at grassroots level, such as users' and consumers' cooperatives and small business associations that are designed to develop an alternative to the market economy (Parker 2006).

The two notions of civil society are conceptually and analytically different. Their political practices, however, cannot effectively be separated from each other. While the *crowds in the streets* can in certain circumstances be the result of a spontaneous popular reaction to political events, in practice mass political action almost always requires some level of organization and coordination. As noted above, in Venezuela mass political mobilization has its roots in the extra-institutional forms of political mobilization that grew as a result of the failure of political parties and social movements to channel popular demands in the 1980s and 1990s. While in opposition, Chávez attracted the support of the informal networks of groups and activists that were behind the politics of social activism. Since gaining office, he has combined the continuous support of these loose networks with the active promotion and financing of new grassroots movements so as to organize and mobilize his supporters in the streets.

Anti-party rhetoric, polarized civil society and grassroots social organizations do not ensure regime continuity or indeed its legitimacy, particularly in a country which, however discredited its political parties, has a long tradition of representative democracy. Chávez has sought to combine political mobilization and social activism with new institutions and symbols of nationhood in order to ensure both the continuity and the legitimacy of his Bolivarian Revolution. The most important of these new institutions is the 1999 Bolivarian Constitution, enshrining the foundational symbols and principles of the new political order. The constitution combines representative bodies typical of liberal democracy and new forms of exercising popular sovereignty that are characteristic of participatory democracy. In a definition that is not short of adjectives, it defines the government as 'democratic, participatory, elective, decentralized, alternative, responsible and pluralist, with revocable mandates'.[4]

The constitution places a strong emphasis on citizens' participation in public affairs, 'either directly or through their elected representatives', and establishes a new 'citizens' power' alongside the traditional liberal democratic division of powers between the executive, legislative, judicial and electoral branches of the state.[5] The rhetoric of the constitution is as significant as its institutional dispositions for understanding the politics of Chavismo. The change of name of the country from the Republic of Venezuela to the 'Bolivarian Republic of Venezuela' grounds the new political order in the mythology of 'Bolivarianism' that represents Chávez's version of radical nationalism. It also marks a break with the previous political order by connecting Chavismo directly with the nineteenth-century independence hero. No fewer than 110 out of 350 articles of the constitution are devoted to listing different types of rights, including human and political rights typical of a liberal-individualist conception of rights combined with social and family rights, educational rights, economic rights, rights of native people and environmental rights, characteristic of collective conceptions of human rights.

The approval of the constitution was the first step in a process of institutionalization and legitimization of the new political order which was followed by a number of electoral victories for the president and the political forces associated with his government. These included, among others, the recall referendum of August 2004, promoted by the opposition according to the dispositions of the new constitution (won by Chávez with 59 per cent of the vote); the elections for the National Assembly in December 2005, which were boycotted by the opposition and gave Chávez total control of the legislative; and the presidential election of December 2006, which he won with 63 per cent of the votes. Paradoxically, a political order that defined as its legitimizing principles the new constitution, periodical elections, plebiscites and popular participation in public affairs has become inseparable from the figure of Chávez himself. Chávez's centrality in Venezuela's new political order derives from three different elements: first, from his direct, personal relationship with the people and his undisputed leadership of the *Chavista* movement; second, from the constitution itself, which, while promoting citizens' participation and the separation of powers, contains provisions that reinforce the discretional power and autonomy of the executive; and third, from his deliberate strategy of polarizing the political field between himself and his opponents and presenting opposition to himself as an attack on the nation.[6]

Chávez's 'Bolivarian Revolution' has polarized not just the Venezuelan people, but also scholarly opinion about the nature of his regime. For his supporters, he has radically democratized Venezuelan society, improving the lot of the poor, giving voice to the excluded and promoting direct democracy from below. For his opponents, he is an elected autocrat who has destroyed liberal democracy and used the country's oil wealth to promote a megalomaniac project of personalistic rule. Between these extreme views, there are several shades of grey, which are coloured by the unfinished nature of Chávez's political project, by internal contradictions within the Bolivarian movement and by Chávez's combination of rhetorical radicalism with tactical flexibility.

The intense politicization of the debate about Venezuela makes it difficult to establish social trends with any degree of accuracy. It appears, however, that there has been a decline in poverty in recent years following a period of rapid expansion in the first half of the 2000s. According to different statistics, poverty has fallen from over 50 per cent of the population in 1999 to between 42 per cent and 33 per cent in 2007, and absolute poverty from around 20 per cent to between 17.6 per cent and 9.4 per cent over the same period (Riutort 2007: 124). Increases in real wages, a fall in unemployment and informality and social programmes targeted at the poor are the main causes for the decline in absolute and relative poverty. At the heart of the government anti-poverty strategy are the so-called *misiones* (missions), which aim at bringing subsidized food, education and healthcare benefits to the barrios (poor neighbourhoods). These programmes operate outside the jurisdiction of relevant ministers and are funded from a special fund for social investment established by Petróleos de Venezuela (PDVSA, the state oil company). Critics argue that the *misiones* should be integrated into existing public institutions, in order to improve administrative capacity and oversight (Economist Intelligence Unit 2008c). More broadly, critics argue that the government's entire economic and social programme is dependent on high oil prices and an unsustainable increase in public spending that have brought high inflation, hurting the poor most, and that high rates of crime and corruption continue to blight the everyday lives of the Venezuelan people.

While there is need for more empirical work on Chávez's attempts at promoting political participation from subordinated groups, it seems clear that he has given political voice to sectors of Venezuelan society that felt unrepresented by the old parties. The *Chavista* discourse of people's empowerment and the activity of community groups and social movements have enhanced the self-confidence, pride and sense of efficacy of groups such as women, Afro-Venezuelans and indigenous people (Ellner 2007b: 11; Motta 2007a). The community focus of the government's social programmes has incorporated the barrios and shanty towns into political life for the first time. Community bodies, such as the Comités de Tierra Urbana (CTU, urban land committees), set up in 2002 to struggle for the legalization of land ownership in the barrios, have developed into powerful grassroots movements: more than 6,000 CTUs have been set up nationally (Motta 2007a).

Critics of the Bolivarian Revolution argue, however, that grassroots organizations are not truly autonomous from the state and that they are effectively dependent on Chávez's charismatic leadership and patronage. The state has played a decisive role in the organization and financing of grassroots associations, which is rather far from the way grassroots organizations are supposed to originate and survive. The so-called *Círculos Bolivarianos* are a case in point. Set up in 2001, the *Círculos* played an important role in thwarting the April 2001 coup, and subsequently proliferated throughout the country. At the peak of their activity, they were the subject of considerable controversy that was symptomatic of political polarization in Venezuela, with the opposition claiming that they were the storm troops of Chavismo used by the president to intimidate his opponents, while supporters of the movement argued that the Circles were peaceful grassroots organizations aiming at promoting political participation in local communities.[7] The Circles, however, did not become consolidated, nor did they develop an autonomous national leadership. They became involved in, and absorbed by, activity sponsored and financed by the state; and since 2004, they have experienced a significant decline in activity. A similar condition of deinstitutionalization and decay has affected other social organizations set up by Chávez (Ellner 2007b: 10; Hansen and Hawkins 2006; Raby 2006: 166).

The effects of Chávez's personalistic leadership on democracy have also been the subject of political and scholarly controversy. Critics of Chávez accuse him of being an authoritarian caudillo in the Latin American populist tradition, with little respect for democratic institutions. Answering critics of Chávez, Laclau (2006: 60) argues that political leadership is central not only to Venezuela, but to many other democratic political regimes, and that accusing Chávez's leadership of being anti-democratic reveals an ideological bias. Defenders of Chávez also note that, in the early stages of periods of radical change, political leadership normally eclipses institutions and organizations, which take time to develop. The controversies that characterize analyses of Chavismo are illustrated by the conflicting interpretations of his 2007 and 2009 attempts to amend the constitution to allow for indefinite presidential re-election. For Chávez's opponents, the amendment was yet another proof of Chávez's undemocratic drive to perpetuate himself in power. Defenders of the initiative argue, however, that many democratic countries, such as France, allow for the indefinite re-election of the president and that, in the USA, indefinite re-election was allowed well into the twentieth century.

Whether indefinite re-election is democratic or not cannot be asserted in separation from the quality of the checks and balances that ensure that the powers of the presidency are limited by other institutions of the state, and that the presidency cannot use the financial and political resources of the state to further the holder's electoral chances. Chávez's personalistic rule has undermined the independence and authority of other powers of the state, and thus democracy itself (López-Maya and Lander 2006). Illustrative of this trend is that the president has sought and has twice been granted extraordinary powers to legislate by executive decree in spite of enjoying total control of the National Assembly.[8] It has also been noted that personalism has affected internal democracy within the Bolivarian movement, as Chávez's status as undisputed leader of the *Chavista* movement undermines internal dissent and debate on strategy and ideology. As a result, he has adopted many key decisions in the 'revolutionary process' with little or no previous consultation within the *Chavista* movement or the nation as a whole (Ellner 2007b: 8–9; López-Maya and Lander 2006).

Perhaps the most serious objection to the democratic nature of the Bolivarian Revolution is the argument that, by undermining liberal democracy, Chávez has undermined democracy itself. At the heart of this argument is a normative debate about the nature of democracy. Michael Coppedge (2005: 291) puts it in a particularly forceful way:

> Chávez claims to be deepening democracy not destroying it. By his account and that of many of his supporters, Venezuela was not a democracy before 1998, rather it was a corrupt, irresponsive *partidocracia*. Therefore, he argued, all the transformations he achieved ... were necessary steps to uproot the old, undemocratic bosses and make the government responsive to the great, long-suffering, and much-abused majority. Although there is some truth in the argument, the emphasis on executing the will of the current majority distracted attention from a more important and more conventional version of democracy – liberal democracy.

Defenders of the democratic nature of the Bolivarian Revolution point out that there are many mixed models of democracy, and that the Bolivarian Revolution favours a mix of representative, participatory and direct forms of democracy. They further argue that the 1999 constitution, far from abrogating liberal democracy, includes several representative bodies, such as the National Assembly, Regional and Municipal Legislative Councils and *Juntas Parroquiales* (Borough Councils), and that there are no plans for doing away with these bodies (Reyes 2006).

The listing of the representative bodies of the 1999 constitution is not, however, enough to elucidate relations between the Bolivarian Revolution and liberal democracy. The history of Latin America's constitutionalism is full of fine legal dispositions that only contribute to highlighting the gap between the 'real country' and the 'legal country'. The issue at stake in the analysis of the Bolivarian Revolution is not just the existence of representative bodies, but the extent to which the weakening of institutional checks and balances has eroded the civil liberties and political rights that are essential for the working of democracy. A main concern in this regard is the blurring of the political, personal and institutional boundaries between the state, the government and the *Chavista* movement. An example of this tendency, which amounts to the political privatization of state resources to put them at the service of a political movement, is a speech made in November 2006 by the president of the national oil company, Petróleos de Venezuela (PDVSA), and Minister of Energy and Petroleum Rafael Ramírez, in which he asserted that all PDVSA workers and managers should be committed to the Bolivarian revolutionary project, and that the company should be '*roja, rojita*' ('red, reddish', the colours of the Bolivarian movement). Similar demands of political allegiance to the Bolivarian Revolution have been made to members of the armed forces and other state employees. When the minister's comments were made public, President Chávez backed the claim and was quoted as saying that both the oil workers and the members of the national armed forces should identify themselves with the (political) process led by him, and that if they didn't like it they should go to Miami.[9]

There are other examples of the lack of checks and balances, the political allocation of state resources and low-level harassment of opposition supporters, all of which undermine important liberal democratic principles.[10] Particularly disturbing was the expulsion, in September 2008, of two representatives of the human rights organization Human Rights Watch, hours after they held a news conference in Caracas to present a report alleging that the government of President Hugo Chávez has weakened democratic institutions and human rights guarantees in Venezuela (Human Rights Watch 2008). And yet, Venezuela retains a robust democratic culture and there is no evidence that the erosion of liberal democracy in the country is either terminal or irreversible. It is also important to take into account the fact that a politicized state was a feature of Venezuelan politics under the *partidocracia*, and that undemocratic attitudes are not exclusive to Chavismo: between 2001 and 2004, most sectors of the opposition refused to accept the legitimacy of Chávez's government and backed the failed military coup of April 2002, as well as the oil workers' and managers' strike of December the same year aimed at removing Chávez from office by unconstitutional means. The opposition also refused to participate in the December 2005 election for the National Assembly. Since then, however, while political polarization remains acute, important sectors of the opposition have started to accept the legitimacy of the new political institutions and to play more the role of a loyal opposition. This shift was exemplified by the December 2006 presidential election in which the opposition candidate, Manuel Rosales, acknowledged Chávez's electoral victory.

In short, Chávez represents a project of radical, eclectic, experimental change (Ellner 2007a) that has generated strong political polarization. He has encouraged the organization and mobilization of subordinate sectors, and has given them a political space they lacked before. There are also, however, powerful counter-tendencies that promote the personalization of politics and limit the autonomy of grassroots organizations (Ellner

2007b). And while he has given voice and participation to sectors of Venezuelan society that felt unrepresented by the previous political order, he has undermined some fundamental principles of liberal democracy and maintained the country's tradition of a politicized state. Yet, in spite of the high levels of polarization, political conflict has so far remained within the country's constitutional limits.

Lula da Silva's Brazil: the politics of accommodation

Luiz Inácio Lula da Silva's triumph in Brazil's presidential election of October 2002 invoked the image of a radical turn in the country's politics, perhaps comparable only to the triumph of Chile's Unidad Popular in 1970 (Panizza 2004a: 465). Since then, however, the Brazilian president has followed a path of political moderation that has disappointed his left-wing supporters and gained the praise of many who feared he would put Brazil on a path of radical change. As we saw in Chapter 8, Lula da Silva and President Chávez have often been contrasted as de facto leaders of two opposite versions of Latin America's left turn: a moderate, social democratic type represented by President Lula, and a radical populist variety headed by the Venezuelan president. And yet a comparison between the two governments shows a more complex pattern of differences and similarities that helps put the thesis of the 'two lefts' into a degree of perspective.

Presidents Lula and Chávez were both re-elected in 2006 with healthy majorities. As was the case in the re-election of President Chávez, the electoral victory of President Lula showed significant social polarization in voting patterns. Although class polarization in Brazil's 2006 election was not near the levels of the election in Venezuela in the same year, the poor voted overwhelmingly for President Lula da Silva's re-election while a majority of the middle classes supported the candidate of the opposition, Geraldo Alckmin. Moreover, Lula da Silva's victory represented a dramatic shift in his traditional base of support, from the urban progressive middle classes and the organized working class of the relatively more affluent and industrialized states of Brazil, such as São Paulo and Rio Grande do Sul, towards lower-income voters in the relatively less developed areas in the north and north-east of the country. In the less developed half of Brazil's municipalities, President Lula beat Alckmin by 66 per cent to 30 per cent, building up an advantage of almost eight million votes, which more than compensated for his loss of 1.3 million votes in the more developed half of the country, where Alckim won by 45 per cent to 43 per cent (Zucco 2008: 31).

In contrast to the Venezuelan president's progressive political radicalization, Lula da Silva has travelled an opposite path, from radicalism to moderation. Moreover, while Chávez, who had no organized social base of support during his first electoral campaign, has since promoted the organization and mobilization of the popular sector, Lula da Silva, who has his political roots as leader of the Metallurgic Workers' Union of São Paulo, and whose party, the PT, had strong links with organized civil society, has witnessed a process of demobilization of many of the social organizations that were particularly active in the earlier years of the PT. What accounts for the similar processes of social polarization and contrasting processes of political polarization in Venezuela and in Brazil? To answer this question, we need first to look at the evolution of the PT since its creation in 1980, and at the political and institutional settings that shaped the political strategies of the party and its leader, Lula da Silva.

Since its foundation in 1980 until 2002, the PT distinguished itself from other political parties in Brazil. In a country where parties are characterized by being catch-all, elitist, parliamentary-based, lacking in internal discipline and relying on state patronage and clientelism to attract political support (Mainwaring and Scully 1995), the PT operated on a different set of principles (Branford and Kucinski 2003; Hunter 2007). Three distinctive characteristics differentiated the PT from other mainstream parties in Brazil. First, the party combined internal pluralism and a notable absence of ideological dogmatism with strong internal discipline and the advocacy of a programme of radical reforms for Brazil's economy and society. Second, the PT had since its inception strong links with the country's thriving social movements. The creation of a group of union leaders and left-wing intellectuals of the state of São Paulo, the PT benefited from the support of grassroots Catholic Church groups inspired by liberation theology and other civil society organizations. Third, while the party acted within the country's political system, it was always highly critical of it, and made a conscious effort to mark its distance from the system. As much as a matter of ideology, these differences were of a political and ethical nature. Politically, the party systematically refused to enter into the kind of opportunistic electoral alliances that are integral to Brazil's electoral game. As a self-proclaimed 'ethical party', the PT systematically denounced the other parties' lack of principles, their corruption, their unprincipled alliances and their willingness to exchange political support for material benefits (*fisiologismo*). Also part of the party's moral and political outlook was a strong commitment to social justice and economic redistribution (Hunter 2007).

The PT was never a revolutionary party, and its radical rhetoric was always tempered with respect for the democratic rules of the game and a considerable dose of pragmatism (Nylen 2000). The party's popular roots, however, and its links with radical social movements, gave the PT political message a hard edge that set it apart from the catch-all, centrist political forces that had traditionally dominated Brazilian politics. It took thirteen years, from Brazil's first direct presidential election since the return to civilian rule in 1989 to the presidential election of 2002, for the PT's leader, Lula da Silva, to win the presidency. During this time, the PT evolved from a small but highly organized leftist party into the largest political party in Congress in 2002 (Couto and Baia 2006). During these years, the PT made steady electoral progress at local, state and national levels. At municipal level, the party won control of a number of important towns and cities, including state capitals, particularly in the south and south-east of the country. The control of local governments had three important consequences for the PT. First, it gave party leaders experience in government and the chance to better understand the constraints and possibilities of administering a public body and show their administrative competence; with time, many local mayors became important leaders at state and national levels. Second, it allowed the party to develop and promote new forms of local democracy with the participation of grassroots organizations, some of which, such as the city of Porto Alegre 'participatory budget', became worldwide examples of participatory democracy (Baiocchi 2003). Third, the PT used these experiences to promote what it called 'the PT way of governing', which was meant to combine administrative efficiency, ethical principles and new forms of democratic participation.

The PT also made steady gains at national level, increasing its congressional representation in every election it contested. The electoral progress of its presidential candidate, Lula da Silva, however, was less linear. In 1989, Lula da Silva narrowly lost to Fernando Collor de Mello in a run-off presidential election, suggesting that it was possible for the candidate of a radical party of the left to gain the presidency without watering down

213

his party's programme or abandoning its ethical principles. Yet, by the mid-1990s, it had become apparent that there were clear limits to the party's chances of steady political and electoral progress towards national government (Hunter 2007). Even if Lula da Silva had narrowly lost the 1989 presidential election, his vote in the second round was swollen by a strong rejection of Collor among many non-PT voters. Moreover, in a country where regional diversity and electoral rules promote a highly fragmented party system, Lula da Silva's appeal remained limited mainly to the PT's regional and social base of support in the south and south-east of the country.

More importantly, the country began to change in the 1990s. As was seen in the case of Venezuela, economic and political volatility favour anti-status-quo candidates and support for radical change. This was not the case of Brazil in 2002. After a decade of political and economic volatility, between the mid-1980s and the mid-1990s Brazil became steadily more stable in both areas (Panizza 2000c). Crucial for the new stability was the 1994 *Real* Stabilization Plan, which secured the electoral victory of its political architect, Fernando Henrique Cardoso, and brought a second consecutive defeat for Lula da Silva (the PT had misread the political and economic effects of the *Real* and opposed the plan). Four years later, in 1998, the election was still largely fought on the four-year success of the *Real* Stabilization Plan and on the fears that a PT government would return the country to the economic disorder of the recent past. President Cardoso was re-elected, with 53 per cent of the vote, on his record in office and on the grounds of his greater experience to face the looming impact of the Asian and Russian economic crises on the Brazilian economy. Lula da Silva came second, with 31 per cent of the vote (ibid.: 510–11).

After eight years of governments led by President Cardoso, the 2002 election had all the characteristics of a plebiscite on his government. This was clearly the political dividing line around which all the opposition candidates, including Lula, chose to campaign. But it was an election fought within an increasingly institutionalized political system. While the system had in the past proved to be vulnerable to populist outsiders or pseudo-outsiders, such as Collor de Mello, the 2002 electoral contest was an election in which all the main presidential candidates were political insiders backed by established political parties against a government whose legitimacy was not in question, which by Brazilian standards had

214

relatively low levels of corruption, and which had managed to maintain at least a semblance of economic stability (Panizza 2004a).

Lula made 'change' the nodal point of his campaign. He strongly attacked the neoliberal economic model, but he also made explicit his commitment to achieving the International Monetary Fund's (IMF) agreed targets for the budget primary surplus necessary to honour the country's external debt, thus committing himself to tight control of public expenditure, and pledged to preserve economic stability, both of which were important elements of the Cardoso government economic model. No promises were made on traditional left-wing policies, such as increasing public spending, the renationalization of privatized utilities or the return to the policies of state economic intervention. Even the financial sector, the bogeyman of the left during the Cardoso years, was spared in the PT's electoral campaign, as Lula met bankers to reassure them that they had nothing to fear from a future PT-led government (ibid.).

What made Lula abandon so many elements of the radical political programme that his party had sustained for more than two decades? Political learning was clearly one factor in Lula da Silva's shift to the centre, as three consecutive electoral defeats made him reassess his electoral tactics. As Wendy Hunter (2007: 469) puts it, in 1994 the evaporation of Lula's early lead over Fernando Henrique Cardoso with the success of the inflation-reducing *Plano Real* suggested that the PT's promises to combat deep structural causes of poverty and inequality (for example, unequal land distribution) were much less attractive to poor voters than immediate, albeit limited, improvements. An equally important learning factor was the PT's experience of local and state government. The assumption of local governmental responsibilities made it difficult for party leaders – particularly those in governmental positions – to advocate economic policies that would be detrimental to their administration's financial health (Couto and Baia 2006: 25). Not by chance, Antonio Palocci Filho, the architect of the PT's 2002 economic programme and the first PT government finance minister, cut his political teeth as mayor of Riberão Preto, a medium-size city in the state of São Paulo.

Institutional factors also played an important role in the PT's path towards political moderation. The federal nature of the country's constitutional system and the structure of the party system mean that it is difficult for a presidential candidate to run as the candidate of a single party, leading to the establishment of pragmatic multiparty electoral alliances around the main candidates, often composed of parties with considerable politico-ideological differences among themselves. So, while presidential elections may favour the division of the political space into two opposite camps, the wider electoral rules of the game limit the inbuilt polarization resulting from the nature of presidential contests and transform elections into a complex game of intersected alliances that often change from state to state. In 2002, the PT abandoned its traditional reluctance to forge electoral alliances with parties other than small fringe left-wing parties and campaigned in alliance with the centre-right Liberal Party (PL). President Lula also chose as his vice-president the PL leader, José Alencar, a well-known businessman. If presidential candidates require multiparty support to fight an election, elected presidents need to form large multiparty coalitions to control Congress, which usually include parties of different ideological leanings brought together by the distribution of the spoils of office (Abranches 1990). In office, President Lula da Silva broadened his electoral alliance with the PL to include other parties of the centre and the centre-right, which further conditioned the government's political agenda.

Economic constraints are the third factor in explaining Lula da Silva's moderation. The so-called '*Carta ao Povo Brasileiro*' ('Letter to the Brazilian People'), issued at the height of the 2002 electoral campaign, was seen by many PT supporters as making public the PT's abandonment of its radical economic agenda. While formally addressed to the people, the letter was actually designed to calm the markets' apprehension about a future PT administration. It was published while the outgoing government of President Cardoso was engaged in delicate negotiations with the IMF for emergency financial assistance to prevent the worsening of an unfolding financial crisis. A public commitment from all main presidential candidates that a future government would abide by the terms of the agreement was set by the IMF as a condition for the success of the negotiations. The letter, issued when Lula da Silva was ahead in the polls, confirmed that a future PT administration would comply with the IMF's conditions. The decision to abide by the terms of the agreement between the government of President Cardoso and the Fund was seen by the party's leadership as the only option to avoid a major financial crisis for the new government (Panizza 2004a; Tavolaro and Tavolaro 2007).

Lula da Silva's commitment to economic orthodoxy could be seen as a case of a left-wing leader abandoning radical policies under overwhelming economic constraints. Pressure from the markets and the IMF, however, comprised only one explanatory factor in the PT candidate's opting for macroeconomic orthodoxy. As important, or more so, in explaining his abandonment of previous radical policies was the realization that Brazilian citizens wanted a change of government that did not put at risk the gains made under the presidencies of Cardoso, particularly in terms of economic stability. The lessons from the 1994 and 1998 defeats had truly been learned.

The 2002–06 PT-led administration effectively honoured Lula da Silva's electoral commitment to macroeconomic orthodoxy with the fundamental goals of keeping inflation under control and generating the necessary financial resources to pay the public debt. The economic strategy disappointed traditional PT militants and contributed to the formation of a breakaway party, the Partido Socialismo e Liberdade (PSOL, Socialism and Liberty Party). Equally disappointing for many PT supporters was the party's abandonment of its ethical principles, as the PT was the subject of serious allegations of corruption in 2005. President Lula denied any knowledge of the party's wrongdoings and made the typical populist argument that accusations against him were part of an 'elites' conspiracy' against a president supported by the people. Yet he also justified the PT's corruption by arguing that all parties were involved in similar practices (Folha de São Paulo 2006; Hunter and Power 2007: 11), an argument that effectively destroyed the party's claim to be an 'ethical party' and showed that the PT had fully embraced the (informal) rules of the game of a political system that it had so much denounced in the past.

'The PT's way of governing' was also undermined by the government's failure to set up effective participatory policies at federal level. The PT-led government created some participatory institutions, including a national development council (CDES, Conselho de Desenvolvimento Econômico e Social), with the involvement of representatives of businesses, unions and other civil associations to discuss issues of economic development. It also set up a consultation process on the government's multi-year public investment plan, comprising meetings between national officials and representatives of non-governmental organizations. Neither of these institutions, however, allows participants to make real decisions about government resources or has a significant impact on the decision-making process (Goldfrank and Schneider 2006: 25). While invoking the language of participation, the CDES and the multi-year investment plan consultation process have unclear mandates, and their resolutions have little impact on government policies, as economic policy and budgeting decisions remain firmly in the hands of politicians and technocrats in the executive, Congress and the Central Bank (Baiocchi and Checa 2007).[11]

In spite of the allegations of corruption, Lula da Silva was re-elected in October 2006, with a 60.8 per cent share of the vote in the second round. The president remained popular during his first four years in office, and the opposition never succeeded in making him responsible for his party's acts of corruption. During the electoral campaign, he increasingly distanced himself from the PT. He abandoned traditional left-wing discourses of structural reform and stressed instead the success of his government's flagship social policy, the *Bolsa Familia* (Family Grant), and his personal commitment to the poor and to social justice. On the economy, he insisted that, unlike Alckmin's alleged 'privatizing programme', his administration's fiscal austerity never implied compliance with neoliberalism (Tavolaro and Tavolaro 2007). President Lula da Silva's charisma and his ability to appeal directly to the people – a trend that has been associated with populism – played a significant role in securing popular support. But the main factor in explaining his victory was the good performance of the economy, which, after a difficult initial period in which the Central Bank used orthodox monetary policies to bring inflation down, grew strongly towards the end of his first mandate.

Falling unemployment, low inflation, a sustained rise in the minimum wage and targeted social policies allowed the poor to benefit disproportionately from economic growth. There are contending arguments about which of these factors played a more important role in lifting the income of the poor (Carraro et al. 2007; Hunter and Power 2007; Zucco 2008), but altogether the gains of the poorest sectors of the population were significantly higher than those of the middle classes: according to an economic research agency, the Instituto de Pesquisa Econômica Aplicada (IPEA, Institute for Applied Economic Research), between 2001 and 2005 the aggregate income of the poorest 10 per cent of Brazilians grew by 35.9 per cent, or approximately 7.9 per cent a year. The total increase in income between 2001 and 2005 for the poorest 50 per cent of Brazilians was 16 per cent. In contrast, those in the upper 20 per cent of the income distribution saw their aggregate income decline (–0.5 per cent) over these four years, and for the top 10 per cent the decrease was sharper (–1.3 per cent) (IPEA 2006, cited in Hunter and Power 2007: 16).

In this re-election campaign President Lula da Silva received a much larger share of the vote than his party did in the congressional election. To a certain extent, this is a natural occurrence in Brazilian elections, particularly taking into account the fact that the president's re-election was supported by a large multiparty coalition and not just by the PT. As the country's best-known politician and the incumbent president, Lula da Silva had an inbuilt electoral advantage over his party. His personal charisma and his connection with the popular sectors, which regarded Lula as 'one of them', were also important contributing factors to his margin of victory. To the extent that electors punished anybody for corruption, it was the PT rather than Lula da Silva which was blamed, but the wide margin of difference between the presidential and the congressional vote underlines the growing political autonomy between Lula da Silva and the party he co-founded and led for over two decades: in 2002, the PT's congressional vote represented around 40 per cent of the votes for Lula da Silva; by 2006, the proportion had fallen to just 30 per cent. What is even more remarkable is the differences in the electoral bases of Lula da Silva and the PT: while both Lula and the PT traditionally performed better in the relatively more developed and urban regions of the country, and the party continued to do so in the 2006 elections, Lula, for the first time, drew much more support from the poorest regions of the country and among rural voters, areas that in the past have backed candidates representing local oligarchies (Hunter and Power 2007; Zucco 2008: 32–3).

Comparing Venezuela and Brazil

We can now draw some comparisons between Venezuela and Brazil and explore their wider implications for LOC politics in Latin America. As seen above, social polarization among the electorate was common to both Venezuela and Brazil, with the poor voting overwhelmingly for Chávez and Lula da Silva, and the middle and upper classes favouring the opposition candidates. There appears to be a common element that explains social polarization in spite of the two presidents' divergent ideological trajectories: namely, the increase in the well-being of the lower-income sectors of the population as a result of their governments' social policies (the so-called 'missions' in Venezuela and the Family Grant in Brazil), and the gains made by the poor from general economic growth. While not falling into vulgar economism or ignoring other contributing factors such as the two leaders' personal charisma, we can say that social conditions rather than ideology emerge as the main explanation for social polarization in the electoral processes. Similar factors related to economic conditions could also help to explain the survey findings cited in Chapter 8 which show that the turn to the left in Latin America has not been paralleled by any significant ideological radicalization among the electorate.

Institutional and socio-economic factors must be taken into consideration in explaining political polarization in Venezuela and the moderation of political antagonisms in Brazil. At times of political instability, presidential elections have an inbuilt plebiscitarian element that favours political polarization and the promise of a break with the status quo (Mangabeira Unger 1990). This was the situation of Venezuela in 1998, when Chávez was first elected president. Brazil went through its own decade of political and economic instability between the country's return to democracy in 1985 and the 1994 general election. The first direct presidential election after the retreat of the military, in 1989, saw the victory of a right-wing populist, Fernando Collor de Mello, who had no organized party support and ran as an anti-establishment candidate. As noted above, however, the 1990s was a period of progressive economic stabilization and institutional sedimentation, and by the mid-1990s there was already little chance of a return to populism. The main candidates in the four presidential elections between 1994 and 2006 represented the two main political parties (the PT and the PSDB), and fought the elections within the limits of an increasingly narrow political and ideological spectrum. Significantly, following the corruption scandals of 2005, Lula da Silva's 2006 electoral campaign had many elements of the populist mode of identification (see Chapter 8), such as personalism, a direct appeal to the people and the use of targeted social programmes to secure the political support of the economically excluded. And yet, the different institutional contexts in which Chávez and Lula operated mean that, while radical populism can be regarded as a defining characteristic of Venezuela's political order under Chávez, in Brazil populist appeals operate at the margins of a highly institutionalized political system of which Lula da Silva is an integral part.

Economic factors also contribute to a better understanding of the contrasting politico-ideological trajectories of Chávez and Lula da Silva. The two leaders were under different economic constraints: economic resources for Chávez's social programmes came from oil revenue, while the financing of the Lula da Silva administration's social policies was based on general taxation, which is highly sensitive to the working of the market economy. More generally, Lula da Silva's moderate economic policies reflect the not negligible legacy of popular support for the economic project of stabilization and economic modernization of his predecessor, Fernando Henrique Cardoso, even after the economic downturn of Cardoso's second mandate. No such legacy was evident in Venezuela in 1998, when the dominant popular perception was of a failed project of top-down economic reform.

Participatory democracy has been at the heart of both the Bolivarian Revolution and the PT's 'way of governing'. In Venezuela, participatory politics was meant to differentiate the new political order from the old *'partidocracia'*. In Brazil, demands for more participatory forms of democracy made up the legacy of the prominent role played by civil society organizations in the struggle against the dictatorship. Demands for participatory politics were incorporated into the 1988 constitution mandate for political participation in the policy-making process at different levels (Zaluar 2007). In both Venezuela and Brazil, there have been innovative experiences of popular participation at local level. Participatory forms of local democracy, however, have also found obstacles in both countries. In Venezuela, local forms of participatory democracy have proved vulnerable to changes of policies from the top, as seen in the case of the demise of the Bolivarian Circles. Grassroots organizations have also been captured by local political figures from the *Chavista* movement who control and use the movements through new forms of patronage politics (Ellner 2007b: 11). In Brazil, the PT's pioneer participatory budget in the city of Porto Alegre incorporated civil society organizations into the policy-making process and contributed to the allocation of resources to disadvantaged areas of the city according to their inhabitants' priorities. The project proved vulnerable to its own raised expectations, however: it failed to sustain the image of clean government, brought tax increases along with fiscal insecurity and left unfulfilled participants' expectations for targeted investments (Goldfrank and Schneider 2006: 24). At national level, the limits to participatory democracy are more obvious in both countries, but they also reflect different institutional environments. In Venezuela, the main limit to participation is the personalization of politics in the figure of President Chávez. In contrast, in Brazil, the PT federal administration's failure to set up proper participatory arenas of decision-making reflects the political centrality of Congress in the policy-making process, and the priority assigned by the PT government both to working with its multi-party political alliances in Congress and to avoiding potential conflict between representative and participatory institutions.

Conclusions

Finally, we can draw some general conclusions about LOC politics and democracy in Latin America. The coming-to-office of LOC parties in Latin America represents a significant democratic advance in the region. By offering the electorate broader political choices, LOC parties have revitalized the democratic process. The ascent of the left can be seen as part of a new wave of political and social incorporation into the democratic process of previously excluded social sectors (Roberts, K. M. 2008). At elite level, representatives of historically subordinated and discriminated social sectors, such as Lula da Silva in Brazil and Evo Morales in Bolivia, have reached their countries' highest office, breaking deep-rooted cultural prejudices and formidable political obstacles. At the political level, parties that were banned until the latest wave of democratization, and whose militants were jailed and murdered just over a quarter of a century ago in countries under military dictatorships, are now in office. At the social level, ethnic groups and other subordinate sectors are now a powerful presence in their countries' public life.

As noted in the introduction to this chapter, democratic change entails conflict and confrontation. Political conflict could be a necessary aspect of the new wave of inclusion and institutionalization, or lead to further instability, left-wing authoritarianism or a right-wing backlash. So far, political polarization has not led to new democratic breakdowns in Latin America, as has been the case throughout the region's history. As noted elsewhere in this book, democratic continuity reflects the weakening of anti-democratic forces and the underlying strength of democracy, as well as the high costs of authoritarianism (Mainwaring and Pérez-Liñán 2005: 49).

The level of political polarization brought about by the rise of the left has varied significantly throughout the region. In the countries where change has been more radical and conflict more acute – such as Venezuela, Bolivia and Ecuador – the forces of the left have not sought a revolutionary rupture with the political order, but rather its refoundation on different principles. To this purpose, left-wing governments in these countries have promoted the convocation of constituent assemblies aimed at a symbolic break with the political order of the 1990s and at the setting-up of new political institutions that combine representative and participatory democracy. The new constitutionalism has the potential to relegitimize the countries' democratic orders. A constitutional order that is not grounded on some shared minimum agreements among a significant majority of citizens, however, can also crystallize deep-seated political, social and ethnic divisions that could make it difficult to achieve the balance between conflict and consensus characteristic of a democratic order. And the promotion of participatory democratic institutions sits uneasily with initiatives to centralize power in the executive and the blurring of the legal and political dividing line between the presidency as an institution and the persona of its holder.

Meanwhile, parties of the left in Chile, Uruguay and Brazil have become increasingly integrated into the existing political system and have moved from the radical left towards the centre-left. The contrast between the trajectory of the left in these countries and that of the radical left in Venezuela, Ecuador and Bolivia reflects the higher economic stability and relative strength of the state and representative political institutions in the first group of countries (Hunter 2007; Roberts, K. M. 2008), which, in the case of Chile and Uruguay, is grounded in the two countries' history of democracy, and in Brazil in the gains in political and economic stability of the 1990s. It also reflects the much stronger political impact of the military dictatorships of the 1970s in Uruguay, Chile and Brazil which made the left highly conscious of the dangers of political radicalization. The electoral victories of the left have contributed to a further consolidation of liberal democracy in countries where its institutions already enjoyed strong legitimacy. As seen in the episodes of corruption in Brazil that involved the PT, however, opting for the politics of accommodation over the politics of antagonism also has potentially high costs for the forces of the left. This is the case if accommodation becomes a barrier to the left's promises of democratic change, leading instead to politics as usual. A consequence of this strategy is that LOC governments risk facing the disenchantment of their traditional rank-and-file supporters, as has been evident in Chile and Brazil over the past years.

Finally, the left's attempts at deepening democracy through the promotion of participation raises questions about the relation between participative and liberal democracy. As the case of Brazil shows, participation is much easier to implement at local level than at national level, where the aggregation of interests is more complex and the symbolic economy of information provided by political parties is more relevant for making informed choices. Moreover, as an alternative to liberal democratic institutions, so-called participatory democracy presents well-known problems of legitimacy, mobilization bias and representation. It is also prone to capture by special interests or manipulation by populist rulers. This does not amount to underestimating the importance of participatory institutions in a democratic order, but to claiming that truly participatory institutions require well-working democratic institutions, and vice versa. The next chapter looks at the LOC governments' economic constraints and policy choices.

10 | Left governments, economic constraints and policy choices

International and domestic constraints

We have seen in previous chapters that while in opposition the left systematically denounced the injustices of neoliberalism and its failure to fulfil its promises of economic development. How has the left, on reaching office, approached the task of promoting an alternative, more equitable, model of economic growth?

In addressing this question we have first to consider the constraints and choices that shape government policies. In coming to office, left-of-centre (LOC) forces faced some common constraints while others were specific to their countries' political and economic circumstances. Among the common ones were those derived from the international economic environment. These include binding bilateral and multilateral trade agreements, such as the World Trade Organization (WTO) anti-discrimination rules that limit the countries' scope for alternative trade and industrial policies, the need to access financial markets to finance public debt and investment, the leverage exercised by highly mobile financial capital on fiscal and macroeconomic policy, and the volatile export price of commodities and its impact on trade balances and current accounts. Last but not least, all countries of the region had to face up to the impact of globalization, particularly to the rise of new economic powers such as China and India, and the implications that economic competition from these countries has for economies characterized by low labour productivity, low institutional capabilities and dependency on commodity exports (Abugattas and Paus 2007).

Among the domestic constraints that LOC governments needed to take into account were long-term deficits of physical and human capital, particularly in education, infrastructure and technology, and the shorter-term legacy of the free market reformation on economic growth, poverty and inequality. The latter not only weakens the effects of economic growth on poverty reduction, but poses serious political obstacles for LOC governments' attempts at promoting equality through, for instance, higher progressive taxation or the redistribution of assets, as resistance to these measures is likely only to underlie the power asymmetry that perpetuates inequality in the first place (Skinner and Torras 2006: 5). Moreover, governments depend on the private sector for the generation of jobs and investment, as well as for tax revenue, and while in contrast to past experiences, such as that of the Allende government in the 1970s, on the whole the private sector does not regard the new LOC governments as presenting the same level of threat to its fundamental interests, it none the less retains the power to disinvest in a country's economy unless offered the right economic incentives.

Some of the most significant domestic constraints are of a political and institutional nature. As noted in Chapter 8, few LOC governments have enjoyed parliamentary majorities in their own right, having instead to rely on coalitions with parties of the centre and the centre-right. The popular sectors are often regarded as the natural allies of LOC governments, but relations can be quite fractious. Unions perceive the coming to office of LOC governments as an opportunity to press for demands that may not be easy to contemplate or may be contrary to more socially pressing priorities. This is particularly the case of public sector unions that often enjoy relatively privileged conditions on issues such as pension rights and job security. The quality of public institutions also represents a major limitation to the policies usually favoured by LOC governments. The left has historically favoured a more interventionist state and higher public spending across different policy areas. But the effects of state intervention depend not only on the quality of the policies being implemented but on the capabilities of the state to enact policy in a timely and efficient way. As shown in more detail in previous chapters, the state in Latin America is characterized by institutional weaknesses, high levels of politicization and low levels of tax revenue, all of which affect the state's ability to intervene in economic and social matters efficiently and in the public interest.

Economic, political, social and institutional constraints and capabilities vary significantly throughout the region. Several comparative indices have been compiled by international organizations which measure an array of indicators in an attempt to give a picture of a country's standings on issues relevant for economic development. Indices are problematic and may suffer from imperfect data collection and ideological and methodological biases, but overall they are useful for appreciating the significant differences in the constraints and capabilities of countries controlled by LOC governments. If we take as examples Argentina, Brazil, Bolivia, Chile, Ecuador, Paraguay, Uruguay and Venezuela, the South American countries that in 2008 were under LOC governments, the World Economic Forum's *Global Competitiveness Report 2007–2008* shows that most of these countries did not have particularly competitive economies. Chile – ranked 26 among 131 countries listed in the table – was the only economy positioned among the most competitive economies in the world. It was followed by Brazil (72), Uruguay (75), Argentina (85) and Venezuela (98), with Ecuador (103), Bolivia (105) and Paraguay (121) near the bottom of the table (World Economic Forum 2008). Social conditions vary considerably among the countries under consideration. The Human Development Index compiled by the United Nations Development Programme shows Argentina (38), Chile (40), Uruguay (46) and Brazil (70) classified as countries with 'high human development', while Venezuela (74), Ecuador (89), Paraguay (95) and Bolivia (117) are considered as having medium human development status (UNDP 2007). Institutional capabilities are more complex and thus more difficult to rank. The World Bank's Governance Indicators measure governance capabilities along six dimensions: voice and accountability, political stability and the absence of violence, government effectiveness, regulatory quality, rule of law, and control of corruption, and rank countries on each of these variables. As for competitiveness and social conditions, the tables reveal wide differences among the countries under consideration: Chile and Uruguay top the rankings in all dimensions, with positions either in the highest or second-highest quartiles, followed by Brazil and Argentina ranked around the middle of the tables and Ecuador, Paraguay, Bolivia and Venezuela ranked among the bottom quarter of nations in most dimensions (World Bank 2008a).

Constraints and capabilities are not fixed for ever, as economic conditions can change quite substantially in relatively short periods of time. Between 2003 and 2008, and coinciding with the wave of electoral victories of the left in the region, a commodities boom prompted the strongest years of economic growth in Latin America in recent times: 2008 was the sixth consecutive year in which regional average growth exceeded 3 per cent, the highest rate in the past forty years of the region's history. Largely because of the benefits of economic growth, unemployment has fallen and poverty declined by more than nine percentage points between 2002 and 2008. There has also been a reduction in inequality. The region's fiscal solvency has improved, leaving more resources available for public investment and social spending. Buoyant external accounts have allowed the Latin American countries to accumulate reserves and reduce their external debts, including the full repayment of obligations to the IMF by Argentina, Brazil and Uruguay, thus increasing the margins of policy autonomy of national governments (ECLAC 2008a).[1]

Ideas, interests and policy choices

As the considerable variation in economic policies among different LOC governments in the region makes evident, decisions are not just dictated by the constraints within which governments operate, but by the choices and strategic calculations that governments make. More importantly, economic and political constraints are not immovable objects but are themselves defined and redefined by the strategic choices that they inform. Beyond the changing impact of structural factors, such as commodity prices and the size of internal markets, there is a vast field of alternatives in which choices and constraints are defined and redefined by the political struggles through which actors constitute their identities, define their interests and pursue their strategic choices, or to put it in slightly different terms, constraints are not defined just in terms of objective factors, but as part of competing narratives about the desirability and feasibility of contending political goals (Hay 2001: 203). The fact that constraints are as much politically constructed as the choices actors make does not make those constraints any less compelling or real than money, physical bodies, weapons or raw materials. It simply means that we have to be aware that constraints crystallize past and current strategic choices, and are grounded on certain ideas about both the means and the ends of government and the political construction of interests that are not always made explicit when constraints (or the lack thereof) are considered (Panizza 2008: 176–7).

Crucial for any possibility of choice is the availability of alternative visions concerning economic development. It was argued in Chapter 1 that economic ideas crystallize into policy-making decisions in response to deeply felt political demands that require the backing of powerful interests in order to be addressed. It was also shown in the same chapter how in the late 1980s free market economics offered embattled democratic governments a clear diagnosis of the economic problems of the time and an agenda for the restoration of political and economic order.

228

There is of course no lack of diagnoses of the failures of neoliberalism and there is a rich repository of economic principles and policy suggestions alternative to the orthodoxy of the WC that were explored in Chapters 6 and 7. But helpful as these may be, the accumulation of diagnoses and policy suggestions does not add up yet to an alternative economic model.

There have been a number of attempts at codifying a new consensus on economic development that could play a similar role to Williamson's 1990 seminal opus on the Washington Consensus. In October 2003 the then presidents of Argentina, Néstor Kirchner, and of Brazil, Luiz Inácio Lula da Silva, published a joint document entitled 'The Consensus of Buenos Aires', with the obvious intention of providing an alternative political and economic framework to the WC. The document's proposals are broader and set at a much higher level of generalization than Williamson's development decalogue. Among the points of agreement summarized in the document's twenty-two statements on democracy and development are a commitment to implement public policies 'aimed at achieving sustainable development and the equitable distribution of its benefits [...]', the need to go beyond palliative social assistance programmes and take action to reduce unemployment by generating conditions favourable to the development of trade and productive investment, together with the importance of strengthening state institutions and professionalizing the public administration. Other issues included in the Buenos Aires Consensus are: the priority assigned to education as a tool for social inclusion; a commitment to honour international agreements on the environment, such as the Kyoto Protocol and the Rio Declaration on the Environment and Development; and the consideration of regional integration as 'a strategic option to strengthen our countries' insertion in the world, increasing their negotiating capacity and decision-making autonomy'.[2] The long list of topics covered by the document, however, read more as statements of good intentions than as a strategy for economic development and, as the considerable differences in economic policies between the two governments show, even the signatories to the Buenos Aires Consensus have interpreted it in different ways. In short, the Consensus never caught the public imagination and had little political impact.

Other international documents have also sought to define new terms of consensus on economic development. In March 2002, a UN-sponsored

International Conference on Financing for Development met in Monterrey, Mexico, and produced a document entitled 'The Monterrey Consensus'. The declared goals of the Consensus are to 'eradicate poverty, achieve sustained economic growth and promote sustainable development as we advance to a fully inclusive and equitable global economic system' (United Nations 2002). The tone of the document is captured in Article 4 of the Declaration:

> Achieving the internationally agreed development goals, including those contained in the Millennium Declaration, demands a new partnership between developed and developing countries. We commit ourselves to sound policies, good governance at all levels and the rule of law. We also commit ourselves to mobilizing domestic resources, attracting international flows, promoting international trade as an engine for development, increasing international financial and technical cooperation for development, sustainable debt financing and external debt relief, and enhancing the coherence and consistency of the international monetary, financial and trading systems. (Ibid.)

As is the case with other similar international documents, the Monterrey Consensus is long on lofty goals and short on the means to achieve them.

Off-the-shelf alternative economic models are difficult to find and even more difficult to implement. The quest to replicate the impact of Williamson's decalogue by publishing alternative versions of a development consensus is based on a profound misunderstanding of processes of hegemonic construction. Agreements on paper between countries, political leaders, intellectuals or economists are only statements of shared beliefs among their signatories, and more often than not their generalities barely conceal fundamental disagreements on how to translate principles into practices. Moreover, the quest for an alternative ready-made model to the WC betrays an idealist and idealized notion of what a model is and how it comes to life. The countries of Latin America started implementation of protectionist economic policies in the 1930s, well before Raúl Prebisch published his 1949 manifesto, and in Chile the government of General Pinochet radically liberalized the economy a decade before Williamson's decalogue crystallized the WC. Economic policies, such as those that characterized Import Substitution Industrialization, and the free market model were originally implemented by governments as ad hoc, practical responses to economic crises that gained the support of powerful political and economic actors and a considerable degree of social acceptance in the process of becoming more structured economic models.

The PWC agenda outlined in Chapter 7, which decries one-size-fits-all economic models, argues that economic development should include equity as well as growth, and advocates that the combination of market forces and an enhanced role for the state could provide a broad framework for the LOC governments' development agenda. There are, however, significant differences in LOC governments' application of PWC principles to issues such as the mix of state/market incentives, the role of state institutions, the scale of welfare spending, and the relationship with foreign investors (Helleiner 2003). As explored in more detail below, there are also a number of LOC governments that have departed from the broad principles of the PWC in significant aspects of their economic strategies.

In taking a distance from the free market reforms of the 1990s, there has been a new emphasis on the social and economic role of the state. In its PWC version, state intervention has come to mean less control over the commanding heights of the economy and more a combination of selective protectionism and targeted state intervention, with a drive for the state to carve out independent courses of action in the global economy (Grugel and Riggirozzi 2007: 100; Helleiner 2003: 689–90). These changes resonate with the developmentalist economic policies of the 1960s, to the extent that some scholars regard neo-developmentalism as informing a new development consensus among LOC governments.

Neo-developmentalists claim that they have learned from the failures of both 1960s developmentalism and 1990s neoliberalism to produce a distinctive national development strategy suitable for the twenty-first century, particularly for industrialized, medium-developed countries such as Brazil and Argentina. They criticize traditional developmentalism for its inward-oriented growth strategy based on indiscriminate protectionism and its emphasis on public spending to stimulate demand with no regard for fiscal equilibriums. They attack neoliberal orthodoxy for the premature opening of the capital accounts, indiscriminate and unilateral trade liberalization, dependence on foreign capital for domestic investment, and the reliance on an overvalued exchange rate for controlling inflation. They share with traditional developmentalism the belief in state investment and state intervention, but emphasize that intervention and investment should be selective and that public investment requires the control of current spending and the achievement of fiscal surpluses to render low inflation compatible with high levels of productive investment based on domestic savings, low interest rates and a competitive exchange rate. They share with neoliberal orthodoxy a preference for export-oriented growth and a belief in the importance of macroeconomic stability, but argue that economic opening should be based on negotiation and reciprocal concessions, and that macroeconomic policy should aim not just to control inflation but to ensuring a stable balance of payments and an exchange rate attractive to export-oriented industrial growth, as well as high employment. Among neo-developmentalism's macroeconomic proposals are the selective and time-limited closure of capital accounts, which entails awarding central banks regulatory powers to deter short-term capital inflows. Microeconomic proposals include a new type of industrial policy that allocates public funding across sectors to promote value-added exports, and tax reforms that both increase tax revenue and promote distributive incomes (Bresser Pereira 2007; Ffrench Davis 2006; Mollo and Saad Filho 2006).

Neither the PWC nor developmentalism, however, provides a common ideational framework for the LOC governments' visions of development. The variety of economic policies among these governments reflects significant differences in strategies of development, with Chile's Concertación working predominantly within the free market legacy of the government of General Pinochet and making it more socially equitable while Chávez's Venezuela promotes a yet to be fully specified 'twenty-first-century socialism', with other LOC governments somewhere in between. The array of strategies also reflects different policy options in different areas of economic policy, as well as changing balances of constraints and choices over time. A brief comparison between the economic policies of the LOC governments of Brazil and Argentina can aid a better understanding of the constraints and choices that have shaped these governments' economic policies.

Brazil: keeping the confidence of the markets *and* the support of the people

Against the notion of model change and a blank rejection of the economic liberalization policies of the 1990s, some LOC governments have established a more nuanced relation with the free market reformation. This relation can be summarily described as a strategy of adopting, adapting and correcting the policies commonly associated with what the left in the 1990s rather indiscriminately labelled neoliberalism. While the government of the Concertación in Chile was committed to a market economy prior to its first electoral victory in 1989, in the case of the PT a strategic turn towards market-friendly economic policies with social inclusion became apparent only in the run-up to the 2002 electoral victory. While the party fought previous elections on the alternative of 'keeping the markets happy' *or* promoting social justice, in 2002 the PT electoral campaign was based on a platform of keeping the markets happy *and* promoting social justice. As happened with political moderation, economic moderation was born out of a mixture of structural constraints, strategic calculations and negative as well as positive learning.

As noted in Chapter 9, the possibility of an electoral victory of Lula da Silva in the 2002 election raised considerable alarm in the markets, which materialized in a run on the currency, the real, and a jump in the country's external debt risk ratings in the run-up to the election.[3] Lula da Silva sought to reassure the markets by publicly committing a future PT government to following the same orientation in crucial areas of macroeconomic policy as the outgoing administration of President Cardoso (Chapter 9). The PT's presidential candidate adoption under economic duress of significant elements of the economic programme his party had previously denounced as neoliberal and unfair encapsulated the dilemma between keeping the confidence of the markets that wanted policy continuity and the support of the people who had voted for change: if forfeiting the confidence of the markets threatened economic governability, betraying the wishes of the people threatened political governability in a country where parliamentary support for the executive depends to a considerable extent on the support of public opinion.

Honouring his campaign commitments, President Lula da Silva's government followed a macroeconomic policy of fiscal austerity and high interest rates that was more orthodox than that pursued by the previous administration (Paiva 2006: 202). While high interest rates and fiscal austerity contributed to the maintenance of low inflation and a healthy external balance, they had a negative impact on growth, employment and investment, particularly in 2003 and early 2004 (Aman and Baer 2007). Negative socio-economic outcomes were perceived by observers as at least partially responsible for the PT's relatively poor showing in the mid-term municipal elections of 2004. The government's macro-economic orthodoxy also raised tensions between the administration and the PT, as well as within the government itself. At the end of 2003, the National Directorate of the PT published a resolution that called on the government to 'make a major inflexion in economic policy in the sense of prioritizing measures aimed at retaking [economic] development, and promoting the creation of jobs and income redistribution'.[4] The statement was followed by a resolution by the party's executive in March 2004 that called for changes in economic policy and stated that the party would work for the government 'to make 2004 the start of a new cycle of sustainable social and economic development, made possible by changes in economic policy necessary for the implementation and consolidation of all our social, economic and administrative programmes'.[5]

Continuity in macroeconomic policy did not, however, mean policy continuity in all aspects of President Cardoso's programme of free market economic modernization. In contrast with the continuity in the macro-economic framework, the government of President Lula da Silva was more circumspect in adopting the WC's agenda of structural reforms. The only major part of the reform agenda that was completed during his government's first term in office was the reform of the pension regime, which put the government in conflict with one of its main constituencies, the public sector employees who were negatively affected by the reform. Other aspects of economic policy were closer to the PT's traditional values. There were no major privatizations during President Lula's first term in office. On economic integration, the government effectively buried the proposed Free Trade Area of the Americas (FTAA) in favour of south–south trade cooperation and state-led regional integration.

In the first years of his second term in office, President Lula da Silva's government signalled a shift towards a more mixed model of economic development. It combined the maintenance of fiscal discipline and infla-tion targeting, typical of macreoeconomic orthodoxy, with forms of state intervention in line with neo-developmentalist thinking. Symbolic of this shift was the change in framing of the economic agenda away from the *structural reforms* characteristic of the WC towards *programmes* of state intervention in economic and social affairs (Tavolaro and Tavolaro 2007). The government's flagship economic programme was the so-called *Programa de Aceleração do Crescimento* (PAC, growth acceleration pro-gramme). Launched in 2007, the PAC was a programme of public and private investment in infrastructure aimed at increasing the country's growth rate by financing public works (Economist Intelligence Unit 2008a). The government also promoted a more proactive industrial policy through subsidized loans and investments by the National Development Bank, BNDES, and sought to increase the public sector stake in privatized utilities through the participation of the BNDES and the pension funds of the employees of said utilities in companies' takeovers.[6] In 2008, the government also announced that it was considering the creation of a public sovereign fund and the setting-up of a new state-owned oil company to manage recently discovered oil deposits.[7]

Socially and politically, the most import programme of President Lula da Silva's two terms in office has been the *Bolsa Familia* (Family Grant) (Hall 2006). The history of the *Bolsa Familia* is illustrative of the strategy of *adopting and adapting* policies originated in the WC and first implemented by the previous administration. The programme's conditional cash transfer (CCT) format has its origins in the early 1990s targeted emergency social funds promoted by the IFIs to alleviate the transition costs of the free market reforms in a cost-effective way. Emergency funds were later developed by the PWC into more permanent social programmes incorporating direct cash payments to the poor in exchange for socially desirable returns by the recipients. The first Lula da Silva government initially pursued a Zero Hunger campaign, which ultimately succumbed to policy deficiencies and administrative difficulties (Burton 2008). It was succeeded by the *Bolsa Familia* programme, created in 2003 from the consolidation of four social security programmes that originated in the Cardoso administration. The programme provides cash transfers ranging from 15 to 95 reals per month depending on the level of family income and the scale of previous benefits. Access to the benefits is conditional on parents maintaining their children in school and ensuring that they undergo regular medical check-ups. The coverage of the *Bolsa Familia* rose from 3.6 million families in 2003 to 11.1 million in 2006. This meant that by 2006 44 million Brazilians were covered, roughly one quarter of the entire population (Aman and Baer 2007).

Lula da Silva's 2002 electoral campaign for change in the economic model, which was followed by significant elements of policy continuity once he was in office, is reminiscent of similar volte-faces in the early 1990s of presidential candidates campaigning on an anti-neoliberal discourse only to enforce harsh neoliberal economic policies once in government, Alberto Fujimori and Carlos Menem being cases in point (see Chapter 3). And yet the parallels are not wholly justified. As noted in the previous chapter, while promising change, Lula da Silva had already made clear during the electoral campaign his commitment to the IMF's macroeconomic conditions and generally moderate economic policies. In short, if the PT's 2002 moderate programme arguably represented a betrayal of the party's socialist roots, at least Lula da Silva performed the 'betrayal' during the electoral campaign, instead of waiting to get into government à la Menem or Fujimori (Panizza 2004a: 468).

Nevertheless, the 2003–06 PT-led administration's economic orthodoxy surprised many observers and dismayed those on the left, both within and outside the party, who had well-founded expectations of a more radical course of action. Justifications for the government's moderation varied from an emphasis on the overwhelming constraints imposed by the leverage of the markets and the denial that the policies were 'neoliberal', to the argument that the policies in force represented only a transitional stage towards a more radical economic model.

President Lula da Silva himself used some of these arguments in a partially contradictory mix of rhetoric and political realism. He qualified the development model in force until 2002 as an 'evil model that wrongly separated economic from social development, and opposed [economic] stability to [economic] growth', while pointing out that 'it was humanly impossible for the PT in government to maintain the discourses it held while in opposition'. Meanwhile, some of his ministers maintained their rhetorical critique of the neoliberal model while claiming that the government was already implementing a new development model or arguing that it was setting the financial conditions for transition towards a more radical one.[8]

The justifications and arguments of President Lula da Silva and his ministers are not completely unwarranted. Parties' options when in government are necessarily different from when they are in opposition. While the economic and social policies of the government of President Lula da Silva did not differ in essence from those of the Cardoso administration, the PT government substantially expanded the social policies of the previous government and, together with President Lula da Silva's emphasis on social justice, this made for a more integrated development agenda. The transition argument is also at least partially justified by the high inflation and delicate financial situation inherited by the PT government in 2003, and by the rather more heterodox policy mix that followed when financial constraints were less pressing at the beginning of President Lula da Silva's second term in office.

Financial constraints, the hard realities of political office and the need for a transition period are not, however, full explanations for the government's choice of policies. A better understanding of why the PT-led government adopted and adapted substantial elements of the programme of economic modernization of the previous administration has to take on board not just economic constraints and political realities, but also some issues familiar to this book, namely the role of ideas and interests in policy options. An interview with President Lula da Silva's first finance minister, Antonio Palocci Filho (2003–05), gives a good insight into the thinking behind the policy choices of the first Lula da Silva administration, or at least of the thinking of the group of policy-makers that controlled economic policy with the backing of President Lula da Silva during his first three years in office. Asked why the government's policies lacked a utopian element, Palocci answered that, for him, utopia was 'ten years of economic growth with income distribution' and contrasted the government's allegedly rational economic policies with 'magical approaches' to economic policy-making. Underlying the importance of political learning, he argued that Brazil had tried alternative economic policies that had all ended in failure: 'I don't know any country that has attempted so many [policy] alternatives as Brazil. If they had produced good results, I would have no problems in adopting them. But they haven't.' Palocci stressed his firm belief in economic orthodoxy by reaffirming that the government was undertaking 'a classical economic adjustment' that had strong resonances with the agenda of the PWC: 'We are going to pay our bills, balance the budget, fight inflation and drive Brazil towards economic growth. We are going to make institutional changes and strengthen the rules for the enforcement of contracts. And the state is going to take care of infrastructure and education.' He stressed the government's commitment to fighting poverty and inequality and argued that 'the [then] current macroeconomic restrictions will set up the conditions for an expansion in health and education spending in the medium term'. While noting that no country had achieved economic development with social inclusion by conducting the type of economic adjustment undertaken by the government, he mentioned Chile as an example of success. Palocci further claimed that the PT's experience in governing municipalities and states produced an evolution in the party's thinking, but not a change in sides. He argued that all government policies had a pro-poor dimension but that the government was conscious of the high risks of a process of abrupt change: 'That [abrupt change] was not President Lula's option. That was not my option,' he remarked, stressing the element of choice in the government's economic strategy (Folha de São Paulo 2004).

Governments' choices are not just influenced by ideas and political learning, but must take into account the weight of interests affected by any given course of action. Mollo and Saad Filho (2006) highlight the importance of interests when they argue that alternative policies were and remained feasible, but their implementation required confrontations with 'the market' and the imposition of costs on specific social groups, especially those that had gained most from the neoliberal re-regulation of the economy. As they put it: 'The government's reluctance to pursue this change of course has had severely negative consequences for the majority of the population, especially the poorest social groups. These are precisely those that had expressed hopes that Lula's election would bring about social, political and economic change in Brazil' (ibid.: 99). Mollo and Saad Filho are right in arguing that the abandonment of neoliberalism required affecting powerful interests, particularly those of the financial sector, which continued to reap huge profits from the policies of high interest rates pursued by the first Lula da Silva administration. The question, however, is whether left-wing critics of the PT-led administration were also right in their argument that the costs of not upsetting the markets have been paid by the majority of the population, especially by the poor.

Figures for the initial years of the first Lula da Silva administration appeared to sustain the left-wing critics' argument, as the contractionary policies of the first year of the new administration reduced GDP growth to 0.54 per cent (−0.9 per cent per capita) in 2003. Even if economic performance improved in the following years, average economic growth during President Lula da Silva's first presidential mandate was below the country's historical average, below that of the Latin American average, and lower than that of other major emerging economies (ECLAC 2008a). Another disappointing outcome was the low investment rate, which hovered around 19–20 per cent of GDP. This was due to subdued foreign direct investment and to low investment by the government. Much-needed investment in infrastructure was forgone, while low economic growth restricted investment in health and education and led to rises in unemployment and underemployment (Aman and Baer 2007). Disappointing economic growth also appeared to give credence to left-wing critics' arguments that the choice of economic policy was unlikely to bring down unemployment, reduce poverty and inequality, or permit a sustained period of economic growth in the years ahead. These predictions proved, however, to be at least premature. As noted in Chapter 9, by the election year of 2006, three consecutive years of moderate economic growth and increasing social spending had brought down unemployment and made the poor better off, helping President Lula da Silva to a commanding electoral victory. The trend has continued in the first years of President Lula da Silva's second term in office, and by 2008 Brazil was halfway through former finance minister Palocci's aforementioned 'utopia' of 'ten years of [moderate] economic growth with income distribution'.

According to a study by the Instituto de Pesquisa Econômica Aplicada (IPEA, the applied economic research institute), the number of people living below the poverty line in the main metropolitan regions almost halved from 44 per cent in 1990 to 35 per cent in 2003, and to 24.1 per cent in 2008. The fall in poverty has been accompanied by a fall in inequality and a rise in the number of Brazilians joining the middle classes. After remaining basically static at 0.6 between 1970 and 2000, the Gini index of inequality has fallen from 0.627 in April 2002 to 0.58 in April 2008; a not inconsiderable improvement, particularly in the Brazilian context. Also as noted in Chapter 9, between 2001 and 2005 the income of the poorest sectors of the population rose at a high average rate, while that of the middle classes remained static. Between 2006 and 2008, however, all sectors of Brazilian society were enjoying steady levels of income growth, as a result of which in 2008, for the first time in the country's history, over half of the population (51.89 per cent) was classified as belonging to the middle class (ibid.; Neri 2008; Paes de Barros et al. 2006).

The above figures suggest that economic stability, targeted social policies and the rise in formal employment, itself the result of economic growth, have improved the well-being of the majority of Brazilians, particularly that of the poorest sectors of society. Studies show that a variety of factors account for the improvement in social conditions. In the 1990s, the period in which the fall in poverty was more concentrated was between 1993 and 1995, which coincided with the introduction of the *Real*

Stabilization Plan (Aman and Baer 2007: 11). About one-third of the fall in inequality between 2001 and 2004 was the result of non-employment-generated income, mainly contributory and non-contributory social security payments, among these the *Bolsa Familia* (Paes de Barros et al. 2006: 31). Job creation in the formal sector and increases in employment-related income have, however, been the main determinants in the reduction in poverty and inequality in Brazil in the new century (Neri 2008). Significantly, no government since 1995 can claim sole responsibility for the improvement in social conditions. Stability was first achieved by the Real plan of 1994. It was maintained by President Cardoso and, at a high initial social and political cost, also by the governments of President Lula da Silva. Targeted social programmes were originated by the government of President Fernando Henrique Cardoso and expanded during the administrations of President Lula da Silva. Economic growth was low between 1995 and 2002 and has gathered momentum only since 2004, but arguably higher growth rates are at least partly the result of the economic reforms of the previous decade.

Economic and social trends placed a different complexion on arguments about the continuity of a neoliberal economic policy framework between the administrations of presidents Fernando Henrique Cardoso and Lula da Silva, as well as to counter-arguments that the PT-led administrations have effectively broken with the neoliberal economic model of the previous government. Alternatively, it could be argued that improving social trends within the framework of a market economy reveal the continuity not of neoliberalism, but rather of a broad social democratic consensus masked by the political rivalries between the PT and the PSDB.

Against the arguments of left-wing critics of the PT government, economic growth and improved social indicators appear to show that it is possible to better the condition of the people without upsetting powerful economic interests, and that economics, like politics, does not need to be a zero-sum game. This claim needs, however, at least to be qualified. Like the rest of Latin America, Brazil benefited between 2003 and 2008 from exceptionally favourable external economic circumstances. Taking advantage of this environment, it has been possible for the government to raise revenue and simultaneously please different constituencies without the need for hard choices: high fiscal primary surpluses have allowed a reduction in the external debt at the same time as increases in current spending have paid for higher wages in the public sector, pork barrel for politicians and pro-poor social programmes. The markets, the PT historical social base in the public sector and President Lula da Silva's 'new electoral constituency' of the poor all have reasons to be pleased.

The fact that towards the end of the first decade of the twenty-first century Brazil is less poor and unequal than in the 1990s should not detract from the country's still stark socio-economic problems. Brazil likes to see itself as part of the elite group of emerging economies that are striving for a place at the top of the development table. But its growth rate is still lower than that of the other so-called BRIC[9] group of developing nations, and still too dependent on volatile commodity prices. Brazil remains one of the most unequal societies in the world, and ranks only eighth among the Latin American nations in the UNDP's Human Development Index (UNDP 2007). A more substantial reduction in inequality will not be easy to achieve. Over the span of the country's history, income inequality has been underpinned by an accentuated concentration in assets, and any administration faces the substantial challenge of redistributing assets if inequality is to be reduced in the long run (Aman and Baer 2007: 13). In education, a key element for both social and economic development, Brazil has been positioned at the bottom or near the bottom among countries entering the Organisation for Economic Co-operation and Development (OECD) Programme for International Student Assessment (PISA).[10] To overcome these challenges, Brazil needs further economic and social reform. This should include policies for a continuous reduction in inequality and more and better-quality public investment in research and development, infrastructure, health and education. Of equal or more importance is the reform of public institutions to promote a less corrupt and more accountable political system, and a system of justice that truly enforces the principle of equality before the law. It remains to be seen to what extent this can be done without affecting powerful political and economic interests, and whether the country's elite would be willing to pay for its costs (Morais and Saad Filho 2003: 22).

The return of the repressed: national-popular politics and policies

In the previous section it was shown how, by adopting, adapting and correcting the legacy of the economic reforms of the previous decade, the development strategy of the LOC government of Brazil was broadly in line with the prescriptions of the PWC. In contrast, other LOC governments in the region have sought to implement policies that in many aspects represent a more radical departure, not just from the WC but also from the broader principles of the PWC. Among these governments are the administrations of Presidents Néstor Kirchner in Argentina, Evo Morales in Bolivia, Rafael Correa in Ecuador and Hugo Chávez in Venezuela. Just as Chile's Concertación was the inspiration for the newly found moderation of the PT and the FA, Chávez's Venezuela has played a significant political and economic role in promoting and supporting more radical alternatives. As was the case in Brazil and Uruguay, however, international and domestic constraints and opportunities as well as political choices were more important than foreign influences in explaining policy options.

There are significant differences in the economic policies pursued by the above-mentioned governments, ranging from the neo-developmentalism of the government of President Kirchner to the 'twenty-first-century socialism' of Chávez. The claim that these administrations' economic policies go beyond the PWC should also be qualified by noting that by definition the PWC is not an economic model, but a rather inchoate set of principles, that none of these governments has sought to implement ground-zero economic policies, and that, as usual, there is a considerable gap between rhetoric and reality. What these governments have in common, however, is a much more politicized approach to the economy that blurs the dividing line between politics and markets that was the key principle of the free market reformation and downplays the importance of institutions, perhaps the most crucial addendum of the PWC to the free market agenda of the WC. An example of the erosion of the dividing lines between politics and markets is the questioning of the technocratic neutrality of institutions, such as central banks and regulatory agencies, and the intervention of the state in the formation of prices. The politicization of economic relations also derives from the vindication of a more active role of the state in economic affairs, which, as a general principle, is shared with other more PWC-aligned LOC governments, although the aims, means and limits of intervention can be significantly different.

In reaction against the embracing of globalization by both the WC and the PWC, there has been a revival of economic nationalism, manifested in the practical abandonment of the free trade agenda of the 1990s, in a more confrontational attitude towards foreign companies, particularly in the mineral resources sectors, and in the selective renationalization of some of the utilities privatized in the 1990s. The new nationalism cannot be separated from appeals to new popular identities, which in the case of these governments comprise policies aimed at contemplating the demands of both the collective actors mobilized against neoliberalism in the late 1990s and early 2000s, such as the *piqueteros* in Argentina and the social movements of El Alto in La Paz, Bolivia, and, more generally, the losers from the free market reformation.

As Carlos Vilas (2006: 245) suggests, the new nationalism and the attempts at constituting a new popular base of support have similarities with the national-popular regimes of mid-twentieth-century Latin America during the ISI era. But there are also significant social, political and economic differences between the early-twenty-first-century national-popular left-wing governments and their mid-twentieth-century predecessors. As in the case of any other retro look, the new nationalism is not just a nostalgic trip to the past but a combination of the old and the new. The new nationalism has led to clashes between government and international financial and industrial investors, for instance in relation to the debt default in Argentina and the nationalization of oil and gas companies in Venezuela and Bolivia. In the short term at least, LOC governments have been able to impose their will on international investors by renegotiating contracts, partially or totally expropriating foreign companies, or imposing new conditions for their operations in their countries. This outcome shows the rebalancing of power relations between governments and markets in favour of the nation-state, and a relative weakening of international capital in the early twenty-first century when compared to the 1990s, and thus the relative increase in the margins of autonomy enjoyed by governments across the region.

A number of reasons make the analysis of the economic strategy of the government of President Néstor Kirchner in Argentina particularly relevant for a better understanding of the constraints and choices that define more radical alternatives to the PWC. In contrast to Venezuela, Bolivia and Ecuador, Argentina is not a major oil and gas exporter and has not enjoyed the windfall gains accruing to those countries, which according to Weyland (2007: 2) discredited the neoliberal insistence on constraints, suggested the availability of great opportunities, and thus stimulated radicalism and voluntarist attacks on the established socioeconomic political order. Compared to Venezuela's rentier state economy (Karl 1997), Argentina has a more complex productive structure. Also in contrast with Venezuela's oil-funded 'twenty-first-century socialism', Argentina has adopted an economic strategy that has elements of the neo-developmentalist proposals that in many aspects overlap with the principles of the PWC. But there have also been significant differences between the economic policies of the administration of President Kirchner and those of the LOC governments of Brazil, Chile and Uruguay: Argentina's economic strategy has been more statist and less institutionalized, and its implementation has led to confrontations with powerful international and domestic economic actors that have been largely absent in the other countries of the Southern Cone. On the whole, the economic polices of the Kirchner administration amounted to a stronger rejection of neoliberalism, and an analysis of them illustrates how Argentina's political and institutional legacy has shaped its LOC government's policy options differently from those of neighbouring countries.

After the collapse of the economy in 2002 and the political instability that ensued (see Chapter 6), the imperative for any government in Argentina was the restoration of economic and political governability. The interim administration of President Eduardo Duhalde (2002/03) and his economics minister, Roberto Lavagna, took some important initial steps towards these goals. The government did so by rejecting an orthodox stabilization plan in line with traditional IMF recommendations and distancing itself from the free market economic policies of the Menem era. Instead, the new economic strategy was based on abandoning convertibility, which amounted to an effective devaluation of the currency with the effect of stimulating exports and protecting domestic industry, while taxing commodity exports to finance social programmes. The new government also introduced price controls to bring down inflation and conducted an aggressive and highly successful renegotiation of the external debt, which included a 70 per cent reduction in the debt to private creditors. Politically, the government sought to re-establish its links with social sectors by promoting dialogue with a broad range of actors across society, including labour, business, NGOs, social movements, political parties and religious groups. To address the social emergency it set up a social programme based on a conditional cash-transfers format, the *Jefes y Jefas de Hogar* (Heads of Household), partially financed by export taxes (Grugel and Riggirozzi 2007: 95–6).

While the government of President Duhalde achieved remarkable success in stabilizing Argentina's political and economic situation in its short period in office, his successor, Néstor Kirchner (2003–07), took further steps to reconstruct the authority of the state and redefine Argentina's socio-political matrix farther away from the legacy of neoliberalism. On assuming office, President Kirchner had to face the country's still-dire social and economic situation from a position of political weakness. The new president had no control over the Justicialista (Peronist) party political machine and lacked a majority of his own in Congress. Ideology, politics and economics were combined in the service of a project aimed at strengthening the authority of the state and the power of the presidency and at implementing an economic strategy that retrieved elements of Argentina's national popular tradition.

Ideologically, Kirchner set up a discursive dividing line according to which the 1990s (the Menem era) were defined by anti-national neoliberal policies of deindustrialization, corruption, speculation and social exclusion. Moreover, by tracing the origins of the neoliberal model to the military dictatorship of the 1970s, Kirchner discursively constructed an uninterrupted line of political responsibility for the effects of the neoliberal model from the military regime of the 1970s to the democratic governments of the 1980s and 1990s. The demonization of the country's recent history allowed Kirchner to frame his government's alternative economic and political project with reference to Argentina's national-popular roots of the 1960s and 1970s (Slipak 2007).

Politically, President Kirchner reconstructed the historical relation between the Justicialista party and the unions and sectors of business, as well as co-opting the *piquetero* movement and other social organizations through a mixture of state funding and political control.[11] He took advantage of the institutional weakness of Argentina's Congress to claim extraordinary powers to legislate by decree, and of the political weakness of the opposition to construct political alliances across party lines. Economic as well as political power was concentrated in the presidency. In line with the neo-developmentalist macroeconomic framework – and ironically also with the prescriptions of Williamson's decalogue – the government followed a weak currency policy to stimulate economic growth through export competitiveness and import substitution. The extra income for exporters generated by the weak currency and the rise in commodity prices was taxed by the government and the revenue used to help maintain a healthy fiscal balance and to cross-subsidize the utility companies, whose prices were frozen following the breakdown of convertibility. The revenue generated by the export taxes was also used to partially fund social programmes and for discretionary transfers by the executive to provincial state governors in exchange for their support, thus providing the economic foundations for the president's expanded social and political base. The heterodox policy mix of fiscal orthodoxy and an activist state was compounded by the renationalization of several state companies and by a series of ad hoc measures, including semi-voluntary price agreements and food export bans, in order to increase domestic supply so as to prevent inflation from rising. As part of its anti-inflationary strategy the government also intervened in the Instituto Nacional de Estadística y Censos (INDEC, the national statistics agency), hence raising claims that it had resourced the manipulation of the consumers' price index.

President Kirchner's hybrid economic strategy of fiscal orthodoxy, economic nationalism and state intervention seemed to pay off both economically and politically. Partly as a rebound from the recession of 1998–2002 and prompted by high commodity prices, the economy expanded by nearly 50 per cent and poverty and unemployment halved during his term in office. Facing a weak and divided opposition, his wife, Cristina Fernández de Kirchner, won the presidential election in 2007 under the slogan 'change is just beginning'.

By 2008, the Argentinian economy was enjoying its sixth consecutive year of growth averaging over 8 per cent, faster than any big economy except China. By the same time, however, the Kirchners' economic strategy was facing political and economic problems reminiscent of past periods of state economic intervention that polarized society in the late 1960s and 1970s. This period was characterized by a pattern of conflicts in which economic gains and losses resulting from politically mediated forms of economic intervention in a weakly institutionalized political environment led to an accumulation of sectoral conflicts around governments' decisions (Cavarozzi 1992). Representative of these conflicts in the twenty-first century were a series of farmers' strikes early in 2008 that followed the introduction of a new sliding scale for export taxes on grains and oilseeds. The government decision, initially taken by executive decree, precipitated a wave of protests by rural producers joined by the middle and upper classes in major towns and cities (Economist Intelligence Unit 2008b). The protests weakened the government of Fernández de Kirchner, leading to its defeat in Congress, which voted down the tax increases. Economically, the rise in inflation, which the government sought to mask by manipulating official statistics, threatened to undermine the social gains of the first years of her husband's administration and popular support for the government. A sharp fall in the popularity of the president, together with the institutional weaknesses of the Argentine economy, as exemplified by the allegations about the political manipulation of the inflationary figures, has generated a climate of uncertainty about the future of the Argentine economy, which has not yet been able to attract the levels of investment necessary for sustained, long-term economic growth.

Conclusions

This chapter has sought to analyse how international and domestic constraints and choices shaped the economic strategies of LOC governments in the region, and the ideas and interests that informed the search for alternative economic policies. It was assumed in the 1990s that the structural power of global financial capital, the influence of the IFIs and of the US government and the political hegemony of centre-right governments left little margin for alternatives to the Washington Consensus. Conditions in the early twenty-first century changed significantly both economically and politically. Between 2003 and 2008 the IFIs largely lost their economic influence and intellectual authority; the USA was distracted by its own domestic and international problems; and the commodities boom provided LOC governments with more financial resources and broader margins of policy autonomy than they had thought possible only a few years earlier.

As noted above, however, long-standing social, political and economic constraints remain in place in spite of the more permissive economic and political environment. These constraints pose serious obstacles for equitable social development and define the development agenda for the future: the state apparatus in most Latin American countries suffers from major institutional and financial shortcomings that need to be overhauled if it is to be used as an efficient instrument for economic development. Overcoming high levels of inequality and low levels of education is a long-term enterprise that cannot be accomplished in the short time span of an electoral cycle. Significant structural differences also define the nature of the constraints facing different LOC governments. Countries such as Brazil that have a large domestic market and a sophisticated industrial base have considerable scope for inward-oriented growth. Oil-rich countries, such as Venezuela, have a very different margin of autonomy from external constraints to small, open, commodity-exporting economies such as Chile and Uruguay. In turn, Uruguay and Chile have better-quality public institutions than Venezuela, Bolivia, Argentina and Ecuador.

Within these constraints, ideas about development shape governments' choices of development strategies. What united LOC parties and popular protest movements in the late 1990s was not a ready-made alternative to the status quo, but the view that failed neoliberal prescriptions should be replaced with more socially oriented and nationalist policies, and a more central role for the democratized state (Sandbrook et al. 2007: 234–5). Even within these broad parameters there were always significant differences on issues such as the boundaries of state intervention and attitudes towards foreign capital. It would not be feasible or desirable for LOC governments to follow a uniform alternative economic model that would result in replicating the WC's assumption that there is a set of development policies that are right independently of context and history. Instead, LOC governments have relied on a mix of economic principles and policies drawn from different approaches to development, including neo-developmentalism and the PWC, and implemented them in the context of their countries' changing political and economic environments.

Moreover, as shown in Chapter 9, the balance between class conflict and compromise underlying the LOC governments' economic policies has varied significantly from country to country. Any alternative development model requires the building of a new social consensus that makes development politically sustainable. In the 1970s the ISI economic model was grounded on a corporatist social consensus comprising the state, industrialists, the new industrial working class and important sectors of the middle classes. As noted in Chapter 3, support for the policies of the WC in the early 1990s was based on a precarious alliance between a modernizing technocratic elite, neo-populist leaders, sectors of the business community and the poor, who benefited from the fall in inflation. In the early twenty-first century, LOC governments face the challenge of building a new social consensus around a project of economic growth and social justice in fragmented and unequal societies. LOC governments have followed different strategies of consensus-building, from the social democratic compact based on strict limits to reforms on the part of left-wing forces in exchange for the political allocation of the economic surplus in favour of the poor (ibid.: 236) characteristic of the governments of Chile, Brazil and Uruguay, to the confrontation of economic power holders by more radical projects of redistribution of assets in Bolivia, Ecuador, Venezuela and, to a more limited extent, Argentina.

Finally, for all the significant differences in economic strategies between LOC governments, attempts at dividing them into two mutually exclusive models of development frozen in time are only relatively helpful. A more detailed analysis of the LOC governments' economic policies than allowed by this book would show significant differences between the economic strategies of governments that are classified as belonging to the same development camp, as well as elements in common between the opposite camps: targeted social programmes being a case in point. The economic projects of LOC governments are works in progress that respond to political calculations as much as to economic principles, and are open to challenges and redefinitions both from within and from outside the parties in power. As happened to the LOC governments' approaches to democracy, national history and institutions weigh heavily in the choices of economic policies.

Conclusions

This book began by mapping the emergence of the free market reformation in Latin America, and is being concluded in late 2008 at a time in which the US financial system is undergoing its worst systemic crisis since the 1930s. In September 2008, in an extraordinary turn of events, the US government was forced to nationalize some of the country's main financial institutions and to pump billions of US dollars of public money into the system in an attempt to prevent the collapse of the entire financial edifice upon which the country's economy depends. The gravity of the crisis, which has also spread to the developed economies in Europe and elsewhere, was vividly summarized by the British Chancellor of the Exchequer (finance minister) Alistair Darling's claim that Britain was facing 'arguably the worst' slump in sixty years (Oakeshott and Smith 2008). If this assessment proves to be the case globally, perhaps historians will set the date of the death of the free market, financially driven, casino capitalism that has dominated the world economy for the past quarter of a century at some time in September/October 2008. In any case, there is little doubt that we are facing epoch-changing times.

In the midst of the storm that is battering the financial markets worldwide, it is difficult to anticipate its likely implications for Latin America, and more specifically for the LOC governments that are the subject of this book. Financial crises are sadly familiar to the countries of Latin America, and, contemplating the developed world's frantic efforts to weather a crisis of its own making, some Latin American leaders could not resist turning the tables on the very same governments and financial institutions that in the past lectured their countries about the goodness of the markets and were now experiencing their unforgiving fury. Addressing the 63rd Session of the United Nations General Assembly on 23 September 2008, President Cristina Fernández de Kirchner of Argentina said that the world could no longer speak of the Tequila effect, which indicated that the crisis came from emerging countries and spread to the centre. She suggested that if a name were to be given to the current crisis it should be called 'the jazz effect', meaning that it emanated from the first economy of the world to the rest. Speaking to the same gathering, President Lula da Silva blamed 'speculators', 'adventurers' and 'opportunists' for an economic and financial crisis that, he claimed, had spawned 'the anguish of entire peoples'. More radically, President Evo Morales of Bolivia claimed that the General Assembly was meeting at a time of rebellion against misery and poverty, and against the effects of climate change and privatization policies throughout the world (United Nations General Assembly 2008a, 2008b).

LOC Latin American leaders may be justified in noting that speculative financial attacks safeguard no country, not even the USA, and that, as President Lula da Silva put it, 'we must not allow speculators' profits always to be privatized, while their losses are invariably socialized' (United Nations General Assembly 2008b). And yet, LOC leaders have no reason to feel smug, not least the Argentinian president. One element that weaves together the financial crises of Latin America, Asia and Russia of the 1990s and that of the USA and Europe in 2008 is the extraordinary volatility of global financial capitalism. While the economies of Latin America appeared to have been relatively little affected by the initial effects of the so-called credit crunch that brought the economies of the developed world to a stop, soon the impact of the global crisis was being felt throughout the world.

As examined in the body of this book, the extraordinary favourable international economic conditions of the half-decade from 2003 to 2008 offered LOC governments in the region the opportunity to gain higher levels of policy autonomy from international financial institutions and to combine economic growth with social policies that have reduced poverty and inequality. A deterioration in the economic environment is likely to place new constraints on these governments' policy options and limit their ability to address social demands. More fundamentally, a change in the economic environment is likely to put an end to the paradox, brought about largely by the commodity boom, of Latin American economies experiencing high levels of growth almost irrespective of their economic policy orientations. If this proves to be the case, the new economic climate may bring a return to the need to make more difficult choices.

As in any crisis, the economic and political outcome of the 2008 financial crisis will not be determined by economic conditions alone. In what has been one of the main arguments of this book, crises are not defined in terms of objective factors, but in subjective terms, in the form of a crisis narrative that makes sense of current problems and offers a credible promise of decisive action for a better future. On the surface, the financial crisis of 2008 may drive the final nail into the coffin of free market economics and favour alternative approaches to economic policy-making. The episodes of 2008 have brought the state back into economic management with a vengeance, and have put free marketeers on the defensive everywhere. As President Lula da Silva put it in his address to the United Nations General Assembly (ibid.): 'Indispensable interventions by state authorities have defied market fundamentalists and shown that this is a time for political decisions.'

And yet there is no guarantee that the narrative of the left will be best placed to frame a vision of the future in the new economic environment. The cleavage between government and opposition that, as shown in Chapter 8, favoured the rise of the left in the late 1990s and in the early years of this century could now turn against LOC incumbents. Moreover, the crisis still leaves open the question of whether LOC governments have an alternative to the free market reformation. It could be argued that the idea of a new model of development is in itself misguided. Benjamín Arditi (2008: 68) notes that the difficulty of generating clear policy choices should certainly be addressed, but that actual policies usually arrive after a new political imaginary gains a foothold in the public imagination.

Moreover, the cupboard of policy alternatives is less bare than is argued by market fundamentalists. We examined some of the alternatives to the Washington Consensus in Chapters 7 and 10 within the loosely bound framework of the post-Washington Consensus (PWC). But the PWC, however broadly we define its limits, does not address the more fundamental political question that divides LOC governments in the region and resonates throughout the history of the left. This division can be summarized in the contrast between the claim by Brazil's former finance minister, Antonio Palocci Filho, quoted in Chapter 10, that for him utopia was 'ten years of economic growth with income distribution', and President Chávez's proclamation of 'twenty-first-century socialism' as the goal of the Bolivarian Revolution; a desire to transcend capitalism that has been echoed by Presidents Morales and Correa, although what is meant by 'twenty-first-century socialism' and how capitalism is to be transcended remains unclear.

In 2008, a twenty-one-member World Bank Commission on Growth and Development published its findings after two years of consultation and deliberation. Their report (World Bank 2008c) argues that successful, high-growth economies share the characteristic of credible, inclusive and pragmatic governments. As the political and economic successes of the Concertación government in Chile and of President Lula da Silva in Brazil show, there is much to be said for a combination of economic pragmatism and social inclusion. Any model of economic development needs to be sustainable, both economically and politically. It must address the relationship between wealth creation, productivity, efficiency and competitiveness (Weyland 2007), together with the social aspects of development, particularly questions of equity, the building of human capabilities and the protection of the more vulnerable sectors of the population against both economic change and economic volatility. Both excessive pragmatism and unguarded utopianism, however, pose their own dangers for LOC governments. Devoid of the left's transformative promise, LOC governments run the danger of becoming disconnected from their grassroots supporters and of falling into their own versions of technocratic managerialism that render the left indistinguishable from other political alternatives. Utopian economics that rely on political will in order to ride roughshod over economic fundamentals end up hurting those very same social sectors that they are meant to protect.

Latin American economies have enjoyed high levels of economic growth in the second half of the 2000s. Joining the club of developed nations is, however, a long-term process that cannot depend on repeatedly winning the commodities lottery. Since the Second World War, only thirteen countries in the whole world have achieved a growth rate of more than 7 per cent year for periods of more than twenty-five years (World Bank 2008c). Among the countries of Latin America, only Brazil achieved these levels of growth between the 1950s and the mid-1970s, and as we know, it has not been able to maintain them since.

The same tensions between pragmatic gradualism and utopian foundationalism traverse the left's project of deepening democracy. Two interrelated questions are behind these tensions. The first is that in countries such as Bolivia, Ecuador and Venezuela, political institutions lost legitimacy because of their inability to represent the people and address their demands. Crises of representation in these countries gave way to the deinstitutionalization of democracy expressed in the politics of mass protest and the rise of new leaders who have given voice to those who did not feel represented by the old political order. Democratically elected political leaders have the legitimate right to promote radical changes in their countries' ineffectual and discredited political institutions. Constitutional reforms in those three countries have sought to mark a new beginning and to set up new, more democratic and more inclusive political orders. But processes of constitutional reform have also laid bare deep political divisions that could make it difficult for the new constitutional orders to bridge the gap between the republican principle of the primacy of institutions and claims to the unmediated exercise of popular sovereignty by personalist leaders or the politics of mass protests.

When a political leader occupies the presidency under liberal democratic principles, the leader is only temporarily endowed with legitimate authority by virtue of his/her institutional investiture. The concentration of power in the presidency puts this principle into question. Moreover, in a republican setting a democratically elected president can claim to be the leader of the plebs ('the people as the underdogs') but he is the president of the demos ('the citizens'). How the leader/president negotiates the chasm between the plebs and the demos is of the essence of democracy. As the clashes between supporters of the autonomic claims of the departments of the east and defenders of the Morales government in August and September 2008 in Bolivia show, the left has no monopoly of the politics of mass protests. A shared sense of citizenship requires legitimate institutions that are able to strike a balance between conflict and accommodation, which, in the argument of this book, is characteristic of a democratic order.

The second question at stake in the arguments about LOC governments and democracy concerns the relationship between different forms of political representation in a democratic polity. As noted in Chapter 8, party, personalist and social forms of political representation are present in different combinations in all modern democracies and express different traditions within the left. In a well-functioning democracy, different forms of political representation check and complement each other. There could be no change without visions of the future, and political leaders are often those best positioned to convey these visions. As explored in this book, popular leaders can also give voice to those who do not have institutional channels through which to express their demands. Political parties are necessary to channel citizens' preferences and to negotiate and generalize sectoral interests; and grassroots organizations are key actors through which to channel social demands and ensure political accountability.

If left unchecked, however, each of these forms of political representation can become a threat to both the quality and the survival of democracy. For instance, in Chile the predominance of party forms of political representation has resulted in a perception of the political game as dominated by a political and technocratic elite that has produced considerable levels of political alienation. In Brazil, the dominance of congressional politics has led to the institutionalization of corruption and to the colonization of the state by political clienteles. By contrast, in Bolivia the predominance of social forms of political representation perpetuates social fragmentation, makes governmental action difficult, and endangers the integrity of the state. And in Venezuela, the personalist leadership of Hugo Chávez has led to an excessive concentration of political resources in the executive and to a weakening of mechanisms of democratic control.

How can these dangers be avoided in a project of democratization of democracy? According to certain visions of the left, the deepening of democracy requires giving so-called participative democracy priority over representative democracy. As discussed in Chapter 9, however, this is a misleading way of looking at the relations between the two visions. Instead, it is the balance between different forms of political representation which is key. As noted, again in Chapter 9, participatory democracy is not an alternative but a complement to representative democracy, as truly participatory institutions require well-working democratic ones, and vice versa. The balancing of different forms of political representation in order to deepen democracy presents LOC governments in Latin America with a common task to be implemented differently in accordance with each country's political context. The principles for the construction of a more democratic order are the same for all countries, but strategies for deepening democracy vary according to the relative strengths and weaknesses of different forms of political representation.

There is no guarantee that the projects of economic development and political change represented by the different strands of the left in Latin America will succeed in promoting equitable development and a more democratic order, and there are good reasons to fear some setbacks in these areas. Nevertheless, we cannot forget that the rise of the left in Latin America is the result of more than two decades of political advances under democracy, advances that cannot be so easily reversed.

Notes

1 Paradigm found

1 The resolution of the issue is not helped by Williamson's contradictory claims regarding what the WC is supposed to be about. On the one hand he says that it was an attempt to summarize the policies that were widely viewed as supportive of development. And yet in the same document he claims that the WC consists of 'the set of policies endorsed by the principal economic institutions located in Washington: the US treasury, the Federal Reserve Board, the IMF and the World Bank' (Williamson 2000: 257). Further on he says that they were 'a lowest common denominator of the reforms that I [John Williamson] judged "Washington" could agree were needed in Latin America as of 1989' (ibid.: 254). Clearly the three claims are very different in nature.

2 The following overview of Brazil's ISI development is based on Panizza (1999).

3 I have borrowed the quote from a speech by Brazil's former Central Bank president, Gustavo Franco, reproduced in Folha de São Paulo, 20 August 1997.

4 R. Alfonsín, 'Llamado a la ciudadanía del Señor Presidente de la Nación, Doctor Raúl Alfonsín', 14 June 1985, quoted in Barros (2002: 111).

5 Politically, the crisis was difficult to attribute to a specific type of government or even political regime. In countries such as Brazil, Argentina and Uruguay the crisis was construed as the legacy of the military regimes. In Mexico it was framed as the consequence of the fiscal profligacy and economic mismanagement of the populist governments of Luis Echeverría (1970–76) and José López López Portillo (1976–82). Meanwhile, in Peru and Bolivia the crisis coincided with the administrations of the democratically elected governments of Fernando Belaunde Terry (1980–85) and Hernán Siles Suazo (1982–85).

2 The organic intellectuals

1 The IMF and the WB are distinct organizations with different goals and corporate cultures, which need to be acknowledged. In the 1980s and early 1990s, however, they worked increasingly together in the promotion of free market reforms. The Inter American Development Bank (IADB) also played an important role in the region over the period. It was often the outlier in its approach to reforms. The role of the IADB is not, however, a part of this chapter.

2 As the World Bank's documents put it, SALs became a fundamental instrument for the dialogue between the Bank and the recipient country on various aspects of development policy, and on the nature and scope of changes to be supported (World Bank 1988: 10).

3 As defined by Antonio Gramsci (1971) in his *Prison Notebooks*, organic intellectuals are particular strata of intellectuals that are con-

nected to the dominant social class and act both as their public intellectuals and organizers, helping the dominant sectors to develop a coherent world view and put it into practice. According to Gramsci, while traditional intellectuals were 'men of letters', organic intellectuals are mostly technocrats and professionals. Arguably in the 1990s the IMF and the World Bank played the role of organic intellectuals of Latin America's political and economic elite by spreading the free market ideas that became dominant throughout the region and promoting their implementation through financial assistance and the conditions attached to it.

4 The following narrative is based on Boughton (2001: 516–17, 694).

5 Perez's letter and Camdessus's response were published in IMF (1989: 82).

6 Established in 1960, the International Development Association is a World Bank institution that supports the development of the poorest countries with interest-free loans (credits), or grants.

7 The case of Bolivia prompted the setting up of a then pioneer Emergency Social Fund that supported a raft of small projects presented by communities and non-governmental organizations (NGOs). The Fund served as a model to similar projects elsewhere in Latin America that were the first initiatives to address the social costs of free market reforms.

8 The narrative for Mexico is taken from Woods (2006: 84–103).

9 World Bank/OED, Memorandum to the Executive Directors and the President, I, 2001 (cited in Woods 2006: 99).

10 The use of these terms is borrowed from remarks made by former US Defense Secretary Donald Rumsfeld at a Department of Defense news conference briefing in February 2002: 'There are known knowns. These are things we know that we know. There are known unknowns. That is to say, there are things that we know we don't know. But there are also unknown unknowns. There are things we don't know we don't know.'

11 For a critique of Pastor's findings, see Edwards (1989).

12 Some internal studies, however, reached more favourable conclusions as they compared economic performance within countries between periods with and without Fund-supported programmes (Boughton 2001: 615).

13 For a summary of the Fund's official position on its role in dealing with poverty, see Development Committee (1989, 1990).

14 For an overview of studies on the effect of conditionality in the 1970s and early 1980s that reached similar conclusions about the mixed record of conditionality and its limited power to influence policy trajectories, see Kahler (1992).

3 The ascent of free market economics

1 As defined by the *Oxford Dictionary of Economics*, rent-seeking is understood as spending time and money not on the production of real goods and services, but rather on trying to change the rules so as to make one's business more profitable. This can take various forms, including subsidies on the outputs or the inputs of business, ensuring monopolist or oligopolist privileges, or persuading the government to keep out competitors, etc.

2 *Patria contratista* and p*atria privatista* are popular expressions to signify the economic sector that benefited respectively from state contracts during the Import Substitution Industrialization phase and from state privatization during the 1990s in Argentina.

3 'Votação é última chance para negociação', *Folha de São Paulo*, 19 March 1998.

4 The parties were Paz Estenssoro's Movimiento Nacional Revolucionario (MNR), Hugo Banzer's Acción Democrática Nacionalista (MNR) and Jaime Paz Zamora's Movimiento de Izquierda Revolucionaria (MIR).

4 Democracy and its promises

1 The transition towards electoral politics included an armed group in Colombia, the M-19, which was incorporated into a peace process in the 1980s.

2 Surveys showed that the percentage of those who agreed that democracy was preferable to any kind of government declined from 61 per cent in 1996 to 53 per cent in 2004 (Latinobarómetro 2004).

3 In 1983, the government of President Alfonsín set up the Comisión Nacional sobre la Desaparición de Personas (CONADEP), led by Argentine writer Ernesto Sábato.

4 In Brazil, the Congress in 1979 had voted an amnesty law for crimes committed between 1964 and 1979 that was widely accepted in both civilian and military society as a mutual amnesty (Stepan 1988).

5 The mode of transition refers to the fact that, in Argentina, the military regime collapsed as a result of its defeat in the 1982 Falklands/Malvinas war. This left the military with less capacity to resist the newly elected government's determination to punish at least some of the officers involved in crimes against human rights. In contrast, in Brazil, Chile and Uruguay, transition was negotiated between the military and representatives of political parties, which allowed the military to impose explicit or implicit constraints to any attempt to bring to justice perpetrators of human rights abuses. For an analysis of the political implications of different modes of transition, see O'Donnell and Schmitter (1986).

6 Even in Argentina, the only nation at the time that prosecuted military officers for their responsibility in the 'dirty war', the quest for justice was truncated by the Punto Final ('Full Stop') and Obediencia Debida ('Due Obedience') laws of the late 1980s, which effectively ended prosecutions for human rights crimes. In October 1989, President Carlos Saúl Menem (1989–95; 1995–99) pardoned more than two hundred military officers accused of human rights abuses and aiding military rebellions, alleging that the move was essential for national reconciliation. The laws were repealed by Argentina's National Congress in August 2003, which allowed for the reopening of cases of alleged crimes against humanity.

7 In Portuguese this refers to the term *Novo Sindicalismo*, the independent trade union movement which emerged in Brazil in the 1970s.

5 Democracy and markets

1 According to O' Donnell's (1973) argument about the deepening of industrialization, in the 1970s the bureaucratic authoritarian state project required the political repres-

sion of an increasingly active and militant working class.

2 Institutionalized party systems can also be detrimental for democracy, however, by becoming *partidocracias*; that is, entrenched political machines that colonize the state and operate to serve the interests of the party elite and their captive constituencies with scant consideration for the general welfare of the population.

3 The trend, however, was not uniform, with Brazil and Mexico evolving towards the more stable party systems of Uruguay, Costa Rica and Chile, showing their resilience over time.

4 This does not mean that trade unionists, human rights activists and other social and political leaders were not subject any more to extrajudicial executions and other forms of human rights violations in many countries of the region, particularly in Colombia, Mexico and Brazil. But overall the level of violence and harassment against social leaders was much lower than during the years of military dictatorships. For a survey of human rights conditions by country, see www.amnesty.org/en/human-rights.

6 Paradigm lost

1 To back up this statement, the study constructed a structural policy index to measure the advances made by each country in five reform areas: trade, finance, taxes, privatization and labour. The index reflects the freedom that economic policies have granted the market in these areas. It concludes that according to the results of the index, 'structural reforms have made remarkable and sustained progress in the past decade', although 'the fact that the index

stands at 0.60 shows that there is still considerable room for improving the region's structural policies' (IADB 1997: 31).

2 In contrast, Bulmer-Thomas, on the basis of empirical evidence for the period up to the early 1990s, suggests that the results of the so-called New Economic Model were basically regressive in terms of income distribution (cited in Stallings and Peres 2000: 3).

3 This is true even of Chile, which maintained its copper industry within the state sector and implemented heterodox capital controls during the 1990s (Ffrench Davis 2004).

4 The term *dislocations* refers here to those social processes or events that cannot be represented or symbolized within a given interpretative framework, or to put it in slightly different terms, to processes or events (many of them condensed in statistical figures) that cannot be integrated into the dominant narrative of the time.

5 According to a number of studies the negative effects of trade liberalization and economic globalization on income distribution are not limited to Latin America but include developed and developing nations alike. Rodrik (1997) argues that globalization heightens the asymmetry existing between those groups that can most easily cross national borders (capital and skilled manpower) and those that cannot (low-skilled workers). The possibility of relocating production activities increases the elasticity of labour demand in all countries, thus diminishing workers' bargaining power and increasing the instability of labour income in the event of demand shocks.

6 For a full account of Argentina's political and economic crisis of the 1980s, see Chapter 1.

7 The report claims that whatever concerns the Fund had about the viability of the exchange-rate peg, particularly following the devaluation of the Brazilian real in early 1999, these were not raised with the authorities in deference to the country's prerogative to choose an exchange-rate regime to its own liking.

8 Developments leading up to the crisis of December 2002 showed that the IMF misread the economic problems of Argentina, interpreting as a liquidity problem what was in fact a solvency problem, and gave financial support to the country in spite of the continuous weak implementation of the economic programme agreed with the Argentinian economic authorities. Furthermore, the IMF's financial assistance continued in 2001 even after economy minister Cavallo adopted a series of controversial 'market shaking measures' without the consent of the Fund and even with the Fund's opposition (IMF 2004: 5). The disbursement of funds to Argentina continued for several months in 2001, even when there was an increasing recognition within the IMF that Argentina had an unsustainable debt profile, an unsustainable rate peg, or both. In the report's own words: 'To some extent this appears to have reflected the fact that some key decisions took place outside the Board and that some critical issues were judged by management to be too sensitive for open discussion in the full Board' (ibid.: 5).

9 Mr Lavagna contrasts the Fund's continuous financial assistance to Argentina in 2001, when the authorities implemented policies without the consent of the Fund, and even with its opposition, with the more recent experiences of 2002 and 2003, when the authorities were unable to persuade the Fund staff to support the government's economic programme, despite strong evidence that the policies were producing stable and sustainable growth.

7 The opening of a paradigm

1 For John Williamson's view of the perceived failures of the WC and his criticism of 'market fundamentalism', see Williamson (2003b).

2 After contrasting the successful economies of East Asia with the crisis of the welfare state in the industrial countries and the collapse of the command-and-control economies of the former Soviet Union and eastern Europe, the 1997 report remarks: 'This Report shows that the determining factor behind these contrasting developments is the effectiveness of the state. An effective state is vital for the provision of the goods and services – and the rules and institutions – that allow markets to flourish and people to lead healthier, happier lives. Without it, sustainable development, both economic and social, is impossible' (World Bank 1997: 1).

3 For the WB, however, the re-signification of the role of the state does not mean abandoning the free market agenda, but rather articulating free markets to broader social and political themes. The report restates traditional criticisms of monopoly public providers of infrastructure, social services and other goods and services, and suggests that, in order to better allocate scarce public capability, governments should contemplate separating

the financing of infrastructure and services from their delivery, and unbundling the competitive segments of utility markets from the monopoly segments. It also suggests that the state should be subject to more competition, and that, while people should be protected from economic insecurity and social hazards, the state alone must not carry the burden of helping people to cope with risks to their economic insecurity through pensions, health and unemployment insurance (ibid.: 4).

4 The Report promotes a three-way anti-poverty strategy, consisting of promoting material opportunities through economic growth and greater equity; facilitating empowerment; and enhancing security. The Bank sees markets and the state complementing each other in moving towards these ends: market reforms are central to expanding opportunities for the poor, but the reduction of inequality requires action by the state to support the build-up of human, land and infrastructure assets that poor people own or to which they have access. Among the policy inconstancies were: 'inflexible exchange rates not adequately supported by fiscal and structural openness', 'the mismatch between low trade openness and high capital account openness' and 'a weak and volatile macroeconomic environment' (World Bank 2000: 3).

5 Market-liberalizing recommendations include, among others: ensuring fiscal sustainability, improving banking regulation and supervision, greater trade opening, exchange rate flexibility and labour market reforms.

6 Paralleling the WB's 'hearts and minds' participatory agenda, IMF staff papers propose that Fund staff should seek to establish contacts with national congresses to encourage greater understanding of the Fund's policies, as well as contacts with civil society to ensure that the IFIs fully understand the issues facing a country and communicate effectively the logic behind their policies. The role of persuasion, listening and explanation in the building of consensus is to be complemented by internal and external incentives and anchors. Among the former are social safety nets to buy support from the losers of the reforms and a drive to reduce corruption to increase the legitimacy of the reforms. Among the latter are international agreements, such as the North American Free Trade Agreement (NAFTA), that act as catalysts for institutional change by breaking through domestic impediments to reform (Singh 2004; Singh et al. 2005).

7 According to the WB, good governance includes the creation, protection and enforcement of property rights, the provision of a regulatory regime that works with the market to promote competition, sound macroeconomic policies that create a stable environment for market activity, and the absence of corruption, which can subvert the goals of policy and undermine the legitimacy of the public institutions that support markets (World Bank 2002: 99).

8 Tensions between the WB's 'Washington Consensus' objective of fiscal adjustment and the 'post-Washington Consensus' goal of institution-building may also explain the high rate of failure of the WB's sponsored civil service reforms programmes of the late 1990s. As

Notes

Flavio da Cunha Rezende (2001) argues, fiscal adjustments in the context of low productivity require stronger financial and human resources controls over the bureaucracy. In contrast, reforming the civil service requires the loosening of *ex ante* financial controls and the introduction of performance targets and other autonomy-enhancing devices. State agencies that assign a higher priority to fiscal adjustment, such as the ministry of the economy, fear that more autonomous agencies could weaken their control over the allocations of financial and human resources, thus jeopardizing the goal of fiscal adjustment, while strategic actors in the agencies to be reformed fear the loss of privileges based on their traditional status as a public sector organization and the financial uncertainties associated with the agencies' exposure to competition. Within these rules of the game, actors in the agencies to be reformed tend to strategically choose to collaborate with the fiscal adjustment, while maintaining the institutional status quo.

9 'There is, in fact, no single model of economic management that would guarantee macro-economic stability, nor is there one and only one way of integrating into the international economy or of combining the efforts of the public and private sectors' (ECLAC 2001b: 11).

10 'Initial differences in opportunities are perpetuated down through the generations in a vicious circle that reproduces inequality and undermines growth. Once we begin to think of inequality as an obstacle to growth, the trade-off between purely macroeconomic policies and social policies disappears; spending on health and education then ceases to be the nightmare of finance ministers concerned with balancing the budget and instead takes its rightful place as core component of development strategy' (Machinea and Kacef 2007: 8).

11 For more details of ECLAC's policy agenda, see ECLAC (2001b: ch. III).

8 The rise of the left

1 Only in Uruguay, Guatemala and Chile do citizens position themselves left of the centre.

2 Latinobarómetro asked respondents to position themselves in a 0–10 left–right scale in which '0' represented the extreme left and '10' the extreme right. The region's average in 2007 was 5.3; the average of Venezuela was also 5.3 and that of Bolivia 5.2. The most left-leaning electorate was that of Guatemala, with an average of 4.6.

3 See www.socialistinternational. org/viewArticle.cfm?ArticlePageID =927 (last accessed 22 July 2008).

4 That populism is a matter of attribution rather than of self-identification has much to do with the fact that, at least in the common use of the term, populism has a negative normative bias, as it is used as synonymous with demagogy, personalism and following public opinion rather than political principles.

5 Another traditional force of the left has been the armed organizations. It is only in Colombia, and to a much lesser extent in Mexico, however, that armed left movements of any significance are still operative: the Fuerzas Armadas Revolucionarias (FARC) in Colombia and the Frente Zapatista de Liberación Nacional (FZLN) in Mexico; and although they

are significant actors in their countries their regional appeal is limited and I will not look at them in any detail in this chapter.

6 Partido Nacionalista Peruano (2006).

7 Quoted in Costa Benavides (2003).

8 The significance of the government–opposition cleavage to understanding political change in Latin America in the early twenty-first century is confirmed by the correlation between the economic upturn experienced by the region since 2003 and the high proportion of re-elections of presidents and parties in office during the period. Six out of the eleven presidential elections that took place between November 2005 and December 2006 were won by candidates who were submitting themselves for immediate or alternate re-election, and in another (Mexico, in which re-election is not constitutionally allowed), the winner was the candidate of the incumbent party, the Partido de Acción Nacional (PAN). Re-elected presidents, representing political forces of both the centre-left and the centre-right, now govern 40 per cent of the countries of the region (Latinobarómetro 2007).

9 The highly contested and politically loaded meaning of populism is exemplified by the discussions about whether President Chávez can be characterized as 'populist'. Based on an empirical study of grassroots organizations and everyday politics in Venezuela, Sara Motta denies that Chávez is in any way a populist and argues instead that new grassroots forms of organizing power and authority have broken with traditions of Venezuelan politics, of both the left and the right, in which leader-

ship, political lines and political hierarchy were dominant (Motta 2007b: 30–35). Ernesto Laclau (2006: 60), however, who is also sympathetic to Chávismo, believes that the Chávez phenomenon bears all the marks of a populist rupture and that this rupture is positive for the advancement of democracy in the country. For a discussion of Chávez and the populist tradition in Venezuela, see also Buxton (2005).

10 Corporatism has been defined (Schmitter 1974: 93-4) as: 'A system of interest representation in which the constituent units are organized into a limited number of singular, compulsory, noncompetitive, hierarchically ordered and functionally differentiated categories, recognized or licensed (if not created) by the state and granted a deliberate representational monopoly within their respective categories in exchange for observing certain controls on their selection of leaders and articulation of demands and support.'

11 Corporatism can be of a statist or of a societal type. The first one is characteristic of authoritarian states in which the state controls corporatist association through a mixture of repression and co-optation, as was the case in the national-popular, populist Latin American regimes of the 1950s, such as those of Peronismo and Varguismo in Argentina and Brazil and the Partido Revolucionario Institutional (PRI) in Mexico between the 1940s and the 1990s, while the second characterized the social democratic welfare states of northern Europe and Scandinavia in the 1960s and 1970s (Collier and Berins Collier 1998; Schmitter 1974).

12 Kirchner obtained 22 per

cent of the votes in the first-round election which was narrowly won by Carlos Menem with 24 per cent. According to the electoral law the two candidates should have gone to a run-off vote, but facing almost certain defeat, Menem withdrew his candidacy and Kirchner won the election by default.

9 Left governments and democracy

1 Chávez campaigned against neoliberalism although arguably neoliberal reforms were very limited after the failure of President Pérez's shock reform attempt (see Chapter 2).

2 The two notions of civil society described here are very similar to Foley and Edwards's (1996) distinction between 'civil society I' and 'civil society II'.

3 The best analysis of the politics of the crowd in the populist tradition is Laclau (2005b: chs 2 and 3).

4 Constitution of the Bolivarian Republic of Venezuela (1999: Article 6).

5 Article 70: Participation and involvement of people in the exercise of their sovereignty in political affairs can be manifested by: voting to fill public offices, referendum, consultation of public opinion, mandate revocation, legislative, constitutional and constituent initiative, open forums and meetings of citizens whose decisions shall be binding among others; and in social and economic affairs: citizen service organs, self-management, co-management, cooperatives in all forms, including those of a financial nature, savings funds, community enterprises, and other forms of association guided by the values of mutual cooperation and solidarity.

6 This third element was evident, for instance, in the 2006 electoral campaign in which President Chávez claimed that there were only two candidates, himself and President Bush, whom he labelled 'Mr Devil', arguing that a vote for the opposition was a vote for Bush.

7 Hansen and Hawkins's (2006: 104) empirical study of the *Círculos* concluded that they did not conform to either of the two stereotypes. On the one hand, members of the *Círculos* generally did not advocate violence and had a high level of democratic values. They were also involved in a variety of significant efforts to reach into Venezuelan shanty towns, with government programmes and principles of democratic organization. On the other hand, the study found that the *Círculos* failed to herald a new form of participatory democracy. The *Círculos* studied by the authors lacked one of the most fundamental attributes of a civil society capable of sustaining participatory democracy: autonomy from the state. In addition, through their uncritical acceptance of government aid programmes, members of the Circles participated in a system with strong clientelistic overtones that undermined the principle of citizenship essential to democracy.

8 In November 2000, the National Assembly granted President Chávez sweeping powers to issue decree laws in a wide range of areas. The president used these powers to pass forty-nine reform laws, including land and oil industry reforms. Following his victory in the presidential election of December 2006, in January 2007 the National Assembly granted President Chávez sweeping powers to rule by decree for the next eighteen months.

9 *El Nacional*, 3 November 2006, and aporrea.org, cited in López-Maya and Lander (2006).

10 A case in point is the alleged use of the list of those who had signed the petition to hold a recall referendum against President Chávez in 2004 to bar them from public employment and other state benefits. Another example of legal harassment of the opposition is the barring of opposition candidates under allegations of corruption from contesting regional elections in November 2007, even if the candidates had not been convicted in court. Article 65 of the Venezuelan constitution states that only persons that have been found guilty of crimes committed in the exercise of their public duties are banned from running for office. The banning of the candidates was decided by the Contraloría General de la República (the Comptroller General of the Republic) and ratified by the Tribunal Supremo de Justicia (TSJ, the Supreme Tribunal of Justice), both controlled by Chavistas (*Folha de São Paulo*, 12 August 2008).

11 As Paiva (2006: 210–11) points out, there is also a question of legitimacy of the system of representation employed in the building of the CDES. Whereas its members are drawn from the ranks of the elite, the majority of the population is made up of poor people, self-employed workers and members of the informal economy with no access to the representatives of civil society. Second, class-based representatives, by their very definition, are bent on defending the interests of their constituencies. Since some segments of society remain unrepresented, the CDES cannot ensure that its decisions reflect the demands of absent segments.

10 Left governments, constraints and choices

1 In spite of the improvement in economic and social conditions, however, fundamental problems remain. The countries of Latin America are still heavily dependent on foreign investment and levels of social and economic inequality are still extremely high. The quality of education remains poor and markedly segregated in terms of the social sectors that benefit from the best schools. Despite the greater effort being made to finance social policies (especially in the less developed nations), public social spending is still insufficient to address the populations' changing needs (ECLAC 2007a).

2 See www.resdal.org/ultimos-documentos/consenso-bsas.html (last accessed 26 August 2008).

3 Early in 2002, several financial institutions expressed their concerns by refusing to purchase federal securities maturing after 31 December (the last day of Cardoso's presidency). The weekly open market federal security auctions became largely fruitless, as the brokers demanded ever increasing interest rates to roll over the government debt. If these rates were not forthcoming, the brokers liquidated their positions and shifted funds to the dollar market, so devaluing the real. At the same time, their international partners downgraded Brazilian bonds and foreign debt certificates, allegedly because of the perceived lack of policy credibility in the country (Mollo and Saad Filho 2006: 112).

4 *Folha de São Paulo*, 'Sombra no Planalto. Cúpula do PT cobra mudança noa política econômica de Lula', 6 March 2006, available at

www.folha.uol.com.br/ (last accessed 26 August 2008).

5 *Folha de São Paulo*, 'Leia a íntegra da nota divulgada ontem pelo PT', 6 March 2004, available at www.folha.uol.com.br/ (last accessed 26 August 2008). There were also reports of clashes within the administration between the neo-developmentalist sectors represented by planning minister Guido Mantega and the president of the Banco Nacional de Desenvolvimento Econômico e Social (BNDES, the economic and social development bank), Carlos Lessa, and the orthodox wing headed by finance minister Antônio Palocci Filho and the president of the Central Bank, Henrique Meirelles.

6 See *Folha de São Paulo*, 'Nova tele terá forte presence do governo', 20 July 2008, available at www.folha.uol.com.br/ (last accessed 26 August 2008).

7 See *Folha de São Paulo*, 'Governo teme força excessiva da Petrobras', 10 August 2008; *Folha de São Paulo*, 'Governo deixará no exterior parte dos recursos de óleo do pré-sal, diz Mantega', 21 August 2008, available at www.folha.uol.com.br/ (last accessed 26 August 2008).

8 See, for instance, *Folha de São Paulo*, 'Para Lula, modelo perverso vigorou até 2002', 14 January 2004; *Folha de São Paulo*, 'Era impossível manter discurso', 24 January 2004; *Folha de São Paulo*, 'Para Mantega, governo não deve ser neoliberal', 20 July 2004; *Folha de São Paulo*, 'Para Tarso, ver gestão Lula igual à FHC é "má-fé"', 12 November 2004, available at www.folha.uol.com.br/ (last accessed 26 August 2008).

9 Brazil, Russia, India and China.

10 See www.pisa.oecd.org (last accessed 4 September 2008).

11 *Folha de São Paulo*, 'Verba de Kirchner dissolves "piqueteiros"', 26 October 2007, available at www.folha.uol.com.br/ (last accessed 26 August 2008).

Bibliography

Abranches, S. H. (1990) 'Strangers in a common land: executive/legislative relations in Brazil', in S. Marks (ed.), *Political Constraints on Brazil's Economic Growth*, New Brunswick, NJ, and London: Transaction Publishers, pp. 105–29.

Abugattas, L. A. (1987) 'Populism and after: the Peruvian experience', in J. M. Malloy and M. A. Seligson (eds), *Authoritarians and Democrats: Regime Transition in Latin America*, Pittsburgh, PA: University of Pittsburgh Press, pp. 121–43.

Abugattas, L. A. and E. Paus (2007) 'Policy space for a new development strategy for Latin America', Paper prepared for delivery at the 2007 Congress of the Latin American Studies Association, Montreal, Canada, 5–8 September.

Acuña, C. H. (1994) 'Politics and economics in the Argentina of the nineties (or, why the future no longer is what it used to be)', in W. C. Smith, C. H. Acuña and E. A. Gamarra (eds), *Democracy, Markets and Structural Reform in Contemporary Latin America: Argentina, Bolivia, Brazil, Chile and Mexico*, New Brunswick, NJ: Transaction Publishers, pp. 31–74.

Acuña, C. H. and W. C. Smith (1994) 'The political economy of structural adjustment: the logic of support and opposition to neoliberal reform', in W. C. Smith, C. H. Acuña and E. A. Gamarra (eds), *Latin America's Political Economy in the Age of Neoliberal Reform*, New Brunswick, NJ, and London: Transaction Publishers, pp. 17–66.

Acuña, C. H. and C. Smulovitz (1996) 'Adjusting the armed forces to democracy: successes, failures and ambiguities in the Southern Cone', in E. Jelin and E. Hershbergh (eds), *Constructing Democracy: Human Rights, Citizenship and Society in Latin America*, Boulder, CO: Westview Press, pp. 13–38.

Agüero, F. (1998) 'Conflicting assessments of democratization: exploring the fault lines?', in F. Agüero and J. Stark (eds), *Fault Lines of Democracy in Post-Transition Latin America*, Coral Gables, FL: North-South Centre, pp. 1–20.

Ahnen, R. (2003) 'Between tyranny of the majority and liberty: persistence of human rights violations under democracy in Brazil', *Bulletin of Latin American Research*, 22(3): 319–39.

Altman, D. and A. Pérez-Liñan (2001) *Assessing the Quality of Democracy: Freedom, Competitiveness and Participation in 18 Latin American Countries*, available at: www.nd.edu/~daltman/Democratization.htm (last accessed 10 August 2007).

Álvarez, A. E. (2006) 'Social cleavages, political polarization and democratic breakdown in Venezuela', *Stockholm Review of Latin American Studies*, 1 (November), pp. 18–28.

Bibliography

Aman, E. and W. Baer (2007) 'The macroeconomic record of the Lula administration, the roots of Brazil's inequality and attempts to overcome them', Paper prepared for delivery at the 2007 Congress of the Latin American Studies Association, Montreal, Canada, 5–8 September.

Anderson, B. (1996) *Imagined Communities*, London: Verso.

Andrews, G. (1992) 'Racial inequality in Brazil and the United States: a statistical comparison', *Journal of Social History*, 26(2): 229–63.

Angell, A. (1993) 'Chile since 1958', in L. Bethell (ed.), *Chile since Independence*, Cambridge: Cambridge University Press, pp. 129–202.

— (1996) 'Incorporating the left into democratic politics', in J. Dominguez and A. Lowenthal (eds), *Constructing Democratic Governance*, Baltimore, MD: Johns Hopkins University Press, pp. 3–25.

Arce, M. (2006) 'The societal consequences of market reforms in Peru', *Latin American Politics and Society*, 48(1): 27–54.

Arditi, B. (2003) 'Talkin' 'bout a revolution: the end of mourning', *Parallax*, 9(2): 91–5.

— (2008) 'Arguments about the left turns in Latin America: a post-liberal politics?', *Latin American Research Review*, 43(3): 59–81.

Armijo, L. E. and P. Faucher (2002) '"We have a consensus": explaining political support for market reforms in Latin America', *Latin American Politics and Society*, 44(2): 1–40.

Baiocchi, G. (2003) 'Activism, civil society and politics: the Porto Alegre experiment in empowered governance', in F. Fung and E. O. Wright (eds), *Deepening Democracy. Institutional Innovations in Empowered Participatory Democracy*, London: Verso, pp. 45–76.

Baiocchi, G. and S. Checa (2007) 'The Brazilian Workers' Party: from local practices to national power', *Working USA*, 10(4): 411–30.

Baloyra, E. A. (1986) 'From moment to moment: the political transition in Brazil 1977–1981', in W. A. Selcher (ed.), *Political Liberalisation in Brazil: Dynamics, Dilemmas and Future Prospects*, Boulder, CO, and London: Westview Press, pp. 9–53.

Barahona de Brito, A. (1997) *Human Rights and Democratization in Latin America: Uruguay and Chile*, Oxford: Oxford University Press.

Barragán, E. and A. Roemer (2001) *A New Public Management in Mexico: Towards a Government that Produces Results*, Aldershot: Ashgate.

Barros, S. (2002) *Orden, Democracia y Estabilidad. Discurso político en la Argentina entre 1976 y 1991*, Cordoba: Alianza Editora.

Bartelli, E. J and L. A. Payne (1995) *Business and Democracy in Latin America*, Pittsburgh, PA: Pittsburgh University Press.

Bates, R. H. (1994) 'Comment', in J. Williamson (ed.), *The Political Economy of Policy Reform*, Washington, DC: Institute for International Economics, pp. 29–34.

Becker, M. (2008) 'Pachakutik and indigenous political party politics in Ecuador', in R. Stahler-Sholk, H. E. Vanden and G. D. Kuecker (eds), *Latin American Social Movements in the Twenty-first Century. Resistance, Power and Democracy*, Lanham, MD: Rowman and Littlefield, pp. 165–80.

Berins Collier, R. and J. Mahoney (1997) 'Adding collective actors to collective outcomes: labor and recent democratization in South America and southern Europe', *Comparative Politics*, 29(3): 285–303.

Berry, A. (1997) 'The income distribution threat in Latin America', *Latin American Research Review*, 32(2): 3–40.

Bethell, L. and I. Roxborough (eds) (1992), *Latin America between the Second World War and the Cold War*, Cambridge and New York: Cambridge University Press.

Bevir, M. (2005) *New Labour: A Critique*, Abingdon: Routledge.

Blake, C. H. (1998) 'Economic reform and democratisation in Argentina and Uruguay: the tortoise and the hare revisited?', *Journal of Interamerican Studies and World Affairs*, 40(3): 1–26.

Bøås, M. and D. McNeill (2003) *Multilateral Institutions: A Critical Introduction*, London: Pluto Press.

Bobbio, N. (1994) *Destra e Sinistra: Ragioni e significati di una distinzione politica*, Rome: Saggine.

Borzutzky, S. (1987) 'The Pinochet regime: crisis and consolidation', in J. M. Malloy and M. A. Seligson (eds), *Authoritarians and Democrats: Regime Transition in Latin America*, Pittsburgh, PA: University of Pittsburgh Press, pp. 67–92.

Boughton, J. M. (2001) *Silent Revolution. The International Monetary Fund 1979–1989*, Washington, DC: International Monetary Fund.

Branford, S. (2002) *Cutting the Wire: The Story of the Landless Movement in Brazil*, London: Latin American Bureau.

Branford, S. and B. Kucinski (2003) *Policies Transformed: Lula and the Workers' Party in Brazil*, London: Latin American Bureau.

Bresser Pereira, L. C. (2007) 'Estado y mercado en el nuevo desarrollismo', *Nueva Sociedad*, 207 (July/August), pp. 110–25.

Bruhn, K. (1997) *Taking on Goliath: The Emergence of a New Left Party and the Struggle for Democracy in Mexico*, University Park: Pennsylvania State University Press.

Brysk, A. (1994) *The Politics of Human Rights in Argentina: Protest, Change and Democratization*, Stanford, CA: Stanford University Press.

Buckingham, L. (2004) 'Contesting the Post-Washington Consensus in Latin America', MSc dissertation, Department of Government, London School of Economics and Political Science, London.

Buquet, D. (2008) 'El irresistible ascenso de la izquierda al gobierno uruguayo', in C. Moreira, D. Raus and J. C. Gómez Leyton (eds), *La Nueva Política en América Latina. Ruptura y Continuidades*, Montevideo: Editorial Trilce, pp. 251–72.

Burton, G. (2008) 'Social democracy in Latin America: policymakers and educational reform in Brazil and Chile', PhD thesis, Department of Government, London School of Economics and Political Science, London.

Bustos, P. (1995) 'Introducción', in P. Bustos (ed.), *Más allá de la estabilidad. Argentina en la época de la globalización y la regionalización*, Buenos Aires: Fundación Friedrich Ebert.

Buxton J. (2005) 'Venezuela's contemporary political crisis in historical context', *Bulletin of Latin American Research*, 24(3): 328–47.

Camdessus, M. (1993) *IMF Survey*, Washington, DC: International Monetary Fund, 22 February.

— (1998) 'The IMF and good governance', Address by Michel Camdessus, managing director of the International Monetary Fund, at Transparency International, Paris, France, 21 January, available at: www.imf.org/external/np/speeches/1998/012198.htm (last accessed 22 July 2008).

Cammack, P. (1986) 'Resurgent democracy: threat and promise', *New Left Review*, 157 (May/June), pp. 121–8.

— (2001) 'Book review of Gerald M. Meier and Joseph E. Stiglitz (eds), *Frontiers of Development Economics*', *Development in Practice*, 12(5): 661–2.

Camou, A. (1997) 'De como las ideas tienen consecuencias: redes de expertise y reforma económica en la Argentina democrática', Paper prepared for delivery at the XX International Congress of the Latin American Studies Association, Guadalajara, Mexico, 17–19 April.

Campbell, J. L. (2001) 'Institutional analysis and the role of ideas in political economy', in J. L. Campbell and O. K. Pedersen (eds), *The Rise of Neoliberalism and Institutional Analysis*, Princeton, NJ: Princeton University Press, pp. 159–90.

Carraro, A., A. F. Araújo Jr, O. M. Damé, L. M. Monasterio and C. D. Shikida (2007) '"É a economia, companheiro!": uma análise empírica da reeleição de Lula com base em dados municipais', MG Working Paper 41, Minas Gerais: Ibemec.

Carrión, J. F. (2007) 'Authoritarianism and democracy in the Andes. State weakness, hybrid regimes and societal responses', *Latin American Research Review*, 43(3): 223–34.

Castañeda, J. (1993) *Utopia Unarmed: The Latin American Left after the Cold War*, New York: Knopf.

— (2006a) 'Latin America's left turn', *Foreign Affairs*, 85(3): 28–43.

— (2006b) 'Is Evo Morales an indigenous Che?', *New Perspectives Quarterly*, 23(2): 58–60.

Cavarozzi, M. (1992) 'Beyond transitions to democracy', *Journal of Latin American Studies*, 24(3): 665–84.

— (1993) 'La izquierda en América del Sur: la política como única opción', in M. Vellinga (ed.), *Democracia y Política en América Latina*, Mexico: Siglo XXI, pp. 209–30.

— (1997) *Autoritarismo y democracia (1995–1996): la transición del estado al mercado en la Argentina*, Buenos Aires: Ariel.

— (2004) 'Cómo una democracia de libro de texto desembocó en un régimen de partido único ... es el peronismo, estúpido', *Revista Política*, 42, Autumn, pp. 207–20.

CEPAL (1990) 'Balance preliminar de la economía de América Latina y el Caribe 1990', *Notas sobre la economía y el desarrollo 500/501 (diciembre)*, Santiago: Comisión Económica para América Latina, pp. 1–57.

Chalmers, D. (1977) 'The politicised state in Latin America', in J. M. Malloy (ed.), *Authoritarianism and Corporatism in Latin America*, Pittsburgh, PA: University of Pittsburgh Press, pp. 23–45.

Chang, H. J. (2005) 'Kicking away the ladder: "good policies" and "good institutions" in historical perspective', in K. P. Gallagher (ed.), *Putting Development First. The Importance of Policy Space in the WTO and International Financial Institutions*, London and New York: Zed Books, pp. 102–25.

Chávez, D. and B. Franklin (2004) *The Left in the City: Participatory Local Governments in Latin America*, London: Latin America Bureau.

Chilcote, R. H. (1993) 'Left political ideology and practice', in B. Carr and S. Ellner (eds), *The Latin American Left, from the Fall of Allende to Perestroika*, Boulder, CO: Westview Press, pp. 171–86.

Cleary, M. R. (2006) 'A "left turn" in Latin America? Explaining the left's resurgence', *Journal of Democracy*, 17(4): 35–49.

Cleaves, P. S. and C. J. Stephens (1991) 'Businessmen and economic policy in Mexico', *Latin American Research Review*, 26(2): 187–202.

Close, D. and K. Deonandan (eds) (2004) *Undoing Democracy: The Politics of Electoral Caudillismo*, Lanham, MD: Lexington Books.

Cohen, J. N. and M. A. Centeno (2006) 'Neoliberalism and patterns of economic performance, 1980–2000', *Annals of the American Academy of Political and Social Science*, 606(1): 32–67.

Collier, D. and R. Berins Collier (1998) 'Quien hace qué, a quien y cómo. Hacia un análisis comparativo del corporativismo latinoamericano', in J. Lanzaro (ed.), *El fin del siglo del corporativismo*, Caracas: Nueva Sociedad, pp. 169–92.

Collier, D. and S. Levitsky (1997) 'Democracy "with adjectives": finding conceptual order in recent comparative research', *World Politics*, 49(3): 430–51.

Conaghan, C. M., J. M. Malloy and L. Abugattas (1990) 'Business and the "boys": the politics of neoliberalism in the central Andes', *Latin American Research Review*, 29(2): 3–29.

Connolly, W. E. (1983) *The Terms of Political Discourse*, Oxford: Blackwell.

Constitution of the Boliviarian Republic of Venezuela (1999) Available at: www.analitica. com/bitblioteca/venezuela/ constitucion_ingles.pdf (last accessed 22 July 2008).

Conway, P. (1992) 'Debt and adjustment', *Latin American Research Review*, 27(2): 151–79.

Cook, M. L. (2002) 'Labor reform and dual transitions in Brazil and the Southern Cone', *Latin American Politics and Society*, 44(1): 1–34.

Coppedge, M. (2005) 'Explaining democratic deterioration in Venezuela through nested inference', in F. Hagopian and S. Mainwaring (eds), *The Third Wave of Democratization in Latin America*, Cambridge: Cambridge University Press, pp. 289–316.

Cornwall, A. and K. Brock (2005) 'What do buzzwords do for development policy? A critical look at "participation", "empowerment" and "poverty reduction"', *Third World Quarterly*, 26(7): 1043–60.

Corrales, J. (2002) *Presidents without Parties. The Politics of Economic Reform in Argentina and Venezuela in the 1990s*, University Park: Pennsylvania University Press.

Costa Benavides, J. (2003) 'La guerra del gas en Bolivia. Representaciones sobre el neoliberalismo y el rol del estado en la defensa de los recursos naturales en la crisis de octubre de 2003', in D. Matto (ed.), *Políticas de economía, ambiente y sociedad en tiempos de globalización*, Caracas: Facultad de Ciencias Económicas y Sociales, Universidad Católica de Venezuela, pp. 233–51.

Couto, C. G. and P. Baia (2006) 'Lula's administration: the limits of change', Paper prepared to be delivered at the 2006 meeting of the Latin American Studies Association, San Juan, Puerto Rico, 15–18 March.

Crabtree, J. (1998) 'Neo-populism and the Fujimori phenomenon', in J. Crabtree and J. Thomas (eds), *Fujimori's Peru: The Political Economy*, London: Institute of Latin American Studies, pp. 7–23.

— (2005) *Patterns of Protest: Politics and Social Movements in Bolivia*, London: Latin America Bureau.

Crabtree, J. and J. Thomas (eds) (1998), *Fujimori's Peru: The Political Economy*, London: Institute of Latin American Studies.

Cyr, J. (2006) 'The political party system and democratic crisis in Bolivia', Paper prepared for presentation at the Latin American Studies Association (LASA) Conference, San Juan, Puerto Rico, 16 March.

Da Cunha Rezende, F. (2001) 'Entre ajuste fiscal e mudança institucional: por que reformas administrativas falham?', Paper submitted to the Seminário Internacional de Ciencia Política, Porto Alegre, Brazil, October.

Da Silva, L. I. L. (2002) 'Carta ao povo brasileiro', Partido dos Trabalhadores, Dirétorio Nacional, 22 June, available at: 200.205.248.99/site/jornalismo/openew.

asp?IDNews=12822&TPNews=3 (last accessed 5 October 2008).

Dahl, R. (1971) *Polyarchy, Participation and Opposition*, New Haven, CT: Yale University Press.

Daseking, C., A. Ghosh, T. Lane and A. Thomas (2004) 'Lessons from the crisis in Argentina', Occasional Paper 236, Washington, DC: International Monetary Fund.

De Ipola, E. and J. C. Portantiero (1989) 'Lo nacional popular y los populismos realmente existentes', in *Investigaciones Políticas*, Buenos Aires: Nueva Visión.

De La Torre, C. (1997) 'Populism and democracy: political discourses and cultures in contemporary Ecuador', *Latin American Perspectives*, 24(3): 12–24.

De Soto, H., E. Ghersi and M. Ghibellini (1986) *El Otro Sendero*, Lima: Editorial El Barranco.

— (1989 [1986]) *The Other Path*, New York: Harper and Row.

Development Committee (1989) 'Strengthening efforts to reduce poverty', Development Committee Pamphlet no. 19, Joint Ministerial Committee of the Boards of Governors of the World Bank and the International Monetary Fund, Washington, DC.

— (1990) 'Development issues, presentations to the 39th meeting of the Development Committee', Development Committee Pamphlet no. 26, Joint Ministerial Committee of the Boards of Governors of the World Bank and the International Monetary Fund, Washington, DC.

Di John, J. (2004) 'The political economy of economic liberalization in Venezuela', Working Paper no. 46, Crisis States Programme:

Development Research Centre, London School of Economics and Political Science, London.

Di Palma, G. (1990) *To Craft Democracies: An Essay on Democratic Transition*, Berkeley: University of California Press.

Dornbusch, R. and S. Edwards (eds) (1991) *The Macroeconomics of Populism in Latin America*, Chicago, IL: University of Chicago Press.

Dowding, K. (2006) 'Three-dimensional power: a discussion of Steven Lukes' "Power a radical view"', *Political Studies Review*, 4: 136–45.

Drake, P. W. (1991) 'Comment to R. Kaufman and B. Stallings', in R. Dornbusch and S. Edwards (eds), *The Macroeconomics of Populism in Latin America*, Chicago, IL: University of Chicago Press, pp. 35–40.

Dunkerley, J. (1984) *Rebellion in the Veins: Political Struggle in Bolivia 1952–82*, London: Verso.

Eckstein, S. (ed.) (1989) *Power and Popular Protest. Latin American Social Movements*, Berkeley: University of California Press.

ECLAC (1989) *Economic Survey of Latin America and the Caribbean 1988–1989*, United Nations Economic Commission for Latin America and the Caribbean, Santiago, Chile.

— (1995) *Economic Survey of Latin America and the Caribbean 1994–1995*, United Nations Economic Commission for Latin America and the Caribbean, Santiago, Chile.

— (1996) *Social Panorama of Latin America*, United Nations Economic Commission for Latin America and the Caribbean, Santiago, Chile.

— (1997) *Social Panorama of Latin America*, United Nations Economic Commission for Latin America and the Caribbean, Santiago, Chile.

— (1998) *Social Panorama of Latin America*, United Nations Economic Commission for Latin America and the Caribbean, Santiago, Chile.

— (2001a) *Preliminary Overview of the Economies of Latin America and the Caribbean 2001*, United Nations Economic Commission for Latin America and the Caribbean, Santiago, Chile.

— (2001b) *Equity, Development and Citizenship*, United Nations Economic Commission for Latin America and the Caribbean, Santiago, Chile.

— (2002) *Social Panorama of Latin America*, United Nations Economic Commission for Latin America and the Caribbean, Santiago, Chile.

— (2007a) *Preliminary Overview of the Economies of Latin America and the Caribbean 2007*, United Nations Economic Commission for Latin America and the Caribbean, Santiago, Chile.

— (2007b) *Social Panorama of Latin America 2007*, United Nations Economic Commission for Latin America and the Caribbean, Santiago, Chile.

— (2008a) *Economic Survey of Latin America and the Caribbean 2007–2008*, United Nations Economic Commission for Latin America and the Caribbean, Santiago, Chile.

— (2008b) *Statistical Yearbook for Latin America and the Caribbean 2007*, United Nations Economic Commission for Latin America and the Caribbean, Santiago, Chile.

Economist (2008) 'Economics and the rule of law. Order in the jungle', Opinion, 13 March, available at: www.economist.com (last accessed 22 July 2008).

Economist Intelligence Unit (2008a) 'Brazil economy: tightening times', Country Briefing, 15 September, available at: viewswire. eiu.com (last accessed 22 September 2008).

— (2008b) 'Country Report: Argentina (September)', London: Economist Intelligence Unit.

— (2008c) *Venezuela. Country Profile 2008*, London: Economist Intelligence Unit.

Edwards, S. (1989) 'Review essay: the debt crisis and economic adjustment in Latin America', *Latin America Research Review*, 24(3): 172–86.

— (1995) *Crisis and Reform in Latin America. From Despair to Hope*, Washington, DC: World Bank and Oxford University Press.

— (1997) 'Latin America's underperfomance', *Foreign Affairs*, 76(2): 93–103.

— (1999) 'Latin America at the end of the century: more of the same?', Paper presented at the University of California, Los Angeles, 6 September, available at: www.anderson.ucla.edu/ faculty/sebastian.edwards/papers. htm (last accessed 14 July 2006).

Ellner, S. (1993) 'The changing status of the Latin American left in the recent past', in B. Carr and S. Ellner (eds), *The Latin American Left, from the Fall of Allende to Perestroika*, Boulder, CO: Westview Press, pp. 1–21.

— (2007a) 'Politics, protagonism,

and popular accountability in Venezuela', Oral presentation delivered at the meeting of the Latin American Studies Association, Montreal, Canada, 5–8 September.

— (2007b) 'The Movimiento Quinta República (MVR) and the Chavista rank and file', Paper prepared for delivery at the meeting of the Latin American Studies Association, Montreal, Canada, 5–8 September.

Ellner, S. and D. Hellinger (2003) *Venezuelan Politics in the Chávez Era: Class, Polarization, and Conflict*, Boulder, CO: Lynne Rienner.

Ellner, S. and M. Tinker Salas (eds) (2007) *Venezuela, Hugo Chávez and the Decline of an Exceptional Democracy*, Lanham, MD: Rowman and Littlefield.

Enríquez, M. R. (1988) 'The rise and collapse of stabilising development', in G. Philip (ed.), *The Mexican Economy*, London: Routledge, pp. 7–33.

Escobar, A. and S. E. Alvarez (eds) (1992) *The Making of Social Movements in Latin America: Identity, Strategy and Democracy*, Boulder, CO: Westview Press.

Estévez-López, A. (2006) 'Articulating collective action against free trade in Mexico: a human rights discourse approach', PhD thesis, University of Sussex, Brighton.

Etchemendy, S. and V. Palermo (1997) 'Conflicto y concertación. Gobierno, Congreso y organizaciones de interés en la reforma laboral del primer gobierno de Menem', Working Paper no. 41, Universidad Torcuato di Tella, Buenos Aires.

Faoro, R. (1958) *Os donos do poder. Formação do patronato político brasileiro*, Porto Alegre: Editôra Globo.

Feinberg, R., C. H. Waisman and L. Zamosc (eds) (2006) *Civil Society and Democracy in Latin America*, New York and Basingtoke: Palgrave Macmillan.

Feldstein, M. (2002) 'Argentina's fall: lessons from the latest financial crisis', *Foreign Affairs*, 81(1): 8–14.

Ffrench Davis, R. (2004) *Entre el neoliberalismo y el crecimiento con equidad: tres décadas de política económica en Chile*, Buenos Aires: Fundación OSDE-Siglo Veintiuno Editores.

— (ed.) (2006) *Seeking Growth under Financial Volatility*, Basingstoke: Palgrave Macmillan.

Finch, C. D. (1989) 'The IMF: the record and the prospects', *Princeton Essays in International Finance*, 175 (September), Princeton University, Princeton, NJ.

Fine, B. (2001) 'Neither the Washington nor the post-Washington consensus. An introduction', in B. Fine, C. Lapavistas and J. Pincus (eds), *Development Policy in the Twenty-first Century. Beyond the Washington Consensus*, London: Routledge, pp. 1–27.

Flynn, P. (2005) 'Brazil and Lula, 2005: crisis, corruption and change in political perspective', *Third World Quarterly*, 26(8): 1221–67.

Foley, M. and B. Edwards (1996) 'The paradox of civil society', *Journal of Democracy*, 7(3): 38–52.

Folha de São Paulo (2004) 'Entrevista. Utopia é crescer e distribuir renda, diz Palocci', 22 December, available at www.folha.uol.com. br/ (last accessed 26 August 2008).

— (2006) 'Lula diz que, sem reforma, novos escândalos surgirão', 24 July.

Fraga, R. (1996) 'The Menemist movement: sustaining a popular conservative coalition', Centro de Estudios Nueva Mayoría, Buenos Aires.

Franco, G. (1997) 'Leia o discurso de posse de Franco na presidência do BC', *Folha de São Paulo*, 20 August.

Frente Amplio (2003) 'Propuesta de grandes lineamientos programáticos para el gobierno 2005–2010', *Documentos IV Congreso 'Héctor Rodríguez'*, 20/21 December, available at: www. mppuruguay.org.uy/hrodriguez/ grandeslineamientosprog.pdf (last accessed 22 July 2008).

Frieden, J. A. (1991) *Debt, Development and Democracy: Modern Political Economy of Latin America, 1965–1982*, Princeton, NJ: Princeton University Press.

Funk, R. (2004) 'Renovation and continuity. The transition to democracy in Chile revisited', PhD thesis, Department of Government, London School of Economics and Political Science, London.

Gamarra, E. A. (1994) 'Crafting political support for stabilisation: political pacts and the new economic policy in Bolivia', in W. C. Smith, C. H. Acuña and E. A. Gamarra (eds), *Democracy, Markets and Structural Reform in Contemporary Latin America: Argentina, Bolivia, Brazil, Chile and Mexico*, New Brunswick, NJ: Transaction Publishers, pp. 105–28.

Gantman, E. R. (2003) 'The painful way to "capitalist development": structural adjustment and foreignization of the Argentine economy in the nineties', in G. Köhler and E. J. Chaves (eds),

Globalization: Critical Perspectives, New York: Nova Science Publishers, pp. 261–76.

Gardner, H. (1966) *Leading Minds. An Anatomy of Leadership*, London: Collins.

Garretón, M. A. (1994) 'Human rights in processes of democratization', *Journal of Latin American Studies*, 26(1): 221–34.

— (1996) 'Human rights in democratization processes', in E. Jelin and E. Hershberg (eds), *Constructing Democracy. Human Rights, Citizenship, and Society in Latin America*, Boulder, CO: Westview Press.

Geddes, B. (1994) *Politician's Dilemma: Building State Capacity in Latin America*, Los Angeles: University of California Press.

Germani, G. (1962) *Política y sociedad en una época de transición (de la sociedad tradicional a la sociedad de masas)*, Buenos Aires: Editorial Paidos.

Ghersi, E. (1997) 'The informal economy in Latin America', *Cato Journal*, 17(1): 99–108.

Giddens, A. (1998) *The Third Way: The Renewal of Social Democracy*, Oxford: Polity Press.

Gilbert, C. L., A. Powell and D. Vines (2000) 'Positioning the World Bank', in C. Gilbert and D. Vines (eds), *The World Bank. Structure and Policies*, Cambridge: Cambridge University Press, pp. 39–86.

Gillespie, C. G. (1991) *Negotiating Democracy. Politicians and Generals in Uruguay*, Cambridge: Cambridge University Press.

Gills, B. and J. Rocamora (1992) 'Low intensity democracy', *Third World Quarterly*, 13(3): 501–23.

— (1993) 'Low intensity democracy', in B. Gills, J. Rocamora and R. Wilson (eds), *Low Intensity Democracy.*

Political Power in the New World Order, Boulder, CO: Pluto.

Glade, W. (1996) 'Institutions and inequality in Latin America: text and subtext', *Journal of Interamerican Studies and World Affairs*, 38(2): 159–79.

Goldfrank, B. and A. Schneider (2006) 'Competitive institutional building: the PT and participatory budgeting in Rio Grande do Sul', *Latin American Politics and Society*, 48(3): 1–31.

Gonzalez de Olarte, E. (1993) 'Economic stabilization and structural adjustment under Fujimori', *Journal of Interamerican Studies and World Affairs*, 35(2): 51–80.

Gramsci, A. (1971) *Selections from the Prison Notebooks of Antonio Gramsci*, ed. and trans. Quintin Hoare and G. Nowell Smith, London: Lawrence and Wishart.

Gray, V. (2007) 'Politics in the Andes' (review article), *Latin American Politics and Society*, 49(3): 212–16.

Green, D. (1996) 'Latin America: neoliberal failure and the search for alternatives', *Third World Quarterly*, 17(1): 109–22.

Grindle, M. S. (1996) *Challenging the State. Crisis and Innovation in Latin America and Africa*, Cambridge and New York: Cambridge University Press.

— (2001) 'In quest of the political: the political economy of development policymaking', in G. M. Meir and J. Stiglitz (eds), *Frontiers of Development Economics. The Future in Perspective*, New York: World Bank and Oxford University Press, pp. 345–80.

Grugel, J. and M. P. Riggirozzi (2007) 'The return of the state in Argentina', *International Affairs*, 83(1): 87–107.

Guilhot, N. (2005) *The Democracy Makers: Human Rights and International Order*, New York: Columbia University Press.

Gunder Frank, A. (1972) 'The development of underdevelopment', in J. D. Cockcroft, A. Gunder Frank and D. Johnson (eds), *Dependence and Underdevelopment*, New York: Anchor Books, pp. 3–17.

Haas, P. M. (1989) 'Do regimes matter? Epistemic communities and Mediterranean pollution control', *International Organizations*, 43(3): 377–403.

Haggard, S. and R. R. Kaufman (1992a) 'Institutions and economic adjustment', in S. Haggard and R. R. Kaufman (eds), *The Politics of Economic Adjustment*, Princeton, NJ: Princeton University Press, pp. 3–37.

— (1992b) 'Economic adjustment and the prospects for democracy', in S. Haggard and R. R. Kaufman (eds), *The Politics of Economic Adjustment*, Princeton, NJ: Princeton University Press, pp. 319–50.

— (1995) *The Political Economy of Democratic Transitions*, Princeton, NJ: Princeton University Press.

Hagopian, F. (1996) *Traditional Politics and Regime Change in Brazil*, New York: Cambridge University Press.

— (1998) 'Democracy and political representation in Latin America in the 1990s: pause, reorganization or decline?', in F. Agüero and J. Stark (eds), *Fault Lines of Democracy in Post-Transition Latin America*, Coral Gables, FL: North-South Centre at the University of Miami, pp. 99–143.

— (2005) 'Conclusions', in F. Hagopian and S. Mainwaring (eds), *The Third Wave of Democratization in Latin America*, Cambridge: Cambridge University Press, pp. 319–62.

Hall, A. (2006) 'From *Fome Zero* to *Bolsa Familia*: social policies and poverty alleviation under Lula', *Journal of Latin American Studies*, 38(4): 689–709.

Hall, P. (1993) 'Policy paradigms, social learning, and the state. The case of economic policy making in Britain', *Comparative Politics*, 25: 175–96.

Hansen, D. and K. Hawkins (2006) 'Dependent civil society: the "Círculos Bolivarianos" in Venezuela', *Latin American Research Review*, 41(1): 102–32.

Harten, S. (2008) 'Analysis of the dialectic of democratic consolidation, de-institutionalization and re-institutionalization in Bolivia, 2002–2005', PhD thesis, Department of Government, London School of Economics and Political Science, London.

Hartlyn, N., L. Schoultz and A. Varas (eds) (1992) *The United States and Latin America in the 1990s*, Chapel Hill: University of North Carolina Press.

Hay, C. (1999) *The Political Economy of New Labour: Labouring under False Pretences?*, Manchester: Manchester University Press.

— (2001) 'The "crisis" of Keynesianism and the rise of neoliberalism in Britain: an ideational institutionalist approach', in J. L. Campbell and O. K. Pedersen (eds), *The Rise of Neoliberalism and Institutional Analysis*, Princeton, NJ: Princeton University Press, pp. 193–218.

Healey, M. A. and E. Seman (2002) 'The costs of orthodoxy: Argentina was the poster child for austerity and obedience to the IMF formula. Not surprisingly, its economy tanked', *American Prospect*, Winter, p. 34.

Helleiner, E. (2003) 'Economic liberalism and its critics: the past as prologue?', *Review of International Political Economy*, 10(4): 685–96.

Helwege, A. (1994) 'Stabilization policy in Latin America: debates about growth and distribution', in G. Bird and A. Helwege (eds), *Latin America's Economic Future*, London: Academic Press, pp. 145–66.

— (1995) 'Poverty in Latin America: back to the abyss?', *Journal of Interamerican Studies and World Affairs*, 27(3): 99–123.

Herman, E. and J. Petras (1985) '"Resurgent democracy": rhetoric and reality', *New Left Review*, 154 (November/December), pp. 83–98.

Hirschman, A. O. (1981) *Essays in Trespassing*, Cambridge: Cambridge University Press.

Hochstetler, K. (1997) 'Democratizing pressures from below? Social movements in new Brazilian democracy', Paper presented at the Latin American Studies Association XX International Congress, Guadalajara, Mexico, 17–19 April.

Hoff, K. and J. Stiglitz (2002) 'Modern economic theory and development', in G. Meier and J. E. Stiglitz (eds), *Frontiers of Development Economics. The Future in Perspective*, Oxford and New York: Oxford University Press, pp. 389–459.

Hojman, D. (1994) 'The political economy of recent conversions to a market economy in Latin America', *Journal of Latin American Studies*, 26(1): 191–219.

Huber, E., D. Rueschemeyer and J. D. Stephens (1997) 'The paradoxes of contemporary democracy. Formal, participatory and social dimensions', *Comparative Politics*, 29(3): 323–42.

Huber Stephens, E. (1990) 'Democracy in Latin America: recent developments in comparative historical perspective' (review essay), *Latin American Research Review*, 25(2): 157–76.

Human Rights Watch (2008) 'Venezuela: Human Rights Watch delegation expelled', *Human Rights News*, available at: hrw.org/english/docs/2008/09/19/venezu19853.htm (last accessed 12 October 2008).

Hunter, W. (1998) 'Civil–military relations in Argentina, Brazil and Chile: present trends, future prospects', in F. Agüero and J. Stark (eds), *Fault Lines in Post-Democratic Transition in Latin America*, Coral Gables, FL: North-South Centre University Press at the University of Miami, pp. 299–322.

— (2007) 'The normalization of an anomaly: the Workers' Party in Brazil', *World Politics*, 59 (April), pp. 440–75.

Hunter, W. and T. Power (2007) 'Rewarding Lula: executive power, social policy and the Brazilian election of 2006', *Latin American Politics and Society*, 49(1): 1–30.

Huntington, S. P. (1968) *Political Order in Changing Societies*, New Haven, CT: Yale University Press.

— (1991) *The Third Wave: Democratisation in the late twentieth century*, Norman: University of Oklahoma Press.

IADB (Inter-American Development Bank) (1995) 'Overcoming volatility', *Economic and Social Progress in Latin America. 1995 Report*, Washington, DC: IADB.

— (1997) 'Latin America after a decade of reforms. Adjusting. All pain and no gain? Democracy and deficits', *Economic and Social Progress in Latin America. 1997 Report*, Washington, DC: IADB.

— (1999a) 'Facing up to inequality in Latin America', *Report on Economic and Social Progress in Latin America, 1998–1999*, Washington, DC: IADB.

— (1999b) 'Renewing the commitment to development', *Report of the Working Group on the Institutional Strategy*, Washington, DC: IADB, available at: www.iadb.org/exr/corp/ (last accessed 22 July 2008).

— (2002) 'Modernization of the state', Strategy Document Policy and Evaluation Committee, GN-2235, Washington, DC: IADB.

— (2005) 'The politics of policies', *Economic and Social Progress in Latin America. 2006 Report*, Washington, DC, and Cambridge, MA: IADB and David Rockefeller Center for Latin American Studies at Harvard University.

Ianni, O. (1975) *La formación del estado populista en América Latina*, Mexico: Editorial Era.

IMF (International Monetary Fund) (1985) 'Theoretical aspects of the design of Fund-supported issues in the implementation of conditionality: improving program design and dealing with prolonged use', Exchange and Trade Relations Department Report EBS/85/265, Washington, DC: International Monetary Fund, 5 December.

— (1987) 'Theoretical aspects of the design of Fund-supported adjustment programs', IMF Occasional Paper no. 55, Washington, DC: Research Department, International Monetary Fund.

— (1989) *IMF Survey*, 18(6), Washington, DC: International Monetary Fund, 20 March.

— (2004) 'The IMF and Argentina 1991–2001', Washington, DC: International Monetary Fund.

Jessop, B. (2002) 'Liberalism, neoliberalism and urban governance: a state-theoretical perspective', *Antipode*, 34(3): 453–72.

Kahler, M. (1992) 'External influence, conditionality and the politics of adjustment', in S. Haggard and R. R. Kaufman (eds), *The Politics of Economic Adjustment*, Princeton, NJ: Princeton University Press, pp. 89–133.

Kanbur, R. and D. Vines (2000) 'The World Bank and poverty reduction: past, present and future', in C. L. Gilbert and D. Vines (eds), *The World Bank. Structures and Policies*, Cambridge: Cambridge University Press, pp. 87–107.

Kapur, D. (1998) 'The IMF: a cure or a curse?', *Foreign Policy*, 111 (Summer), pp. 114–29.

Karl, T. L. (1997) *The Paradox of Plenty: Oil Booms and Petro-States*, Berkeley: University of California Press.

— (2000) 'Economic inequality and democratic instability', *Journal of Democracy*, 11(1): 149–56.

Kay, B. H. (1995) 'Fujipopulismo and the liberal state in Peru 1990–1995', Paper presented at the International Congress of the Latin American Studies Association, Washington, DC, 28–30 September.

Keck, M. (1989) *The Workers' Party and Democratization in Brazil*,

Bibliography

New Haven, CT: Yale University Press.

Khan, M. and S. Sharma (2001) 'IMF conditionality and country ownership of programs', IMF Working Paper WP/01/142, Washington, DC: International Monetary Fund.

Killick, T. (1995) *IMF Programmes in Developing Countries*, London: Routledge and ODI.

Kingstone, P. R. (1999) *Business Preferences, Political Institutions and Neoliberal Reform in Brazil*, Pennsylvania: Penn State Press.

Kingstone, P. R. and T. J. Power (2000) 'Introduction: still standing or standing still? The Brazilian democratic regime since 1985', in P. R. Kingstone and T. J. Power (eds), *Democratic Brazil. Actors, Institutions and Processes*, Pittsburgh, PA: University of Pittsburgh Press, pp. 3–13.

Kirby, P. (2003) *Introduction to Latin America. Twenty-first Century Challenges*, London: Sage.

Kjær, P. and O. K. Pedersen (2001) 'Translating liberalization: neoliberalism in the Danish negotiated economy', in J. L. Campbell and O. K. Pedersen (eds), *The Rise of Neoliberalism and Institutional Analysis*, Princeton, NJ: Princeton University Press, pp. 219–48.

Knight, A. (1994) 'Latin America: what price the past? An inaugural lecture delivered before the University of Oxford on 18 November 1993 by Alan Knight, Professor of the History of Latin America', Oxford: Clarendon Press.

Krueger, A. O. (2004) 'Meant well, tried little, failed much: policy reforms in emerging market economies', Roundtable Lecture Economic Honors Society, New York University, New York, 23 March, available at: imf.org/external/np/speeches/2004/032304a.htm (last accessed 22 July 2008).

Krugman, P. (1995) 'Dutch tulips and emerging markets', *Foreign Policy*, 74(4): 28–44.

Kuhn, T. S. (1962) *The Structure of Scientific Revolutions*, Chicago, IL: University of Chicago Press.

Kurtz, M. (2004) *Free Market Democracy and the Chilean and Mexican Countryside*, New York: Cambridge University Press.

Laclau, E. (1977) *Politics and Ideology in Marxist Theory*, London: Verso.

— (1990) *New Reflections on the Revolution of Our Time*, London: Verso.

— (2005a) 'Populism: what's in a name?', in F. Panizza (ed.), *Populism and the Mirror of Democracy*, London: Verso, pp. 32–49.

— (2005b) *On Populist Reason*, London: Verso.

— (2006) 'La deriva populista y la centro izquierda Latinoamericana', *Nueva Sociedad*, 205 (Sepember/October), pp. 56–61.

Lakoff, G. (2004) *Don't Think of an Elephant: Know Your Values and Frame the Debate*, White River Junction, VT: Chelsea Green.

Lal, D. (1987) 'The political economy of economic liberalization', *World Bank Economic Review*, 1(2) (January).

Latinobarómetro (1996) *Press Release. Latinobarómetro Survey 1996*, Santiago de Chile, available at: www.latinobarometro.org (last accessed 3 December 2008).

— (2004) *Informe Latinobarómetro 2004*, Santiago de Chile, available at: www.latinobarometro.org (last accessed 22 July 2008).

— (2007) *Informe Latinobarómetro*

2007, Santiago de Chile, available at: www.latinobarometro.org (last accessed 22 July 2008).

Leggett, W. (2007) 'British social democracy beyond New Labour: entrenching a progressive consensus', *British Journal of Politics and International Relations*, 9(3): 346–64.

Levine, D. (1988) 'Paradigm lost: dependency to democracy' (review article), *World Politics*, 40(3): 377–94.

— (2002) 'The decline and fall of democracy in Venezuela: ten theses', *Bulletin of Latin American Research*, 21(2): 248–69.

— (2006) 'Civil society and political decay in Venezuela', in R. Feinberg, C. H. Waisman and L. Zamosc (eds), *Civil Society and Democracy in Latin America*, New York and Basingtoke, Palgrave Macmillan, pp. 169–89.

Levitsky, S. (2003) 'From labor politics to machine politics: the transformation of party–union linkages in Argentine Peronism, 1983–1999', *Latin American Research Review*, 38(3): 4–36.

— (2005) 'Argentina. Democratic survival amidst economic failure', in F. Hagopian and S. Mainwaring (eds), *The Third Wave of Democratization in Latin America. Advances and Setbacks*, Cambridge: Cambridge University Press, pp. 63–89.

Levitsky, S. and M. V. Murillo (2005) *Argentina's Democracy. The Politics of Institutional Weakness*, University Park: Pennsylvania State University Press.

Lewis, P. (1993) *La crisis del capitalismo Argentino*, Buenos Aires: Fondo de Cultura Económica.

Lievesley, G. (1999) *Democracy in Latin America. Mobilization, Power and the Search for New Politics*, Manchester and New York: Manchester University Press.

Lindblom, C. E. (1977) *Politics and Markets*, New York: Basic Books.

Linz, J. J. (1994) 'Presidential or parliamentary democracy: does it make a difference?', in J. J. Linz and A. Valenzuela (eds), *The Crisis of Presidential Democracy: The Latin American Evidence*, Baltimore, MD: Johns Hopkins University Press.

Linz, J. J. and A. Stepan (1996) *Problems of Democratic Transition and Consolidation in Southern Europe, South America and Post-Communist Europe*, Baltimore, MD: Johns Hopkins University Press.

Lipset, S. M. (1959) 'Some social requisites of democracy: economic development and political legitimacy', *American Political Science Review*, 53(1): 69–105.

Llanos, M. (2001) 'Understanding presidential power in Argentina: a study of the policy of privatisation in the 1990s', *Journal of Latin American Studies*, 33(1): 67–99.

López Levy, M. (2003) *We are Millions: Neo-liberalism and New Forms of Political Action in Argentina*, London: Latin America Bureau.

López-Maya, M. (2002) 'Venezuela after the Caracazo: forms of protest in a deinstitutionalized context', *Bulletin of Latin American Research*, 21(2): 199–218.

López-Maya, M. and L. E. Lander (2006) 'Venezuela: las elecciones presidenciales de 2006. ¿Hacia el socialismo del siglo XXI?', Paper presented at the international seminar 'América Latina 2006: Balance de un año de elecciones II', Madrid, 12/13 December.

Lukes, S. (2005) *Politics. A Radical View*, New York: Palgrave Macmillan.

Luna, J. P. (2004) 'Entre la espada y la pared? La transformación de las bases sociales del FA y sus implicaciones de cara a un eventual gobierno progresista', in J. Lanzaro (ed.), *La izquierda uruguaya entre la oposición y el gobierno*, Montevideo: Fin de Siglo, pp. 195–250.

— (2007) 'Frente Amplio and the crafting of a social democratic alternative in Uruguay', *Latin American Politics and Society*, 49(4): 1–30.

Lustig, N. (1998) *Mexico, the Remaking of an Economy*, Washington, DC: Brookings Institution.

Machinea, J. L. and O. L. Kacef (2007) 'Growth and equity: in search of the "empty box"', in R. Ffrench Davis and J. L. Machinea (eds), *Economic Growth with Equity. Challenges for Latin America*, Basingstoke and New York: Palgrave Macmillan, pp. 1–23.

Mainwaring, S. and A. Pérez-Liñán (2005) 'Latin American democratization since 1978', in F. Hagopian and S. Mainwaring (eds), *The Third Wave of Democratization in Latin America*, Cambridge: Cambridge University Press, pp. 14–62.

Mainwaring, S. and T. Scully (eds) (1995) *Building Democratic Institutions: Party Systems in Latin America*, Stanford, CA: Stanford University Press.

Mainwaring, S., A. M. Bejarano and E. Pizarro Leongómez (2006) *The Crisis of Democratic Representation in the Andes*, Stanford, CA: Stanford University Press.

Malekzadeh, S. (2006) 'No one left to argue with: the lack of viable opposition to the PJ and its corrosive effect on Argentina's party system', Paper prepared for presentation at the 2006 meeting of the Latin American Studies Association, San Juan, Puerto Rico, 15–18 March.

Mangabeira Unger, R. (1990) *A alternativa transformadora. Como democratizar o Brasil*, Rio de Janeiro: Editora Guanabara Koogan.

Manning, N. (2000) Public Sector Anchor Group, World Bank, Interview, 20 March.

Margheritis, A. and A. Pereira (2007) 'The neoliberal turn in Latin America. The cycle of ideas and the search for an alternative', *Latin American Perspectives*, 34(3): 25–48.

Marshall, K. (2008) *The World Bank. From Reconstruction to Development to Equity*, London and New York: Routledge.

Massey, D. S., M. Sanchez, R. and J. R. Behrman (2006) 'Of myths and markets', *Annals of the American Academy of Political and Social Science*, 606(1): 8–31.

Matsuda, Y. (2000) Poverty Reduction and Economic Management Unit, Latin America and the Caribbean Region, World Bank, Interview, 24 March.

Mauceri, P. (1995) 'State reform, coalitions, and the neoliberal autogolpe in Peru', *Latin American Research Review*, 30(1): 7–37.

Mayorga, F. (2008) 'El gobierno del Movimiento al Socialismo en Bolivia: entre el nacionalismo e indigenismo', in C. Moreira, D. Raus and J. C. Gómez Leyton (eds), *La Nueva Política en América Latina. Ruptura y Continuidades*,

Montevideo: Editorial Trilce, pp. 125–46.

McCoy, J. and D. J. Myers (2004) *The Unraveling of Representative Democracy in Venezuela*, Baltimore, MD: Johns Hopkins University Press.

Meir, G. M. and J. E. Stiglitz (2001) (eds) *Frontiers of Development Economics: The Future in Perspective*, New York: World Bank/ Oxford University Press.

Méndez, J. E., G. O'Donnell and P. S. Pinheiro (eds) (1999) *The (Un)Rule of Law and the Underprivileged in Latin America*, Notre Dame, IN: University of Notre Dame Press.

Merquior, José G. (1991) 'The other West: on the historical position of Latin America', *International Sociology*, 6(2): 149–63.

Miliband, R. (1989) *Divided Societies: Class Struggle in Contemporary Capitalism*, Oxford: Clarendon Press.

Mollo, M. L. R. and A. Saad Filho (2006) 'Neoliberal economic policies in Brazil (1994–2005): Cardoso, Lula and the need for a democratic alternative', *New Political Economy*, 11(1): 99–123.

Moore, B. (1966) *The Social Origins of Dictatorship and Democracy*, Boston, MA: Beacon Press.

Morais, L. and A. Saad Filho (2003) 'Snatching defeat from the jaws of victory? Lula, the Workers' Party and the prospects for change in Brazil', *Capital & Class*, 81 (Autumn), pp. 17–23.

Morales, J. A. (1994) 'Democracy, economic liberalism and structural reform in Bolivia', in W. C. Smith, C. H. Acuña and E. A. Gamarra (eds), *Democracy, Markets and Structural Reform in Contemporary Latin America: Argentina, Bolivia,* Brazil, Chile and Mexico, New Brunswick, NJ: Transaction Publishers, pp. 129–50.

Morse, R. (1982) *El espejo de Próspero. Un estudio de la dialéctica del Nuevo Mundo*, Mexico: Siglo XXI.

Motta, S. C. (2006) 'Utopias reimagined: a reply to Panizza', *Political Studies*, 54(4): 898–905.

— (2007a) 'The reinvention of the political in Venezuela; the case of the urban land movement (CTU)', Paper presented at the Everyday Life in World Politics and Economics International Conference organized by the LSE Centre for International Studies, London, 11 May.

— (2007b) 'Populism's Achilles heel – popular democracy beyond the liberal state and market economy in Venezuela', Manuscript.

Murillo, M. V. (2001) *Labor Unions, Partisan Coalitions and Market Reforms in Latin America*, Cambridge: Cambridge University Press.

Mussa, M. (2002) *Argentina and the Fund: From Triumph to Tragedy*, Washington, DC: Institute for International Economics.

Naím, M. (1994) 'Latin America: the second stage of reform', *Journal of Democracy*, 5(4): 32–48.

— (2000) 'Fads and fashion in economic reforms: Washington Consensus or Washington confusion?', *Foreign Policy*, 118(86): 87–103.

Navia, P. and A. Velasco (2003) 'The politics of second generation reform', in P. P. Kuczynski and J. Williamson (eds), *After the Washington Consensus. Restoring Growth and Reform in Latin America*, Washington, DC: Institute for International Economics, pp. 265–303.

Bibliography

Nelson, J. (1994) *Intricate Links: Democratization and Market Reforms in Latin America and Eastern Europe*, New Brunswick, NJ: Transaction Publishers.

Neri, M. C. (ed.) (2008) *The New Middle Class*, Rio de Janeiro: Centro de Políticas Sociais, Instituto Brasileiro de Economia, Fundação Getulio Vargas.

Nettl, J. P. (1968) 'The state as a conceptual variable', *World Politics*, 20(4): 559–92.

Newbold, S. (2003) 'The Fujishock: how and why did it occur? An analysis of Alberto Fujimori's policy reversal of 1990', *Entrecaminos* (Spring), Georgetown University, Washington, DC, available at: clas.georgetown.edu/entre2003/Fujishock.html (last accessed 22 July 2008).

Nissenbaum, H. (2000) Consultant, World Bank, Interview, 26 March.

North, D. C. (1993) 'Economic performance through time', Prize Lecture to the Memory of Alfred Nobel, 9 December, available at: nobelprize.org/nobel_prizes/economics/laureates/1993/north-lecture.html (last accessed 10 July 2008).

Novaro, M. (2002) 'La Alianza, de la gloria del llano a la debacle del gobierno', in M. Novaro (ed.), *El derrumbe político en el ocaso de la convertibilidad*, Buenos Aires: Grupo Editorial Norma, pp. 31–105.

Novaro, M. and V. Palermo (1998) *Los caminos de la centroizquierda: dilemas y desafíos del FREPASO y de la Alianza*, Buenos Aires: Editorial Losada.

Nye, J. S. (1990) *Bound to Lead: The Changing Nature of American Power*, New York: Basic Books.

Nylen, W. R. (2000) 'The making of a loyal opposition: the Workers' Party (PT) and the consolidation of democracy in Brazil', in P. R. Kingstone and T. J. Power (eds), *Democratic Brazil. Actors, Institutions and Processes*, Pittsburgh, PA: University of Pittsburgh Press, pp. 126–43.

Oakeshott, I. and D. Smith (2008) 'Labour in turmoil over Alistair Darling gaffe', *Times Online*, 31 August, available at: www.timesonline.co.uk/tol/news/politics/article4641381.ece (last accessed 3 October 2008).

O'Donnell, G. (1973) *Modernization and Bureaucratic Authoritarianism: Studies in South American Politics*, Berkeley, CA: Institute of International Studies.

— (1977) 'Corporatism and the question of the state', in J. M. Malloy (ed.), *Authoritarianism and Corporatism in Latin America*, Pittsburgh, PA: University of Pittsburgh Press, pp. 47–87.

— (1981) 'Las fuerzas armadas y el estado autoritario en América Latina', in N. Lechner (ed.), *Estado y política en América Latina*, Mexico: Siglo XXI, pp. 199–235.

— (1992) 'Transitions, continuities, and paradoxes', in S. Mainwaring, G. O'Donnell and J. S. Valenzuela (eds), *Issues in Democratic Consolidation: The New South American Democracies in Comparative Perspective*, Notre Dame, IN: University of Notre Dame Press, pp. 17–56.

— (1994) 'Delegative democracy', *Journal of Democracy*, 5: 55–69.

— (1999) 'Polyarchies and the (un)rule of law in Latin America: a partial conclusion', in J. E. Méndez, G. O'Donnell and

P. S. Pinheiro (eds), *The (Un)Rule of Law and the Underprivileged in Latin America*, Notre Dame, IN: University of Notre Dame Press, pp. 303–37.

O'Donnell, G. and P. Schmitter (1986) *Transitions from Authoritarian Rule: Tentative Conclusions about Uncertain Democracies*, Baltimore, MD: Johns Hopkins University Press.

O'Donnell, G., P. Schmitter and L. Whitehead (eds) (1986) *Transitions from Authoritarian Rule: Prospects for Democracy*, Baltimore, MD: Johns Hopkins University Press.

Ocampo, J. A. (1998) 'Income distribution, poverty and social expenditure in Latin America', *CEPAL Review*, 65, Washington, DC: ECLAC, pp. 7–14.

Olson, M. (1982) *The Rise and Decline of Nations*, New Haven, CT: Yale University Press.

Paes de Barros, R., M. de Carvalho, S. Franco and R. Mendonça (2006) 'Conseqüências e causas imediatas de queda recente da desigualdade de renda brasileira', *Texto para Discussão*, 1201, Rio de Janeiro: IPEA.

Paiva, P. (2006) 'Lula's political economy: changes and challenges', *Annals of the American Academy of Political and Social Science*, 606(1): 196–215.

Palermo, V. (1999) '¿Mejorar para empeorar? La dinámica política de las reformas estructurales argentinas', in M. Novaro (ed.), *Entre el abismo y la ilusión. Peronismo, democracia y mercado*, Buenos Aires: Grupo Editorial Norma.

Palermo, V. and M. Novaro (1996) *Política y poder en el gobierno de Menem*, Buenos Aires: Grupo Editorial Norma.

Panizza, F. (1999) 'Brazil', in J. Buxton and N. Phillips (eds), *Case Studies in Latin American Political Economy*, Manchester and New York: Manchester University Press, pp. 8–32.

— (2000a) 'Beyond "Delegative Democracy": "Old Politics" and "New Economics" in Latin America', *Journal of Latin American Studies*, 32(2): 737–63.

— (2000b) 'Neopopulism and its limits in Collor's Brazil', *Bulletin of Latin American Research*, 19(2): 177–92.

— (2000c) 'Is Brazil becoming a "boring" country?', *Bulletin of Latin American Research*, 19(2): 501–25.

— (2004a) '"Brazil's need to change". Change as iteration and the iteration of change in Brazil's 2002 presidential election', *Bulletin of Latin American Research*, 23(4): 465–82.

— (2004b) 'A reform without losers: the symbolic economy of civil service reform in Uruguay, 1995–96', *Latin American Politics and Society*, 46(3): 1–28.

— (2005a) 'Introduction', in F. Panizza (ed.), *Populism and the Mirror of Democracy*, London: Verso, pp. 1–31.

— (2005b) 'Unarmed Utopia revisited: the resurgence of left-of-centre politics in Latin America', *Political Studies*, 53(4): 716–34.

— (2008) 'Economic constraints and strategic choices: the case of the Frente Amplio of Uruguay's first year in office', *Bulletin of Latin American Research*, 27(2): 176–96.

Panizza, F. and G. Philip (2005) 'Second generation reform in Latin

America: reforming the public sector in Uruguay and Mexico', *Journal of Latin American Studies*, 37(4): 667–91.

Parker, D. (2006) 'Chávez and the search for an alternative to neoliberalism', in S. Ellner and M. Tinker Salas (eds), *Venezuela: Hugo Chavez and the Decline of an Exceptional Democracy*, Lanham, MD: Rowman and Littlefield, pp. 60–74.

Partido Nacionalista Peruano (2006) 'Ollanta uniendo el Perú. La Gran Transformación. Perú de todos nosotros. Plan de Gobierno 2006–2011', 22 February, available at: www.partidonacionalistaperuano.com/docs/La_Gran_Transformacion.pdf (last accessed 22 July 2008).

Pastor, M. (1987) *The International Monetary Fund and Latin America: Economic Stabilisation and Class Conflict*, Boulder, CO: Westview Press.

Pastor, M. and C. Wise (1992) 'Peruvian economic policy in the 1980s: from orthodoxy to heterodoxy and back', *Latin American Research Review*, 27(2): 82–117.

— (1999) 'The politics of second-generation reform', *Journal of Democracy*, 10(3): 34–48.

Pastor, R. A. (1989) 'Introduction: the swing of the pendulum', in R. A. Pastor (ed.), *Democracy in the Americas. Stopping the Pendulum*, New York and London: Holmer and Meier, pp. 3–10.

Payne, L. A. and E. Bartell (1995) 'Bringing business back in. Business–state relations and democratic stability in Latin America', in E. J. Bartell and L. A. Payne (eds), *Business and Democracy in Latin America*, Pittsburgh, PA:

University of Pittsburgh Press, pp. 257–90.

Peceny, M. (1994) 'The inter-American system as a liberal "Pacific Union"?' (review essay), *Latin American Research Review*, 29(3): 188–201.

Pender, J. (2001) 'From "Structural Adjustment" to "Comprehensive Development Framework": conditionality transformed?', *Third World Quarterly*, 22(3): 397–411.

Perry, G. and L. Servén (2003) 'The anatomy of a multiple crisis: why was Argentina special and what can we learn from it?', Policy research working paper no. 3081, Office of the Chief Economist, Latin America and the Caribbean Region, World Bank, Washington, DC.

Philip, G. (1993) 'The new economic liberalism and democracy in Latin America: friends or enemies?', *Third World Quarterly*, 14(3): 555–71.

— (1994) 'New economic liberalism and democracy in Spanish America', *Government and Opposition*, 29(3): 362–77.

— (1998) 'The new populism: presidentialism and market-orientated reform in Spanish South America', *Government and Opposition*, 33(1): 81–97.

— (1999) 'The dilemmas of good governance: a Latin American perspective', *Government and Opposition*, 34(2): 226–42.

— (2003) *Democracy in Latin America*, London: Polity.

Pinheiro, P. S. (1999) 'The rule of law and the underprivileged in Latin America: introduction', in J. E. Méndez, G. O'Donnell and P. S. Pinheiro (eds), *The (Un)Rule of Law and the Underprivileged in*

Latin America, Notre Dame, IN: University of Notre Dame Press, pp. 1–15.

Pinto, C. R. J. (1989) *Com a palavra o Senhor Presidente José Sarney ou como entender os meandros da linguagem do poder*, São Paulo: HUCITEC.

Pion-Berlin, D. (1991) 'Between confrontation and accommodation: military and government policy in democratic Argentina,' *Journal of Latin American Studies*, 23(3): 543–71.

— (1994) 'To prosecute or to pardon? Human rights decisions in the Latin American Southern Cone', *Human Rights Quarterly*, 16(1): 105–30.

Piven, F. F. and R. A. Cloward (1998) *The Breaking of the American Social Compact*, New York: New Press.

Portes, A. and K. Hoffman (2003) 'Latin American class structures: their composition and change during the neoliberal era', *Latin American Research Review*, 38(1): 41–82.

Prebisch, R. (1949) 'El desarrollo económico de la América Latina y algunos de sus principales problemas', E/CN.12/89, Santiago, Chile: ECLAC.

Przeworski, A. (1991) *Democracy and the Market. Political and Economic Reform in Eastern Europe and Latin America*, Cambridge: Cambridge University Press.

Przeworski, A., M. E. Alvarez, J. A. Cheibub and F. Limongi (2000) *Democracy and Development. Political Institutions and Well-Being in the World, 1950–1990*, Cambridge: Cambridge University Press.

Rabotnikof, N. (2004) 'Izquierda y derecha: visiones del mundo, opciones de gobierno e identidades políticas', in N. García Canclini (ed.), *Reabrir espacios públicos*, Mexico: UAM-Plaza y Valdés, pp. 268–307.

Raby, D. L. (2006) *Democracy and Revolution: Latin America and Socialism Today*, London: Pluto Press.

Rama, G. W. (1987) *La democracia en Uruguay*, Buenos Aires: Grupo Editor Latinoamericano.

Ramírez Gallegos, F. (2008) 'Democracia friccionada, ascenso ciudadano y posneoliberalismo en Ecuador', in C. Moreira, D. Raus and J. C. Gómez Leyton (eds), *La Nueva Política en América Latina. Ruptura y Continuidades*, Montevideo: Editorial Trilce, pp. 171–96.

Reid, M. (2007) *Forgotten Continent. The Battle for Latin America's Soul*, New Haven, CT, and London: Yale University Press.

Remmer, K. (1986) 'The politics of economic stabilization: IMF Standby Programs in Latin America 1954–84', *Comparative Politics*, 19(1): 1–23.

Reyes, O. (2006) 'Sobre el socialismo del siglo XXI en Venezuela', *Stockholm Review of Latin American Studies*, 1 (November 2006), pp. 84–104.

Riutort, M. (2007) 'La economía venezolana en el 2007 y perspectivas para el 2008', *Temas de Coyuntura*, 56: 115–26.

Robbins, D. (1996) 'Evidence on trade and wages in the developing world', Technical Paper no. 119, Organisation for Economic Co-operation and Development (OECD), Paris.

Roberts, B. (1978) *Cities of Peasants. The Political Economy of Urban-*

isation in the Third World, Beverly Hills, CA: Sage Publications.

Roberts, K. M. (1995) 'Neoliberalism and the transformation of populism in Latin America', *World Politics*, 48(1): 82–116.

— (1997) 'Beyond romanticism: social movements and the study of political change in Latin America', *Latin American Research Review*, 32(2): 137–51.

— (1998) *Deepening Democracy? The Modern Left and Social Movements in Chile and Peru*, Stanford, CA: Stanford University Press.

— (2002) 'Social inequalities without class cleavages in Latin America's neoliberal era', *Studies in Comparative International Development*, 36(4): 3–33.

— (2007) 'Latin America's populist revival', *SAIS Review*, 27(1): 3–15.

— (2008) 'The mobilization of opposition to economic liberalization', *Annual Review of Political Science*, 11 (June), pp. 327–49.

Rodríguez, O. (1994) 'Cepal: viejas y nuevas ideas', *Quantum*, 1(2): 37–63.

Rodrik, D. (1997) *Has Globalization Gone Too Far?*, Washington, DC: Institute for International Economics.

— (2007) *One Economics, Many Recipes. Globalization, Institutions and Economic Growth*, Princeton, NJ, and Oxford: Princeton University Press.

Rojas Aravena, F. (ed.) (1993) *América Latina y la Iniciativa para Las Américas*, Santiago, Chile: FLACSO.

Rouquié, A. (1987) *Amérique Latine: introduction à l'Extrême-Occident*, Paris: Editions du Seuil.

Rueschemeyer, D., E. H. Stephens and J. D. Stephens (1996) *Capital-ism, Development and Democracy*, Cambridge: Polity Press.

Sánchez de Losada, G. (1985) 'La nueva política económica (1ra. parte)', *Foro Económico*, 5, Instituto Latinoamericano de Investigaciones Sociales (ILDIS), La Paz.

Sandbrook, R., M. Edelman, P. Heller and J. Teichman (2007) *Social Democracy in the Global Periphery*, Cambridge: Cambridge University Press.

Sanjinés, J. C. (2004) 'Movimientos sociales y cambio político en Bolivia', *Revista Venezolana de Economía y Ciencias Sociales*, 10(1): 203–18.

Santos, B. de S. (2005) *Democratizing Democracy: Beyond the Liberal Democratic Canon*, vol. 1: *Reinventing Social Emancipation*, London: Verso.

Sartori, G. (1976) *Parties and Party Systems: A Framework for Analysis*, Cambridge: Cambridge University Press.

Schamis, H. E. (1991) 'Reconceptualizing Latin American authoritarianism in the 1970s: from bureaucratic authoritarianism to neoconservatism', *Comparative Politics*, 23(2): 201–20.

— (1999) 'Distributional coalitions and the politics of economic reform in Latin America', *World Politics*, 51(2): 236–68.

— (2006) 'A "left turn" in Latin America? Populism, socialism and democratic institutions', *Journal of Democracy*, 17(4): 20–34.

Schedler, A. (1998) 'What is democratic consolidation?', *Journal of Democracy*, 9(2): 108–21.

Scheman, R. (1997) 'Banking on growth. The role of the Inter-American Development Bank',

Journal of Interamerican Studies and World Affairs, 39(1): 85–100.

Schmitt, C. (1996) *The Concept of the Political*, Chicago, IL: University of Chicago Press.

Schmitter, P. (1974) 'Still the century of corporatism?', *Review of Politics*, 36(1): 85–131.

— (1998) 'Continúa el siglo del corporativismo?', in J. Lanzaro (ed.), *El fin del siglo del corporativismo*, Caracas: Nueva Sociedad, pp. 69–119.

Selcher, W. A. (1986) 'Contradictions, dilemmas, and actors in Brazil's Abertura, 1979–1985', in W. A. Selcher (ed.), *Political Liberalisation in Brazil: Dynamics, Dilemmas and Future Prospects*, Boulder, CO, and London: Westview Press, pp. 55–95.

Seligson, M. A. (2007) 'The rise of populism and the left in Latin America', *Journal of Democracy*, 18(3): 81–95.

Sen, A. K. (1999) *Development as Freedom*, New York: Knopf.

Shapiro, I. (2006) 'On the second edition of Lukes' *Third Face*', *Political Studies Review*, 4(2): 146–55.

Sheahan, J. (1999) *Searching for a Better Society. The Peruvian Economy from 1950*, University Park: Pennsylvania State University Press.

Shepherd, G. (2000) Public Sector Management (Latin America), World Bank, Interview, 22 March.

Sieder, R. (2005) 'Challenging citizenship, neo-liberalism and democracy: indigenous movements and the state in Latin America', *Social Movements Studies*, 4(3): 301–7.

Silva, E. (1996) *The State and Capital in Chile: Business Elites, Technocrats and Market Economics*, Boulder, CO: Westview Press.

— (2007) 'Challenging neoliberalism in Latin America', Paper prepared for delivery at the 2007 Congress of the Latin American Studies Association, Montreal, Canada, 5–8 September.

Silva, E. and F. Durand (1998) 'Organized business and politics in Latin America', in F. Durand and E. Silva (eds), *Organized Business, Economic Change, and Democracy in Latin America*, Coral Gables, FL: North-South Center Press.

Silva, P. (1995) 'Empresarios, neoliberalismo y transición democrática en Chile', *Revista Mexicana de Sociología*, 57(4): 3–25.

Singh, A. (2004) 'Latin America: sustaining reforms and growth', Paper delivered at the investors' meeting at the 45th Annual Meeting of the Inter-American Development Bank, Lima, Peru, 27/28 March.

Singh, A., A. Belaisch, C. Collyns, P. de Masi, R. Krieger, G. Meredith and R. Rennhack (2005) *Stabilization and Reform in Latin America. A Macroeconomic Perspective on the Experience since the Early 1990s*, Washington, DC: International Monetary Fund.

Skinner, C. and M. Torras (2006) 'Lula, Chávez, Kirchner: the political economy of contemporary redistribution', Paper prepared for delivery at the 2006 Meeting of the Latin American Studies Association, San Juan, Puerto Rico, 15–18 March.

Slipak, D. (2007) 'Desplazamientos y rearticulaciones del discurso político en la Argentina post-convertibilidad', Unpublished manuscript.

Smith, P. H. (2005) *Democracy in*

Latin America: Political Change in Comparative Perspective, New York: Oxford University Press.

Smith, W. (1989) *Authoritarianism and the Crisis of the Argentine Political Economy*, Stanford, CA: Stanford University Press.

Smith, W. C., C. H. Acuña and E. A. Gamarra (eds) (1994) *Democracy, Markets and Structural Reform in Contemporary Latin America: Argentina, Bolivia, Brazil, Chile and Mexico*, New Brunswick, NJ: Transaction Publishers.

Spanakos, A. P. (2007) 'Adjectives, asterisks and qualifications, or how to address democracy in contemporary Latin America' (review essay), *Latin American Research Review*, 42(2): 225–37.

Springer, G. L. and J. L. Molina (1995) 'The Mexican financial crisis: genesis, impact and implications', *Journal of Interamerican Studies and World Affairs*, 37(2): 57–81.

Stahler-Sholk, R., H. E. Vanden and G. D. Kuecker (eds) (2008) *Latin American Social Movements in the Twenty-first Century. Resistance, Power and Democracy*, Lanham, MD: Rowman and Littlefield.

Stallings, B. (1992) 'International influence on economic policy: debt, stabilisation, and structural reform', in S. Haggard and R. R. Kaufman (eds), *The Politics of Economic Adjustment. International Constraints, Distributive Conflicts, and the State*, Princeton, NJ: Princeton University Press, pp. 41–88.

Stallings, B. and W. Peres (2000) *Growth, Employment and Equity. The Impact of Economic Reforms in Latin America and the Caribbean*, United Nations Economic Commission for Latin America and the Caribbean, Washington, DC: Brookings Institution Press.

Stepan, A. (1985) 'State power and the strength of civil society in the Southern Cone of Latin America', in P. B. Evans, D. Rueschmeyer and T. Skocpol (eds), *Bringing the State Back In*, Cambridge: Cambridge University Press, pp. 317–43.

— (1988) *Rethinking Military Politics: Brazil and the Southern Cone*, Princeton, NJ: Princeton University Press.

Stiglitz, J. (2000) 'Introduction', in C. L. Gilbert and D. Vines (eds), *The World Bank. Structures and Policies*, Cambridge: Cambridge University Press, pp. 1–9.

— (2001) 'More instruments and boarder controls: moving towards the post-Washington Consensus', in H.-J. Chang (ed.), *Joseph Stiglitz and the World Bank: The Rebel Within*, London: Anthem Press, pp. 17–49.

— (2002) *Globalization and Its Discontents*, London: Allen Lane.

— (2005) 'Development policies in a world of globalization', in K. P. Gallagher (ed.), *Putting Development First. The Importance of Policy Space in the WTO and International Financial Institutions*, London and New York: Zed Books, pp. 15–32.

Stokes, S. (1997) 'Democratic accountability and policy change. Economic policy in Fujimori's Peru', *Comparative Politics*, 29(2): 209–26.

— (1999) 'What do policy switches tell us about democracy?', in A. Przeworski, S. Stokes and B. Manin (eds), *Democracy, Accountability and Representation*, Cambridge: Cambridge University Press, pp. 98–130.

— (2001) *Mandates and Democracy: Neoliberalism by Surprise in Latin America*, Cambridge: Cambridge University Press.

Summit of the Americas (1994) 'Declaration of Principles', Miami, FL, 9–11 December, available at: www.summit-americas.org/miamidec.htm (last accessed 13 July 2006).

Sunkel, O. (1973) *El subdesarrollo latinoamericano y la teoría del desarrollo*, Mexico/Argentina/Spain: Siglo Veintiuno de España Editores, SA.

Tavolaro, S. B. F. and L. G. M. Tavolaro (2007) 'Accounting for Lula's second term electoral victory: "leftism" without a political project?', *Constellations*, 14(3): 426–44.

Tedesco, L. (1999) *Democracy in Argentina. Hope and Disillusion*, London: Frank Cass.

— (2002) 'Argentina's turmoil: the politics of informality and the roots of economic meltdown', *Cambridge Review of International Affairs*, 15(3): 469–81.

Teichman, J. (2004) 'The World Bank and policy reform in Mexico and Argentina', *Latin American Politics and Society*, 46(1): 39–74.

Teivainen, T. (2002) 'The World Social Forum and global democatisation: learning from Porto Alegre', *Third World Quarterly*, 23(4): 621–32.

Thirkell-White, B. (2005) *The IMF and the Politics of Financial Globalization. From the Asian Crisis to a New Financial Architecture*, Basingstoke and New York: Palgrave Macmillan.

Thorp, R. and A. Bergés A. (n.d.) 'The historical roots of exclusion in Latin America', Manuscript, Latin American Centre, Oxford University.

Tokman, V. E. (1994) *Generación de empleo en un nuevo contexto estructural*, Lima: ILO Regional Office.

Tommasi, M. and A. Velasco (1996) 'Where are we in the political economy of reform?', *Journal of Policy Reform*, 1: 187–238.

Torfing, J. (1999) *New Theories of Discourse. Laclau, Mouffe and Žižek*, Oxford: Blackwell.

Touraine, A. (1979) 'Introducción al estudio de las clases sociales en una sociedad dependiente', in A. Solari (ed.), *Poder y desarrollo. América Latina. Estudios sociológicos en homenaje a José Medina Echavarría*, Mexico: Fondo de Cultura Económica, pp. 357–76.

Trebilcock, M. J. and J. Daniels (2008) *Rule of Law and Development*, Northampton, MA: Edward Elgar.

Tsebelis, G. (2002) *Veto Players: How Political Institutions Work*, Princeton, NJ: Princeton University Press.

UNDP (2004) *La democracia en América Latina*, New York: UNDP.

— (2007) 'Human Development Report 2007/2008. Fighting climate change: human solidarity in a divided world', New York: United Nations Development Programme, available at: hdr.undp.org/en/reports/global/hdr2007-2008/ (last accessed 22 September 2008).

United Nations (2002) 'Monterrey Consensus', Report on the International Conference on Financing for Development held on 21/22 March in Monterrey, Mexico, New York: United Nations Department of Economic and Social Affairs, available at: www.un.org/esa/sustdev/documents/Monterrey_Consensus.htm (last accessed 26 August 2008).

United Nations General Assembly (2008a) 'Secretary-General calls for "global leadership" to tackle world economic woes, food, energy prices as Sixty-third General Assembly Begins Debate', GA/10749, New York, 23 September, available at: www.un.org/News/Press/docs/2008/ga10749.doc.htm (last accessed 5 October 2008).

— (2008b) 'Statement by H. E. Luiz Inacio Lula da Silva, President of the Federative Republic of Brazil at the General Debate of the 63rd Session of the United Nations General Assembly', GA/10749, New York, 23 September, available at: www.un.org/ga/63/generaldebate/brazil.shtml (last accessed 5 October 2008).

Valenzuela, A. (2004) 'Latin American presidencies interrupted', *Journal of Democracy*, 15(4): 5–19.

Van Cott, D. L. (2005) *From Movements to Parties in Latin America: The Evolution of Ethnic Politics*, Cambridge: Cambridge University Press.

Veliz, C. (1980) *The Centralist Tradition of Latin America*, New York: Oxford University Press.

Vellinga, M. (ed.) (1993) *Democracia y política en América Latina*, Mexico: Siglo XXI.

Vilas, C. M. (2006) 'The left in South America and the resurgence of national-popular regimes', in E. Hershberg and F. Rosen (eds), *Latin America after Neoliberalism. Turning the Tide in the 21st Century?*, New York and London: New Press, pp. 132–70.

Waisman, C. H. (2006) 'Autonomy, self-regulation and democracy: Tocquevillean–Gellnerian perspectives on civil society and the bifurcated state in Latin America', in R. Feinberg, C. H. Waisman and L. Zamosc (eds), *Civil Society and Democracy in Latin America*, New York and Basingstoke: Palgrave Macmillan, pp. 17–33.

Walton, M. (2004) 'Neoliberalism in Latin America: good, bad or incomplete?', *Latin American Research Review*, 39(3): 165–83.

Weber, M. (1991) *From Max Weber: Essays in Sociology*, trans., ed. and with an introduction by H. H. Gerth and C. Wright Mills, London: Routledge.

Weffort, F. (1968) 'O populismo na política brasileira', in C. Furtado (ed.), *Brasil: Tempos Modernos*, Rio de Janeiro: Editora Paz e Terra.

Weyland, K. (1998) 'Swallowing the bitter pill: sources of popular support for neoliberal reform in Latin America', *Comparative Political Studies*, 31(5): 539–68.

— (1999) 'Populism in the age of neoliberalism', in M. L. Conniff (ed.), *Populism in Latin America*, Tuscaloosa and London: Alabama University Press, pp. 172–90.

— (2000) 'The Brazilian state in the New Democracy', in P. R. Kingstone and T. J. Power (eds), *Democratic Brazil. Actors, Institutions and Processes*, Pittsburgh, PA: University of Pittsburgh Press, pp. 36–57.

— (2002) *The Politics of Market Reform Fragile Democracies: Argentina, Brazil, Peru and Venezuela*, Princeton, NJ: Princeton University Press.

— (2004) 'Neoliberalism and democracy in Latin America: a mixed record', *Latin American Politics and Society*, 46(1): 135–57.

— (2007) 'Politics and policies of Latin America's two lefts: the role of party systems vs. resource bonanzas', Paper prepared for delivery at the 26th Congress of the Latin American Studies Association, Montreal, Canada, 5–9 September.

Whitehead, L. (1992) 'The alternatives to "liberal democracy": a Latin American perspective', *Political Studies*, XL, Special Issue, pp. 146–59.

Wiarda, H. J. (1973) 'Towards a framework for the study of political change in the Iberic-Latin tradition: the corporative model', *World Politics*, 25(1): 206–35.

— (1995a) *Democracy and Its Discontents: Development, Interdependence, and US Policy in Latin America*, Lanham, MD: Rowman and Littlefield.

— (1995b) 'After Miami: the summit, the peso crisis, and the future of US–Latin American relations', *Journal of Interamerican Studies and World Affairs*, 37(1): 43–69.

Williamson, J. (ed) (1990) *Latin American Economic Adjustment: How Much Has Happened?*, Washington, DC: Institute for International Economics.

— (1994) 'In search of a manual for technopols', in J. Williamson (ed.), *The Political Economy of Policy Reform*, Washington, DC: Institute for International Economics, pp. 9–28.

— (2000) 'What should the World Bank think about the Washington Consensus', *World Bank Research Observer*, 15(2): 251–64.

— (2003a) 'Overview. An agenda for restoring growth and reform', in P. P. Kuczynski and J. Williamson (eds), *After the Washington Consensus. Restoring Growth and Reform in Latin America*, Washington,

DC: Institute for International Economics, pp. 1–19.

— (2003b) 'Appendix. Our agenda and the Washington Consensus reform', in P. P. Kuczynski and J. Williamson (eds), *After the Washington Consensus. Restoring Growth and Reform in Latin America*, Washington, DC: Institute for International Economics, pp. 323–31.

Wise, C. (1994) 'The politics of Peruvian economic reform: overcoming the legacies of state-led development', *Journal of Interamerican Studies and World Affairs*, 36: 75–124.

Wolfensohn, J. (1999) 'A proposal for a comprehensive development framework', Discussion draft, available at: www.worldbank.org/cdf (last accessed 22 July 2008).

Wolford, W. (2006) '*Sem reforma agrária não há democracia*: deepening democracy and the struggle for agrarian reform in Brazil', in R. Feinberg, C. H. Waisman and L. Zamosc (eds), *Civil Society and Democracy in Latin America*, New York and Basingtoke: Palgrave Macmillan, pp. 139–68.

Woods, N. (2006) *The Globalizers: The IMF, the World Bank and Their Borrowers*, Ithaca, NY, and London: Cornell University Press.

World Bank (1985) *Research News*, 6(1), Washington, DC: World Bank.

— (1987) *World Development Report 1987: Barriers to Adjustment and Growth in the World Economy. Industrialization and Foreign Trade*, Oxford and London: Oxford University Press.

— (1988) 'Adjustment lending. An evaluation of ten years' experience', Policy and Research Series 1, Washington, DC: World Bank.

— (1990) *World Development Report*

1990: Poverty, Oxford and London: Oxford University Press.

— (1997) *World Development Report 1997: The State in a Changing World*, Oxford and London: Oxford University Press.

— (1999a) 'Comprehensive development framework: questions and answers', available at: www.worldbank.org/cdf/cdf-faq.htm (last accessed 22 July 2008).

— (1999b) *World Development Report 1999/2000: Entering the 21st Century*, Oxford and London: Oxford University Press.

— (2000) *World Development Report 2000/2001: Attacking Social Poverty*, Oxford and London: Oxford University Press.

— (2002) *World Development Report 2002: Building Institutions for Markets*, Oxford and London: Oxford University Press.

— (2006) *World Development Report 2006: Equity and Development*, Oxford and London: Oxford University Press.

— (2008a) 'Synopsis of WDRs (1995–2005)', available at: go.worldbank.org/Z2LU71DB90 (last accessed 22 July 2008).

— (2008b) *Worldwide Governance Indicators 1996–2007*, available at: info.worldbank.org/governance/wgi/index.asp (last accessed 26 August 2008).

— (2008c) 'The Growth Report: strategies for sustained growth and inclusive development', Commission on Growth and Development, available at: www.growthcommission.org/index.php?option=com_content&task=view&id=96&Itemid=169 (last accessed 26 August 2008).

World Economic Forum (2008) *The Global Competitiveness Report 2007–2008*, available at: www.ger.weforum.org (last accessed 26 August 2008).

Zàjec, L. (2006) 'Lourdes: Nadie quiere volver a la dictadura y la improvisación', *La República*, 7 April, available at: archivo.larepublica.com.pe/index.php?option=com_content&task=view&id=107090&Itemid=483&fecha_edicion=2006-04-07# (last accessed 13 July 2006).

Zalaquet, J. (1998) 'The ethics of responsibility, human rights: truth and reconciliation in Chile', Washington, DC: WOLA.

Zaluar, A. (2007) 'Democracia participativa?', *Folha de São Paulo*, 1 October.

Zamosc, L. (2007) 'The Indian movement and democracy in Ecuador', *Latin American Politics and Society*, 49(3): 1–34.

Zucco, C. (2008) 'The president's "new" constituency: Lula and the pragmatic vote in Brazil's 2006 presidential elections', *Journal of Latin American Studies*, 40(1): 29–49.

Index